S0-BNS-827

BIRDWATCHING IN NEW HAMPSHIRE

Eric A. Masterson

To Ruth
Good Birding
Eric Masterson

Birdwatching

IN NEW HAMPSHIRE

University Press of New England · Hanover and London

University Press of New England
www.upne.com
© 2013 University Press of New England
All rights reserved
Manufactured in the United States of America
Designed by Mindy Basinger Hill
Typeset in Calluna
For permission to reproduce any of the material
in this book, contact Permissions, University Press
of New England, One Court Street, Suite 250,
Lebanon NH 03766; or visit www.upne.com

Library of Congress Cataloging-in-Publication Data

Masterson, Eric A.
Birdwatching in New Hampshire / Eric A. Masterson.
     pages   cm
Includes bibliographical references and index.
ISBN 978-1-58465-986-0 (pbk.: alk. paper) —
ISBN 978-1-61168-410-0 (ebook)
1. Bird watching—New Hampshire—Guidebooks.
2. Birds—New Hampshire.
3. New Hampshire—Guidebooks. I. Title.
QL684.N4M37 2013
598.072′34742—dc23   2012035742

5   4   3   2   1

PHOTO CREDITS

Page i Prairie Warbler by
Eric Masterson

Pages ii–iii Snow Geese by
Eric Masterson

Page v Loons © Douglas K. Hill,
doughillphoto.com

Page vi Cedar Waxwings
© Stubblefieldphoto,
Dreamstime.com

Page xi Snowy Owl by
Jason Lambert

Page 125 Yellow-rumped Warbler
© Suebakerphotography,
Dreamstime.com

Page 142 Loon © Menno67,
Dreamstime.com

Page 150 Snow Geese © billperry,
123rf.com

DEDICATED TO DAD

Contents

Acknowledgments

I owe a debt to the many birders and ornithologists whose work provided the data that enabled me to write this book. I cannot name them all, but several have contributed an enormous amount to what is known about the birds of New Hampshire. I would be remiss if I did not mention Pam Hunt, Steve Mirick, Bob Quinn, and Becky Suomala. Bob Quinn, especially, provided inspiration to a birder raised in the abundant birdlife of coastal Ireland—and now landlocked in the Monadnock region—by highlighting the diversity of coastal birds that stray inland at times. Bob's inspiration was drawn from Tudor Richards, who was an influential figure in the relatively short time I knew him. Bob also reviewed an early draft of the book, for which I am grateful.

I am likewise grateful to all the photographers whose works appear in the book, including Ralph Eldridge, Catherine Greenleaf, Jim Hully, Scott Young, and the Greenland White-fronted Goose Study. In particular, Jason Lambert and Len Medlock provided a significant number of excellent images from their personal libraries. They have captured some of the finest images of New Hampshire's birds, more of which can be viewed on their Web sites (see Web Resources in the Introduction). All but two of the photographs in the book were taken in New Hampshire or its offshore waters.

Debbie Brewitt, Brian Soares, and the crew of the UNH Marine Program provided me rare access to the area of Jeffreys Ledge during winter, as did Eastman's of Hampton. Star Island Corporation allowed me generous access to Star Island. I am thankful to them all.

Allan Keith and Bob Fox provided valuable data on historical records of New Hampshire's birds by allowing me access to their manuscript, "The Birds of New Hampshire."

Margaret Baker helped with some software issues. Cook Anderson, Phil Brown, Chris Sheridan, and Rob Woodward provided feedback on various aspects of birding in New Hampshire, and Tony Vazzano offered guidance on the influence of weather on bird migration.

I am indebted to Laurie Bryan, Meade Cadot, and the Harris Center, my local regional land trust and employer. Through the Harris Center I had access to mapping software used in the production of the guide, and was provided with the flexibility needed to complete the project.

I would like to offer thanks to Mick Brown, a childhood friend who introduced me to my life's passion; to my parents, for encouraging my passion; and to my friend Eugene, with whom I shared my first decade in the field. Sy Montgomery, Howard Mansfield, and Scott Manning have been constant wellsprings of support through the early days of my writing career.

University Press of New England gave a first-time author a chance, and I am especially grateful to Richard Pult, Peter Fong, Susan Abel, Mindy Basinger Hill, and the other wonderful staff there who helped to smooth the wrinkles and move the project along.

We all owe a debt to the many conservationists who toil for the preservation of birds and their habitat and to landowners across New Hampshire who allow access to their private property for birdwatching and other recreational opportunities. I for one offer them my thanks.

Finally, I am tremendously grateful to my wife Trish for being an unwavering supporter and the love of my life.

BIRDWATCHING IN NEW HAMPSHIRE

Introduction

This is a book about finding birds in New Hampshire. Yet birds are virtually everywhere in the state: in our fields and forests; on our lakes, rivers, and oceans; and atop our mountains. This is not a guide to everywhere, but to the best birding events that New Hampshire has to offer. I use the word *event* deliberately, because good birding involves more than just getting to the right place; it is a function of location, time, and weather. This constellation of factors must align in the right order to produce the most memorable birding moments.

To find a particular species of bird, you must first find the right habitat at the right time of year. Many species occur within broad parameters of time and place, and these are usually the common types with which we are all familiar. Black-capped Chickadee and Blue Jay, for example, occur across a broad spectrum of landscapes, live here year round and, not surprisingly, both are common and familiar. Conversely, Bicknell's Thrush breeds only in spruce-fir forests above 3,500 feet. The more specific a bird's requirements, the rarer it becomes and the harder it is to find.

Black-capped Chickadee and Bicknell's Thrush are but 2 of more than 300 species of birds that occur in New Hampshire each year. This number does not include storm-blown waifs and vagrants, which bring the number of birds recorded in the state to more than 400. Of the regulars, 186 breed here (several more are occasional nesters); about 70 species can be seen year round, while just 30 species occur only in winter.

Most of our birds are migrants, even birds that seem to be permanent fixtures like Blue Jay and American Goldfinch. Other species are more definitive travelers, gracing us with their presence for a few brief weeks in May, August, or September. Individuals of some species move north through the central United States, then take a different route south in the fall that takes them through New Hampshire. A few species rarely make sight of the state's

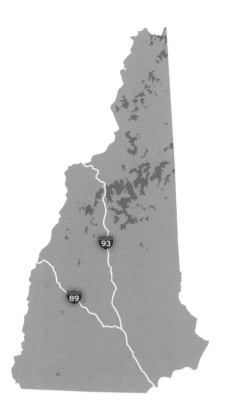

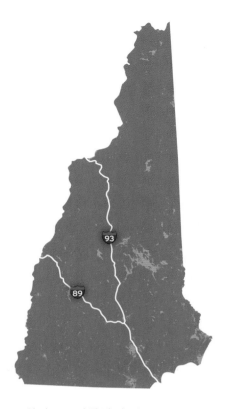

Occurrence of high-elevation spruce-fir forest in New Hampshire. Bicknell's Thrush and Spruce Grouse are seldom found outside this habitat.

Black-capped Chickadee is a generalist, and occurs across a range of habitats, including high-elevation spruce-fir forest, low-elevation spruce-fir forest, Appalachian oak–pine forest, silver maple floodplain forest, hemlock-hardwood-pine forest, northern hardwood–conifer forest, pitch pine forest, and grassland. These habitats are mapped above, showing why Black-capped Chickadee is such a familiar and widespread bird.

eponymous granite at all, choosing instead to remain miles off our coast in the Gulf of Maine.

Some birds occur only in particular locations at specific times, like the handful of Arctic Terns that nest on White and Seavey Islands. Others check all the boxes, occurring statewide and at all times of the year; even here, however, there is nuance. For example, the American Goldfinch is a common visitor at birdfeeders in winter and a common breeder in summer. Yet thousands have been documented migrating south along New Hampshire's coast each fall. Similarly, Canada Geese can be found year round in southern New Hampshire, where they often occur in urban and suburban environments. Yet in spring, individual birds destined for Canada or the rugged wilderness of Greenland pass through the state from their winter quarters along the mid-Atlantic coast. Although these geese appear identical to the ones that remain with us through the summer, they are altogether different and wilder beasts.

Many of New Hampshire's birds are stunningly beautiful; others have songs that are works of art, woven into the fabric of our forests. A few have annual migrations that astonish, then astonish again when they repeat the feat year after year. This book is a collection of the very best sites and the very best times to watch birds in New Hampshire. It is designed to help you find, see, and appreciate these natural wonders. After 30 years of birding throughout Europe, Africa, and North America, I have learned the art of finding birds and, more importantly, of seeing them, not as specks 50 feet high in the canopy, but properly, as their beauty deserves.

Though this guide is filled with maps and directions to birding sites throughout New Hampshire, its purpose is to help you find birds, not birding sites. These often occur together, but not always. In this introduction I attempt to explain the factors that can help bring the two into convergence.

It is impossible to include all good birding locations, even for a small state like New Hampshire, and though the top sites are universally acknowledged, the inclusion or exclusion of others no doubt reflects my own subjective biases.

Many species are easy to find, like Herring Gull, Rock Pigeon, and House Sparrow, and you will not find mention of these in the book except in the species accounts. Instead, the book focuses on the less well-known, the spectacular, the secretive, the rare: in essence, the *good bird*. This will mean different things to different people.

Greater
White-fronted
Goose

Cory's Shearwater

Osprey

Blackpoll
Warbler

Scarlet
Tanager

Bobolink

Great
Shearwater

Hudsonian
Godwit

Wilson's Storm-Petrel
Arctic Tern

Most of New Hampshire's birds are migrants,
and some are world-class travelers.

What Is a "Good Bird"?

Many birders are obsessed with finding rarities. These are the crown jewels of birding, the birds that can turn an ordinary day into a cherished memory. The definition of a rarity is probably best understood by considering two of the most well known in recent history. In January 1975, a Ross's Gull visited Newburyport Harbor and stayed there for several months. Almost three decades later, on August 24, 2004, a Red-footed Falcon was found on Martha's Vineyard; it remained for two weeks. Both species are fairly large birds, both are visually stunning, both come from distant and exotic locations (the Arctic and Eurasia, respectively) and, crucially, both stayed long enough to garner extensive media exposure. These are the ingredients that constitute a modern mega-rarity. Few of us will be lucky enough to find one because there are so few of them—that is why we call them rarities. A career built on the pursuit of rarities alone will be one of infrequent moments of elation interspersed with long periods of frustration. The single-minded obsession with them can grow tedious, and even their attainment can feel anticlimactic; like a drug addict, one is always looking for the next fix.

My own definition of a good bird is a bit more expansive. In addition to the excitement of finding rarities, I enjoy seeing a large kettle of Broad-winged Hawks in September, or experiencing a chance encounter with a flock of shorebirds on an inland pond, away from their more expected coastal habitat.

The following anecdote illustrates my point. I had the good fortune to be on a pelagic trip out of Hyannis, Massachusetts, on August 25, 2007, during which a Barolo Shearwater was seen, the first confirmed sighting of this species in North America. The bird was a mega-rarity of the first order, and I—along with the many other birders on board—was very glad to have seen it. Later that day, as we were steaming north over Nantucket Shoals to return to port, a flock of forty Hudsonian Godwits flew past us, low over the ocean. It was a couple of hours before nightfall and they were heading south over the western Atlantic, next stop: South America. Hudsonian Godwits, though uncommon, are regularly recorded in fall at coastal locations in New England, New Hampshire included. I have seen them on many occasions, but this was the first time I had witnessed their famed ocean crossing. The shearwater was rarer by several orders of magnitude. Yet, in the godwits, I felt as though I was witnessing something truly remarkable. Both were good birds, though of a very different nature.

Whether you seek a Ross's Gull or a Hudsonian Godwit, the practice of finding both remains the same. Without a good understanding of the basic tenets that govern bird occurrence, the hours you spend driving, walking, or canoeing in their pursuit will be less rewarding experiences.

Where to Find Good Birds

This book will direct you to a selection of the best sites in the state but, as your skills improve, you will begin to read the landscape and intuit other likely places to find particular suites of species. In order to find a bird, it is important to develop an understanding of its preferred habitat. Sites change: sod farms become cornfields; beaver ponds become meadows. A rainstorm can turn a stubble field into a muddy pond, a case of "add water to create instant shorebird habitat."

Remember one golden rule: find the habitat, find the bird. This applies everywhere, not just in New Hampshire. One tool that can help tremendously in this regard is Google Earth, which allows you to see the landscape from a bird's perspective. Not only does Google Earth allow you to find previously hidden sites, but you can use it to think like your quarry. An inland waterbird in winter is going to find the only open water, while a shorebird during migration will be looking for an open pasture, field, or lake edge, and so on. By thinking like a bird and then searching for likely habitat, you can dramatically improve your chances of success.

Included in this rule are some other helpful generalities. Some habitats consistently produce good birding for a variety of reasons, chief among these are food availability, shelter, and, for migrant species, visual similarity to the natural habitat of choice.

THE COAST

The coast of New Hampshire offers unparalleled birding opportunities. Coastal marshes, estuaries, bays, and shorelines provide the best habitat in the state for a large number of waterfowl, shorebirds, gulls, terns, and other waterbirds. Wayward land birds from southern and western states also become concentrated on coastal islands and headlands, as the Atlantic Ocean serves as a barrier of sorts during spring and fall migration.

The principal drawback to this area is its high level of development. In addition to impairing the landscape for birds, the human population density creates access difficulties and sometimes extreme traffic congestion. Chapter 5 offers a more detailed examination of some outstanding coastal sites.

INLAND

The terrific potential of coastal birding sites can blind birders to possibilities away from the coast. The following map shows the occurrence of rare birds (species seen 10 or fewer times in the state) by location. Though coastal sites have been most productive, New Hampshire's major population centers also boast significant numbers of records. This is because there are more people to watch for birds in these areas. On the other hand, consider New Hampton, a town with a relatively small population in the state's interior. New Hampton might have been an unremarkable town, from a birding perspective, except for Vera Hebert and Bob Smart—two very active and very competent birders who lived locally during the 1950s and 60s and recorded a long list of unusual birds in the region, including Swallow-tailed Kite, Prothonotary Warbler, Painted Bunting, and Western Meadowlark (see Quinn 2011). Good birding is a function of effort and, if you get out into the field enough, you will have rewarding experiences, regardless of where you look.

Some inland habitat types tend to be more productive than others. I've identified several here.

Wastewater treatment plants Only a few in the state allow access, but they are worth the effort. Pumps and filtration systems often keep the lagoons open in winter, when water bodies elsewhere are frozen, making them ideal for waterfowl. In the fall, the nutrient-rich lagoons support an abundance of insect life for shorebirds, which can be found along the edges of treatment ponds. Late in the season, these sites can still be insect factories, especially on south-facing slopes that catch the sun, making them a good bet for fall vagrants and over-wintering insectivores. Slurry ponds, features of most dairy farms, also fall into this category, as they too are rich with insects. In fact, any site that can sustain an insect population into late fall offers excellent birding potential.

Landfills Landfills are disappearing features of our towns and cities, as the waste stream is increasingly being accommodated through incineration and recycling. Like wastewater treatment plants, landfills usually restrict access. However, they can be excellent spots to find rare gulls during winter. If you cannot gain entry, look for birds roosting or bathing at nearby ponds or reservoirs. Landfills also are good places to find larks, longspurs, and buntings,

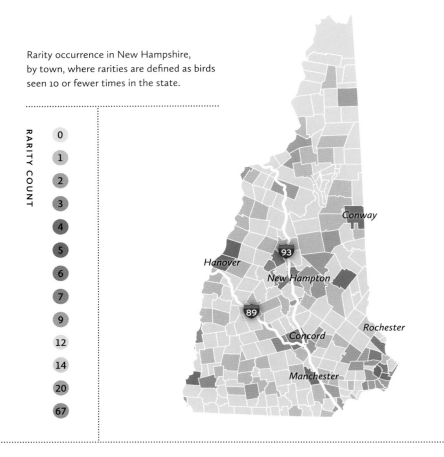

Rarity occurrence in New Hampshire, by town, where rarities are defined as birds seen 10 or fewer times in the state.

RARITY COUNT

0
1
2
3
4
5
6
7
9
12
14
20
67

Conway
Hanover
93
New Hampton
89
Concord
Rochester
Manchester

while Black Vultures occasionally can be found among the more common Turkey Vultures.

Airfields Airfields are the last refuges of several grassland specialists, notably Upland Sandpiper, American Kestrel, Vesper Sparrow, Grasshopper Sparrow, and Eastern Meadowlark. Access can again be an issue, although for more obvious reasons than for landfills and treatment plants. Airfields are best visited early in the morning in late May and early June, while the sparrows are still in song (grassland birds can be surprisingly hard to find otherwise).

Community gardens and market gardens With the rise in interest in locally grown food, more of these gardens are popping up every year. They are excellent places for birding in the fall. Sparrows and buntings love to feed on seeds, while the insects that are drawn to rotting vegetables provide food for warblers. Pumpkin fields in particular offer excellent foraging for seed-eaters. In any such garden, keep an eye out for the rarer sparrows and buntings, especially Clay-colored Sparrow, Blue Grosbeak, and Dickcissel.

Lakes and ponds All good-sized lakes and ponds, though highly variable as birding sites in summer, offer temporary habitat during spring and fall for migrant waterbirds. This is especially true during inclement weather, when they provide a relatively safe haven where birds can wait for the skies to clear. Migrant birds forced into layovers often are uninterested in feeding, especially during spring, and will move on as soon as the bad weather has passed. For the brief period of the storm, however, any body of water offers the potential to host a variety of exciting and unexpected species. Pam Hunt's study of the birdlife of Mascoma Lake in Enfield offers a good example of this potential. From 1989 to 2000, Hunt recorded a remarkable birdlist, including such impressive sightings as Little Gull.

COASTAL BIRDS INLAND Several families of birds readily associated with the coast occasionally occur inland, most particularly shorebirds. Though it is unquestionably easier to find many of these species at Hampton Harbor or along New Hampshire's beaches, it can be exciting to spot them elsewhere. Many shorebirds breed well to the north of New Hampshire, some as far away as Baffin Island or the Canadian Arctic archipelago. To reach these latitudes, the birds often fly over land, but go undetected because they migrate at altitude and at night. When inclement weather forces them to find temporary shelter, shorebirds that favor mudflats, beaches, and marshes at the coast will congregate along inland riverbanks and lakeshores, in flooded fields, and at ponds and wastewater treatment plants.

Particularly memorable was the shorebird fallout that occurred in the Keene area on May 26, 2004, following several days of wet, overcast weather. Local birder James Smith recorded an unprecedented number of shorebirds for an inland location in spring: 12 species and more than 2000 individuals, including 600 Dunlin, 200 Short-billed Dowitchers, and extremely rare inland occurrences of Whimbrel, Ruddy Turnstone, and Red Knot.

In spring, shorebirds tend not to linger. They move on as soon as the weather clears, eager to arrive on the breeding grounds. In fall, shorebirds may occur in greater numbers and remain for longer periods, with adults arriving in New Hampshire as early as mid-July, followed by juveniles in August.

Many inland lakes and ponds host shorebirds only when water levels are low enough to offer an appropriately muddy edge. As the level of many of New Hampshire's water bodies is artificially maintained, the availability of shorebird habitat can be hard to predict. Many ponds are drawn down in the fall, but this usually doesn't happen until October, by which time shorebird migration has ended. Occasionally a lake will be drawn down earlier in the season for dam repair; if this happens in July, August, or September, it can set the table for a shorebirding bonanza. When Powder Mill Pond in Hancock was drawn down in July 2012 to facilitate repairs to a dam on the Contoocook River, 14 species of shorebirds were recorded in a couple of weeks, including rare inland occurrences of Ruddy Turnstone and Sanderling. The New Hampshire Dam Bureau has information on early drawdowns of water bodies under its jurisdiction (see Web Resources). Smaller ponds (less than 10 acres) also may provide potential birding sites. For example, a beaver dam that bursts during spring floods can inadvertently create fall shorebird habitat. A quick Web search can occasionally direct you to a news article or other source noting one of these smaller drawdowns.

Both the Connecticut and Merrimack Rivers are controlled by dams, and their water levels can change surprisingly quickly. I have watched mudflats along the Connecticut River disappear within 30 minutes of dam adjustments made downstream. In spring 2011, on the other hand, I witnessed a flock of Dunlin, Semipalmated Plover, and Least Sandpiper alight on mudflats that had been submerged only moments earlier. They must have been migrating over-head at the time and decided to take quick advantage of the available habitat.

With a little effort and experience, you can begin to intuit when water levels will be low enough to provide shorebird habitat along riverbanks. TransCan-ada operates the dams on the Connecticut River and hosts an information line that provides data on release rates and water levels (see Web Resources).

Sod farms also offer potential inland habitat for shorebirds, as the ground is usually compact enough to form puddles relatively quickly and the short grass can mimic a coastal saltmarsh. American Golden-Plover and Buff-breasted Sandpiper are especially drawn to sod farms during fall. Baird's Sandpiper favors this habitat as well, though the species is very rare inland and rare even on the coast.

When to Find Good Birds

Chapter 8 details the timing of each species' appearance in the state, provid-ing a macro-level answer to the question. Although it can help to know that late October and early November is the prime time to find Golden Eagles in New Hampshire, two weeks is still too long for most of us to devote to searching for a bird. Fortunately, other factors—particularly weather—play

Shorebirds—including Semipalmated Plover, Least Sandpiper, and Dunlin—on the Connecticut River, spring 2011. *Eric Masterson*

important roles in determining when a particular bird will occur within a given timeframe.

TIME OF DAY

Songbirds are generally more active in the morning, making them much easier to find at that time. Though few songbirds remain in New Hampshire during the winter, this rule applies year round and in all habitats.

During migration periods, birders at coastal locations often report "re-orientation flights" immediately following sunrise. (Most species of songbirds are nocturnal migrants and generally make landfall before dawn, then spend the day resting and refueling.) Presumably these migrants are making short-distance flights to more suitable habitats in which to spend the day. I have witnessed this phenomenon most vividly on Star Island, where birds that have almost certainly arrived during the night often leave very early in the morning to fly the 7 miles to the mainland.

Seawatching, a subgenre of birding, is also an early morning activity. I have often arrived at a seawatch 30 minutes after sunrise—thinking I was early—only to curse my laziness. Had I set my alarm for a half hour earlier, I might have arrived in time to witness the beginning of the migration.

When the day is calm and clear—conditions that promote the development of thermals—vultures, eagles, and hawks are often more visible later in the morning, after the ground has heated sufficiently to create rising air currents. This is true even in winter, when a scan of the skyline from a good vantage point will often be rewarded with one or more species.

Evening offers its own rewards. Traditionally, it is a good time to watch birds going to roost, especially those species that favor communal roosts, including waterfowl, herons, swallows, and blackbirds—species that typically are more dispersed during the day. Observing roosts offers an opportunity to make accurate counts and to find unusual birds among the more common species. In May 2011, I observed 150 Chimney Swifts circling over downtown Peterborough at dusk. The swirling mass of birds was circling in an orbit of rapidly decreasing diameter. Just as the light was almost gone, they disappeared down the Town Hall chimney—like a genie disappearing into a bottle—where they roosted for the night. I was particularly intrigued by this sighting as it represented a very large count for a declining species. As it turned out, the high numbers were due to several days of poor weather, which held these birds back in their migration.

TIME OF YEAR

Seasons define the birdlife of New Hampshire. The most exciting times to watch are during spring and fall, when you can witness birds in migration. These also are the times of year when you can expect the unexpected. For this reason, my favorite months are May, September, and October.

A NOTE ON IRRUPTIVE BEHAVIOR

This is not meant to disparage the remaining months of the year. Winter especially can be an exciting time, when visitors from vast Canadian forests and the Arctic tundra fly south to enjoy the relative warmth of New Hampshire. Several winter visitors, especially finches, exhibit what is known as irruptive behavior. For example, Common Redpoll relies on a food resource (seeds of alder, birch, and willow trees) that fluctuates in abundance across its range, forcing the species to undergo periodic massive migrations. This behavior

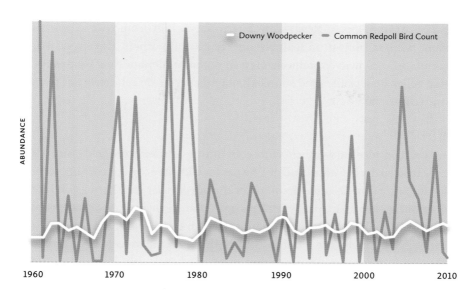

Data for Downy Woodpecker and Common Redpoll from the Christmas Bird Count, 1960–2010. The graph clearly depicts the irruptive nature of Common Redpoll in New Hampshire.

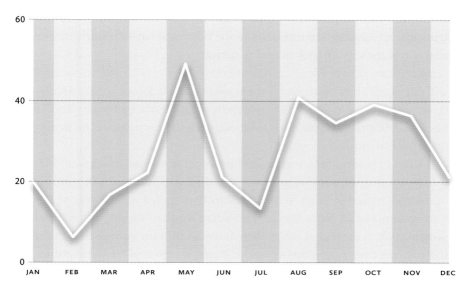

Rarity occurrence in New Hampshire, by month, where rarities are defined as birds seen 10 or fewer times in the state. Unusual birds occur more often during migration, especially in May and from August through November.

causes its numbers in New Hampshire to vary wildly from year to year. In some winters, almost no Redpolls are recorded; in others, thousands. For comparison, Downy Woodpecker is a common resident of New Hampshire that relies on a stable food source. Its numbers remain relatively flat from one year to the next.

WEATHER

I *always* consider the weather before committing to a day in the field—and not only to keep myself warm and dry. Just as location and timing are important for finding birds, an understanding of the effects that weather has on bird distribution can dramatically improve one's chances of observing that special bird. This is especially true from April through early June and from August through November, the months when birds are on the move. My wife jokes that I only get chores done in June and July—after the last bird has arrived on territory and before the first fall migrants appear on the coast.

Before discussing weather patterns that influence bird migration, I want to share a brief explanation of why it is important. What follows is an account of a classic week of birding in the spring of 2011.

A low-pressure system in the western Atlantic created several days of northerly winds over much of the East Coast from May 9 to 13, thus discouraging any appreciable movement of birds. When the weather finally broke, almost a week's backlog of migrants surged north. However, a cold front along the Canadian border created an effective barrier to further movement and put many birds down along the coasts of Massachusetts, New Hampshire, and Maine, including an astounding 150 Northern Parulas and 50 Black-and-White Warblers on Star Island, with similar numbers on nearby Appledore Island.

A series of fronts in the region produced cool northeast winds from May 15 to 18, keeping the weather unsettled and the birds grounded. On May 19, a warm front passed through New Hampshire then stalled against a high-pressure system east of Nova Scotia. The warm southerlies brought migrant shorebirds over the region; when these birds hit the rain associated with the stalled front, they sought shelter across Massachusetts and New Hampshire. The Connecticut River was full to the brim from a combination of rain and spring run-off, denying shorebirds of foraging habitat along the river banks. I guessed that they would be attracted to the many cornfields in the river floodplain, but most had already been ploughed. Two fields in Walpole and

Weather conditions caused a fallout of tropical migrants on Maine's
Machias Seal Island, May 24, 2011. *Ralph Eldridge*

Charlestown had yet to be tilled, however, and these both held inviting
puddles and ponds. The Charlestown site hosted a stunning collection of 9
species, including White-rumped Sandpiper and Red Phalarope, both rare
birds in the interior of New Hampshire, and a female Ruff, a standout rarity
that breeds in northern Europe and Russia and winters in sub-Saharan Africa,
Asia, and Australia.

IDEAL WEATHER FOR SPRING BIRDING The most advantageous conditions
during spring migration obviously involve southerly winds. From late April
through early June—especially mid- to late May—it is worth keeping an
eye on the forecast (see Web Resources). Following a bout of persistent
southerlies, it can be especially rewarding to go birding along the coast,
to Star Island, or to some favorite inland localities. In addition to the expected species that arrive on these tailwinds, you can reasonably hope for
an occasional spring overshoot. These are birds that breed to our south but
occasionally fly beyond their normal spring destination. Every May, a few
Hooded Warblers, Worm-eating Warblers, and Summer Tanagers occur
along the coast of northern New England, along with some other species
with more southerly distributions.

Your chances of success in spring improve greatly when a warm southerly

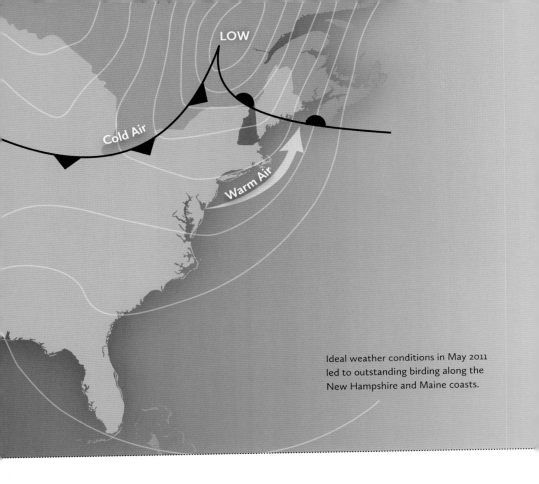

LOW

Cold Air

Warm Air

Ideal weather conditions in May 2011
led to outstanding birding along the
New Hampshire and Maine coasts.

airflow is interrupted by a weather front over New Hampshire. Cold fronts
and warm fronts are the two types that most influence bird migration. A
cold front describes a boundary where a mass of cold air is advancing on a
mass of warm air. In a warm front, the order is reversed; the warm air-mass
is advancing on the cold air.

During spring, warm fronts usually approach New England on south or
west winds. This type of weather pattern is conducive to migration and,
without complicating factors, most birds will continue north. This is good
for birds, because they want to get to their breeding grounds quickly, but bad
for the birders who want to see them. A frontal boundary, however, can bring
rain as well as a change in wind direction. Migrants entering the frontal zone
can experience wet weather, poor visibility, and possibly a headwind—the
proverbial brick wall for a migrating bird. Cold fronts moving in from the

north also can produce headwinds. In either case, the resulting fallout of birds can be stunning when the right factors coalesce at the right time.

Warm fronts from the south also can affect fall migration. During the first week of October 2011, for example, three Worm-eating Warblers, two Hooded Warblers, and two Summer Tanagers were reported along the coast of New Hampshire in the space of a few days—an unprecedented occurrence for that time of year. These migrants had left the southeastern United States, bound for the Gulf, but were caught instead in a strong southeasterly airflow off the southern Atlantic coast. The birds flew downwind, which carried them north to New Hampshire and away from their intended destination (Iliff 2011).

Spring Westerlies Following a May bout of westerlies, a birding trip to the coast—or even an offshore boat trip—can sometimes produce unexpected results. Birds moving north can find themselves blown out to sea by westerly winds, and I have witnessed some unusual sightings on Jeffreys Ledge after such conditions.

Spring Easterlies Prolonged easterlies at this time of year can push migrating birds inland. This was a causal factor in the large number of scoters and shorebirds seen in interior New England during spring 2011.

IDEAL WEATHER FOR FALL BIRDING Many of the general rules that apply in spring also work in the fall, although you should take into account two important differences.

Hooded Warbler, Rye Harbor State Park, October 3, 2011. *Jason Lambert*

Although it hardly needs stating, birds are heading south in the fall; southerly winds therefore represent headwinds at this time of year.

Cold weather acts as an environmental cue for birds. The passage of a cold front is often accompanied by a migration event.

Cold fronts in fall are often followed by clear weather. With nothing to interrupt their migration, birds will keep on moving. Coastlines remain a sort of barrier to many species, however. If northwesterlies or westerlies carry birds out over the ocean during the night, they will reorient themselves in the morning, often heading for the nearest point of land. This can make for good coastal or island birding. In October, persistent and expansive westerlies can be caused by strong low-pressure cells moving through the Midwest and Great Lakes regions. These winds are often associated with the arrival of western vagrants like Ash-throated Flycatcher and Cave Swallow at or near the coast.

In general, a sudden drop in temperature in early fall should inspire you to check for migrants along the coast; in mid-September, watch for Broad-winged Hawks; in late October, be on the lookout for Golden Eagles. An October cold snap with westerly winds is a good time to look for vagrants from the west.

STORM BIRDING Before going any further, let me stress that safety should be of paramount importance during storms. No effort should be made in the pursuit of birds that would endanger the health of any person—or bird.

There is no standout location along New Hampshire's coast for storm birding, but Little Boars Head offers the best combination of proximity, height, and parking (enabling you to seawatch from the shelter of your vehicle). Ragged Neck in Rye is also a good spot. Offshore, the Isles of Shoals are New Hampshire's best storm birding location, but it is practically impossible to get out to the islands in the high winds that create ideal seawatch conditions. However, a good time can still be had along the coast in winds of 30 mph or more out of the south or southeast.

Hurricanes can be equally as devastating to wildlife as people, and are thankfully rare in New England. Several recent hurricane events, however, have left exotic birds in their wakes. For example, Hurricane Irene made landfall in North Carolina as a category I storm, with maximum sustained winds of 86 mph, on August 17, 2011. It continued north, hugging the Eastern Seaboard, before crossing Long Island Sound and heading inland up the Connecticut River Valley. Prior to landfall in the United States, the storm passed over the northern Antilles and the Bahamas, home to several species of tropical birds not normally seen in our region. After the storm dissipated, tropical species were discovered all along the East Coast, deposited by the hurricane in an exhausted state, including the first New Hampshire record of White-tailed Tropicbird (in Claremont), and a Sooty Tern (in Stoddard; Iliff 2011).

Tools for Birders

Modern birders have a wide range of tools available. Some of these have been around for decades, but others are relatively new.

RADAR

Radar can help you to plan your birding activities for the following day. Nexrad, the nationwide network of weather surveillance radar stations, can detect nocturnal bird migrations, enabling you to see large movements of birds in real time. (See Web Resources.)

CANOES OR KAYAKS

Whether at Lake Umbagog, on the Connecticut River, or at Hampton Marsh, a canoe or kayak can help you more fully explore the state's bird habitats. Without one, you will be denied access to some of the best locations, find fewer birds, and be rewarded with poorer views of those that you do find. A canoe allows you to approach some species to a degree that is otherwise impossible. This is especially true with shorebirds, gulls, and terns. After years of hunting, however, waterfowl can be quite wary of humans, whether in a boat or on foot. Common sense is required to minimize disturbance to birds. If an individual appears to be in a state of exhaustion, you should not increase its distress by approaching too closely.

BINOCULARS

If you don't yet own a decent pair of binoculars, you must get one. Birding is now a mainstream hobby and there is a bewildering array of binoculars on offer. I don't recommend any particular brand or model because no one shoe fits all. Some people have a budget, others don't. Some people also watch

Track of Hurricane Irene in August 2011, with accompanying sightings of tropical seabirds. The black dots represent Sooty Terns, while the white dots represent White-tailed Tropicbirds.

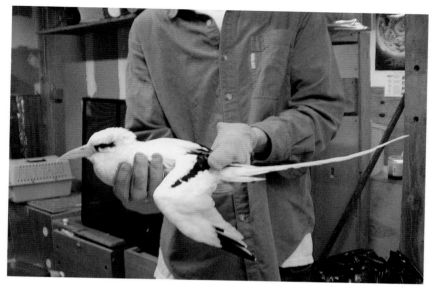

New Hampshire's first White-tailed Tropicbird, found in a Claremont yard and brought to a wildlife clinic in Lyme. *Catherine Greenleaf*

butterflies, others the night sky. There is no substitute for field-testing a range of binoculars to find a pair that best fits your needs.

There are two basic binocular designs: roof prism and Porro prism. Roof prism binoculars consist of two straight barrels that house all of the optical elements (most modern binoculars are of this design). The older, Porro prism binoculars have an extra chamber on each barrel. If your grandfather had a pair of binoculars, they were of this design. Most of today's birders use roof prism binoculars, even though they tend to be more expensive. They are more comfortable to hold, more durable, offer better protection against water damage, and usually have better close-focusing capabilities.

If you have $300 to $500 to spend, you will be able to purchase an excellent new pair of binoculars. If your budget is well short of that, I urge you to seriously consider purchasing a used pair. The quality of a used pair in good condition will almost certainly be better than that of a cheap new pair. I would certainly not purchase anything new for less than $100. Many birders have spent years in the game and have accumulated several pairs of optics. A request on New Hampshire's birding listserv would be a good place to start looking for a quality used pair. (See Web Resources.)

If money is no object, you can spend several thousand dollars on top of the line binoculars. Before you splash the cash, remember that, although optical quality improves with price, it is not a steadily increasing curve. Once past the $500 mark, the rate of improvement declines rather quickly for every extra dollar spent. For example, a pair of binoculars that costs $300 will generally be significantly better than a pair that costs $60, but you are unlikely to see a similar leap in quality by spending $1,000 rather than $300.

Once you have figured out how much you want to spend, you can further refine your search by deciding how powerful you want your binoculars to be. The two numbers that describe every pair of binoculars refer to the magnification and the size of the objective lens. Common combinations include 8×30 and 10×40.

The first number in the combination describes magnification: the higher the number, the more powerful the binoculars, thus 10×40 binoculars are more powerful than 8×40 binoculars.

The second number describes the size of the objective lens in millimeters. A pair of binoculars with a larger objective lens gathers more light and produces a brighter image than an otherwise identical pair with a smaller objective lens. This is an important consideration if you will be birding in low light conditions, early or late in the day or during winter.

More expensive models also can increase light-gathering ability by incorporating special low-dispersion glass in their design; this is a worthwhile investment if you can afford it. Otherwise, a balanced approach is recommended, one that considers power, brightness, and weight. High-powered binoculars can perform poorly in low light conditions and can be difficult to hold steady, while binoculars with bigger objective lenses tend to be large and heavy. My preference is for more brightness rather than more power. There are many cheap but "powerful" models with small objective lenses, for instance, 10×25. Stay away from them. They might suffice as a back-up pair, but not as a first choice.

You should now be ready to enter a store and test several models. As you compare them, consider the following properties.

IMAGE QUALITY This is the most important characteristic of a pair of binoculars. Look for brightness, which is easier to gauge under low light conditions. Look for sharpness, especially toward the edge of the field of view. Pay attention to the color of the image. Some optics impart a color cast to an image, often yellow or blue.

FIELD OF VIEW This is the width of the area that you can see through the binoculars. A narrow field of view makes it more difficult to find a bird, which can be especially troublesome for fast-moving species like warblers.

DEPTH OF FIELD This is the distance between the nearest and farthest objects that remain in focus. If the image is out of focus immediately in front of and behind the object you are looking at, the binoculars have a narrow depth of field. This can be frustrating if you are following moving birds because you will have to keep refocusing.

FOCUSING How many rotations of the focus wheel does it take to get from minimum to maximum focus? The fewer rotations the better—you want to spend more time looking at the bird and less time fiddling with your binoculars.

CLOSE FOCUS If you also plan on looking at butterflies, for example, you will need binoculars that focus at distances as close as 8 feet or less.

EYE RELIEF This is especially important if you wear eyeglasses, because you will need to be able to adjust the distance between your glasses and the binoculars. Some models feature retractable eyecups, but these often are poorly designed. Check to make sure that the eyecups can be easily extended or retracted and that they hold their position when you find the eye relief that works best for you.

WEIGHT Every extra ounce that you feel in the store will be felt doubly in the field. If you are concerned about weight, consider buying a binocular harness to distribute the load more effectively.

TELESCOPES

If you stick with birding, you will eventually want a telescope. Many fascinating aspects of birding are difficult or impossible to enjoy without one, including lakewatching, seawatching, and hawkwatching. Several varieties on the market are totally unsuitable for birding, most obviously astronomical telescopes, which produce an inverted image.

Models suitable for birding don't really come much below $400. High power generally demands high quality (and higher expense), so avoid cheaper scopes that promise 60× magnification or zoom technology. Like higher-quality binoculars, more expensive telescopes also incorporate low-dispersion glass, which transmits more light. These are a good choice if you will be birding in the early morning and late evening, especially in winter, when light levels can be challenging. Regardless of which telescope model you choose, a *good* tripod is essential. Don't skimp on the tripod and put the money saved to a better scope. You will regret it. A good tripod is sturdy, with legs that lock properly, and a head that locks in position, pans smoothly, and allows secure fastening of the scope.

Whether you choose a model with a straight or angled eyepiece is a matter of personal preference. Many top brands offer the same scope in both designs, and there should be absolutely no difference in optical quality between them. An angled eyepiece makes it harder for some people to find the bird, because the eye is not pointing directly at the bird when you are looking through the scope. On the other hand, a straight eyepiece requires the telescope to be raised higher than would be the case with an angled eyepiece. This can increase shake and vibration, though a good tripod should help you avoid that problem. I strongly prefer an angled eyepiece as it is more comfortable on my neck and easier for sharing with a group, but this is a personal choice.

Test several scopes before you buy. Online shopping is only for those who already know what they want. Bird Watchers Supply and Gift on the Route 1 traffic circle in Newburyport, Massachusetts, has been in business for years. The owner is a birder and knows his products. They stock many models and are a good option for a first-time buyer. You can visit the store, test different scopes, and ask for advice. New Hampshire Audubon also sells optics at its Concord location on Silk Farm Road.

Web Resources

The following Web sites offer resources for birdwatchers in New Hampshire and the larger region.

www.ericmasterson.com My personal site, featuring many relevant data about, and images of, New Hampshire's birds, and regional fieldtrips to some of the locations in this guide.

www.nhaudubon.org New Hampshire Audubon is the premier bird conservation organization in the state and offers multiple opportunities to engage with other birders in citizen-science projects. They also sponsor several statewide chapters that offer free programs and field trips. The

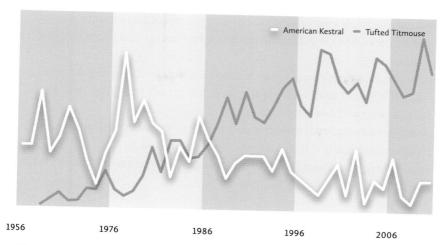

American Kestral — Tufted Titmouse

1956   1976   1986   1996   2006

Christmas Bird Count (CBC) data have documented the decrease of American Kestrel and the increase of Tufted Titmouse in New Hampshire.

Concord location features a store that stocks all bird-related paraphernalia; telephone 603-224–9909.

www.nhbirdrecords.org New Hampshire Bird Records is New Hampshire's definitive ornithological journal.

http://birding.aba.org/maillist/NH NH Birds Google Group is a free online community of the most active birders in the state.

www.audubon.org The National Audubon Society is one of the oldest conservation groups in the United States. Participating in the society's Christmas Bird Count is a great way to learn from more experienced birders, while at the same time conducting useful citizen science to help track the health of our bird populations.

www.pwrc.usgs.gov/bbs/ The Breeding Bird Survey is another terrific citizen science project, but requires considerable field expertise before you will be accepted as a volunteer observer. Joining an established volunteer as a helper is a great way to improve your field skills.

www.ebird.org eBird is an online tool for recording birds, keeping track of bird lists, exploring dynamic maps and graphs, sharing sightings, and contributing to science and conservation.

www.merlinwildlifetours.com This company, based in New Hampshire, specializes in natural history tours.

www.woodcreeper.com Woodcreeper is an excellent and educational site that tracks bird migration along the mid-Atlantic coast using Doppler radar.

www.nhnature.org Squam Lakes Natural Science Center in Holderness offers summer cruises on Squam Lake to see breeding Osprey, Bald Eagle, and Common Loon.

www.reportband.gov The federal government's Patuxent Wildlife Research Center maintains this site for reporting banded birds.

www.aba.org The American Birding Association specifically focuses on the concerns of recreational birders.

NEW HAMPSHIRE BIRD IMAGES

The following sites offer some of the best photographs available of New Hampshire's birds.

www.ericmasterson.com Eric Masterson photography
www.pbase.com/lmedlock/aves Len Medlock photography
www.flickr.com/photos/lmedlock/ Len Medlock photography
www.flickr.com/photos/jlambert614/ Jason Lambert photography
jimhully.smugmug.com Jim Hully photography

WEATHER AND WATER LEVELS

The following sites provide information on weather and water levels that can help you plan your birding activities.

weather.rap.ucar.edu/model/ The National Center for Atmospheric Research provides real-time weather charts.

des.nh.gov/organization/divisions/water/dam/index.htm The New Hampshire Dam Bureau offers information on lake drawdowns around the state.

www.h2oline.com This site provides information on water flows for rivers throughout New Hampshire and the nation.

The water level of Lake Umbagog can be obtained by calling 800-557-3569. Information on water flows and levels in the Connecticut River is available at 800-452-1742. When prompted, enter one of the following six-digit codes.

Station	Code	Information
Connecticut River at Second Connecticut Lake, Pittsburg	335121	(water flow)
Connecticut River at First Connecticut Lake, Pittsburg	335122	(water flow)
Connecticut River at Murphy Dam, Pittsburg	335123	(water flow)
Connecticut River at Moore Dam, Littleton	335124	(water flow)
Connecticut River at Comerford Dam, Monroe	335125	(water flow)
Connecticut River at McIndoes Dam, Monroe	335126	(water flow)
Connecticut River at West Lebanon	331138	(water level)
Connecticut River at North Walpole	331135	(water level)
Connecticut River at Vernon Dam	505123	(water flow)

TRAILS AND ACCESS

These sites offer information on trails in the state, many of which are excellent for birding.

www.nhstateparks.org/explore/bureau-of-trails/recreational-rail-trails.aspx
The New Hampshire Division of Parks and Recreation maintains this portal to the state network of rail trails.

www.nhstateparks.org/explore/state-parks/connecticut-lakes-head waters-working-forest.aspx This site provides information on road closures in the Connecticut Lakes Headwaters Working Forest.

www.fs.usda.gov/whitemountain This U.S. Forest Service site describes road closures in the White Mountain National Forest.

SHOPPING AND ADVICE

www.betterviewdesired.com Offers good advice on optics for birding.
www.birdwatcherssupplyandgift.com This locally owned store (in nearby Newburyport) stocks optics as well as other birding paraphernalia.

Conservation, Birding Ethics, and Birding Safety

Our birdwatching pleasure is dependent on the continued health of bird populations. In New Hampshire and across North America, we have excellent data on our birds thanks to some of the longest running and most innovative bird-monitoring programs on the planet—including the Christmas Bird Count and Breeding Bird Survey—and, more recently, eBird. Birders actively contribute vital data to all of these efforts. The message in New Hampshire is mixed, with many species declining and others increasing (see chapter 8). At least three species that formerly occurred in New Hampshire are now extinct: Great Auk, Eskimo Curlew, and Passenger Pigeon. A fourth extinct species, the Labrador Duck, though never documented, was likely a winter visitor off our coast.

As we approach the centenary of the demise of the world's last Passenger Pigeon—it died at the Cincinnati Zoo on September 1, 1914—laws have been enacted to prevent new extinctions. Yet the overall picture remains troubling, with many of our birds in varying stages of decline. This is often due to factors that occur outside the United States, in countries where our birds spend the winter. Many of these changes happen over too long a span to be detected by any individual eye or ear. We must rely on long-term studies, for example, to tell us that Wood Thrush has declined by at least 40 percent over the past 50 years (Poole 2005). Other changes have been more dramatic. There are still a few active birders who remember when Golden-winged Warblers bred in New Hampshire. The next generation will likely not be so lucky, as the species has largely disappeared from the state. (I have never seen one in New Hampshire.) American Kestrel, Eastern Meadowlark, Rusty Blackbird, and several more species are following this warbler in the severity and steepness of their declines. Be active in the conservation of birds and their habitat.

THE AMERICAN BIRDING ASSOCIATION'S CODE OF BIRDING ETHICS

Everyone who enjoys birds and birding should respect wildlife, its environment, and the rights of others. In any conflict of interest between birds and birders, the welfare of the birds and their environment comes first.

CODE OF BIRDING ETHICS

1. Promote the welfare of birds and their environment.
   a. Support the protection of important bird habitat.
   b. To avoid stressing birds or exposing them to danger, exercise restraint and caution during observation, photography, sound recording, or filming. Limit the use of recordings and other methods of attracting birds, and never use such methods in heavily birded areas, or for attracting any

species that is Threatened, Endangered, or of Special Concern, or is rare in your local area. Keep well back from nests and nesting colonies, roosts, display areas, and important feeding sites. In such sensitive areas, if there is a need for extended observation, photography, filming, or recording, try to use a blind or hide, and take advantage of natural cover. Use artificial light sparingly for filming or photography, especially for close-ups.

    c. Before advertising the presence of a rare bird, evaluate the potential for disturbance to the bird, its surroundings, and other people in the area, and proceed only if access can be controlled, disturbance minimized, and permission has been obtained from private landowners. The sites of rare nesting birds should be divulged only to the proper conservation authorities.

    d. Stay on roads, trails, and paths where they exist; otherwise keep habitat disturbance to a minimum.

2. Respect the law, and the rights of others.

    a. Do not enter private property without the owner's explicit permission.

    b. Follow all laws, rules, and regulations governing use of roads and public areas, both at home and abroad.

    c. Practice common courtesy in contacts with other people. Your exemplary behavior will generate goodwill with birders and non-birders alike.

3. Ensure that feeders, nest structures, and other artificial bird environments are safe.

    a. Keep dispensers, water, and food clean, and free of decay or disease. It is important to feed birds continually during harsh weather.

    b. Maintain and clean nest structures regularly.

    c. If you are attracting birds to an area, ensure the birds are not exposed to predation from cats and other domestic animals, or dangers posed by artificial hazards.

4. Group birding, whether organized or impromptu, requires special care. Each individual in the group, in addition to the obligations spelled out in Items 1 and 2, has responsibilities as a Group Member.

    a. Respect the interests, rights, and skills of fellow birders, as well as people participating in other legitimate outdoor activities. Freely share your knowledge and experience, except where code 1(c) applies. Be especially helpful to beginning birders.

    b. If you witness unethical birding behavior, assess the situation, and intervene if you think it prudent. When interceding, inform the person(s) of the inappropriate action, and attempt, within reason, to have it stopped. If the behavior continues, document it, and notify appropriate individuals or organizations.

SAFETY

The single greatest threat that birding presents to human health is Lyme disease. Lyme disease is widespread in the state and can cause life-changing illness if not taken seriously. First and foremost, focus on prevention before cure. Deer ticks are the vector by which the pathogen enters the human body. Recent tests in Hillsborough and Rockingham Counties have found that 66 percent of deer ticks carry Lyme disease. Some simple steps will help you to avoid getting bitten.

> Unless you have to bushwhack, stick to the paths. Ticks can't jump, so if you do not walk through grass or brush, you can either eliminate or seriously reduce the number of ticks that attach themselves to you.

> Wear long pants and long-sleeved shirts, preferably of light coloring, so you can more easily spot any ticks that find you. Clothes treated with permethrin will further discourage ticks.

> Check yourself after you come in from the field. A tick must be attached to your skin for at least 24 hours before the Lyme bacterium can be transmitted.

If you have reason to believe that you have been bitten by a tick, seek treatment as soon as possible. Early diagnosis and treatment of Lyme disease can lead to a full recovery. Late treatment—or no treatment at all—puts you at risk of developing chronic and potentially life-threatening symptoms.

1 Monthly Guide to the Best of New Hampshire Birding

January

Birding is not at its best in January, but the Superbowl of Birding is a fun way to beat the winter blues and get out with friends in some of the best areas in southeastern New Hampshire. This friendly competition is run by the Massachusetts Audubon Society's Joppa Flats Education Center. Prizes are awarded for most points scored (different species are worth different point totals) in New Hampshire's Rockingham County or Massachusetts' Essex County. See the Mass Audubon Web site (www.massaudubon.org) for details.

February

If you can get out to Jeffreys Ledge toward the end of the month, the number of alcids—including Razorbills, Black Guillemots, and Atlantic Puffins—can be impressive. Access can be difficult during winter, however, and late fall offers more dependable conditions for similar birds (see November).

March

From mid-March through the end of the month, waterfowl migration north through the Connecticut River Valley is outstanding. Several rare species are more likely to be found here than elsewhere in New Hampshire, including Greater White-fronted Goose and Cackling Goose. New Hampshire's first records of Barnacle Goose and Pink-footed Goose were discovered in Hinsdale and Walpole, respectively. The farm fields on both sides of the river, from Hinsdale north to Charlestown, are especially productive. About 25 species of waterfowl are recorded each spring. The Merrimack River Valley and the coast also are excellent at this time, especially the agricultural fields at the Big Bend in Boscawen, Moore Fields in Durham, Great Bay, and Meadow Pond in North Hampton.

April

Waterfowl migration continues into April and is so spectacular that it warrants repeat mention. Some southeastern spots peak in April, including Meadow Pond in Hampton for Green-winged Teal and Powwow Pond in Kingston for Ring-necked Duck. Later in the month, northward migration of Brant, Common Loon, Double-crested Cormorant, and Northern Gannet can be impressive along the coast. April also is when the North Country awakens, especially for waterfowl.

May

The arrival of songbirds from their tropical winter homes peaks in May, typically during the middle of the month. Nowhere in the state is this phenomenon more evident than on Star Island, one of the Isles of Shoals. Nocturnal migrants such as warblers, tanagers, and buntings that find themselves over the ocean as dawn breaks must find the nearest landmass to rest and refuel. The concentration of songbirds on the island is often an order of magnitude greater than at similar locations along the coast. Additionally, there are few large trees on the island in which the birds can hide. Most are so busy feeding that they pay little attention to birdwatchers, allowing the sort of breathtaking views that seldom occur at breeding sites in the interior of the state. Access in May is usually by private charter, with scheduled ferries sometimes available later in the month (see chapter 5).

June

June is a great time to visit the White Mountains and the North Country, including Mount Washington, Pondicherry Wildlife Refuge, Umbagog National Wildlife Refuge, and East Inlet Wildlife Management Area. Pondicherry, located in Jefferson and Whitefield, is one of the crown jewels of New Hampshire's landscape. This 6,000-acre preserve of boreal habitat, fashioned around Cherry and Little Cherry Ponds, includes spruce-fir forest and black spruce–tamarack bog and is a mecca for boreal species (238 species of birds have been recorded). Farther north, Umbagog National Wildlife Refuge in Errol is another northern gem, boasting outstanding habitat for waterbirds and northern boreal specialties. Harper's Meadow, on the western shore of

A Magnolia Warbler on Star Island, May 14, 2011. *Eric Masterson*

the lake, has been designated a National Natural Landmark for its exemplary floating bog. Close to the Canadian border, East Inlet in Pittsburg is a relatively easy place to observe New Hampshire's boreal specialties, particularly for those who don't want to hike the White Mountains. All boreal species that occur in the state have been seen from the area's forest roads, and it is probably the most reliable spot in the state to find Spruce Grouse (though even here it is not guaranteed). June also is the best month to find Bicknell's Thrush in New Hampshire, most easily from the Mount Washington Auto Road or the Cannon Mountain aerial tram.

July

July is the best month to visit the tern restoration project on White and Seavey Islands at the Isles of Shoals, the nesting site of 2,500 pairs of Common Terns, several dozen pairs of federally listed Roseate Terns, and a handful of Arctic Terns. Visits are by specially arranged charter or private transport (see chapter 5).

August

Thirty-four species of shorebirds occur annually in New Hampshire, the majority just passing through on their way to and from their breeding grounds in the boreal forest and the Arctic. In fall, their numbers are swelled by southbound juveniles. Though New Hampshire's short coastline is heavily developed, there are several locations where the incredible diversity and abundance of these birds can be witnessed, including Hampton Harbor and Plaice Cove in Rye.

September

Jeffreys Ledge may be less well known than Stellwagen Bank to the south, but this relatively shallow, offshore bank is comparable in terms of marine life. Early September is a good time to spend a half-day on a whalewatching boat, in search of both whales and birds. Up to four species of shearwaters,

Sedge Wren on Star Island, October 16, 2011. This was the only
New Hampshire record of the year for this rare species. *Eric Masterson*

Wilson's Storm-Petrel, Red-necked and Red Phalarope, all three jaegers, and Atlantic Puffin are among the possibilities in September. The whale show can be even more impressive: Humpback, Fin, and Minke Whales are regularly sighted, while Sei and Northern Right Whales are seen occasionally, and even Blue Whales have been spotted. (See chapter 5.)

Hawk migration is equally compelling in September. Each year about 10,000 eagles, hawks, and falcons pass by New Hampshire Audubon's raptor observatory atop Pack Monadnock in Miller State Park. About 60 percent of Broad-winged Hawks pass the mountain between September 16 and 19, and every year several thousand birds are seen from the observatory on one "Big Day." For birders, it's a matter of rolling the dice and trying to hit the jackpot. Mark these dates on your calendar; when the time approaches, you can improve your odds by watching the weather. Choose a day during this window that is calm and clear, or with light winds out of the north, and you'll have a good chance of success. If you cannot make it to Pack Monadnock, there are several other good hawkwatching sites in New Hampshire, including Little Round Top in Bristol, Carter Hill in Concord (8,000 hawks in fall of 2011), Pitcher Mountain in Stoddard, and Little Blue Job in Strafford. Alternatively, find a spot near your home that has an unobstructed view to the north, and establish your own hawkwatch site.

October

Star Island in October is probably the best location—at the best time—for seeing vagrant birds in New Hampshire, for the same reasons that I described under "May." October access is by special charter only (see chapter 5). The mainland coast, especially Odiorne Point, is the next best option.

November

Severa species of alcids, those endearing birds of the open ocean, breed in vast colonies in Canada and Greenland. In winter, they venture south to the relatively hospitable environment of the Gulf of Maine. They arrive in November, when a visit to Jeffreys Ledge with Eastman's (www.eastmansdocks.com) is often rewarded with views of Dovekie, Common Murre, Razorbill, and Atlantic Puffin. Other seabirds, such as Northern Fulmar and Black-legged Kittiwake, are common as well. This trip also is recommended in February, but transport is more reliable during November. For best results, pick a calm day with wind, if any, out of the west or northwest and less than 10 knots.

December. Join your local Christmas Bird Count, a great way to round out the year, meet fellow birdwatchers, and contribute to the longest-running citizen science project in the world. (See Web Resources.)

2 The Connecticut River Valley

Overview

The Connecticut River links four of New England's six states along its 410 miles, starting at the northern tip of New Hampshire's border with Maine. It flows southward between New Hampshire and Vermont, then through Massachusetts and Connecticut, finally reaching the Atlantic Ocean at Long Island Sound. Like Interstate 91, the river provides a direct north-south corridor through New England—but for birds, not humans. Birds are known to navigate using a variety of methods. Some species use their sense of smell, while others navigate using the earth's magnetic field, but all use visual cues. When the weather is fair, the river valley provides a clear route north in spring and south in fall, even from an altitude of thousands of feet.

The state line between New Hampshire and Vermont follows the low-water mark on the Vermont side of the river. Although most birds seen on the water therefore will be in New Hampshire, several viewing sites included in this guide actually are located in Vermont, including Brattleboro Retreat Meadows, Albee's Cove, Herrick's Cove, Roundy's Cove, White's Cove, and Ompompanoosuc River Flats.

SPRING MIGRATION

The area offers some of the finest birding in New Hampshire, with the section that stretches from the Massachusetts border to Charlestown as good as any. The agricultural fields on both banks provide excellent foraging habitat for waterfowl in the spring. About 25 species of goose and duck are recorded every year, usually including some rare birds like Greater White-fronted Goose, Cackling Goose, Canvasback, or Redhead. This area also furnished the first state records for both Pink-footed Goose and Barnacle Goose.

The Connecticut River would stand out as one of the best spots in the state purely on the basis of the waterfowl migration, but the birding continues to

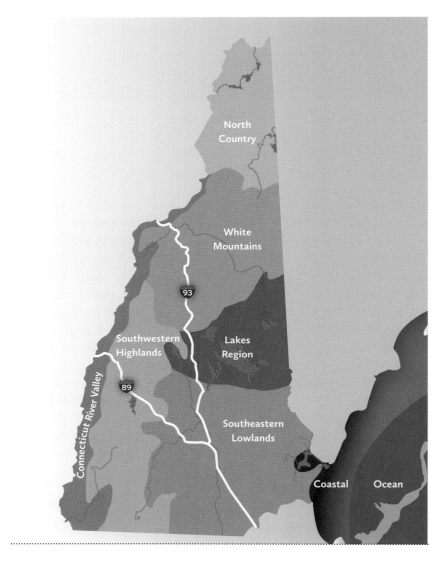

BIRDING REGIONS OF NEW HAMPSHIRE

Canada Goose GJN, with other Canada Geese and some Greenland Greater
White-fronted Geese, in enclosure before banding, Isunngua, Greenland, July 17, 2008.
Greenland White-fronted Goose Study

be excellent right through early June, when swallows, warblers, shorebirds, and terns begin to move north through the valley. By the time that spring gives way to summer, about 165 species of migrant birds will have graced the river or its adjacent fields and woodlands, with about 120 of these staying to breed in the river's marshes, floodplain forests, and other habitats.

WATERFOWL Beginning in late February and early March, the flocks of Canada Geese, Green-winged Teal, and other waterfowl that have crowded mid-Atlantic coastal marshes during winter heed the call of impending spring and start to head north. Though many follow the Atlantic coastal plain, others take an inland route along the Connecticut River Valley. Most birds that pass through the area are heading to various parts of Canada: Quebec, New Brunswick, Nova Scotia, Newfoundland, or Labrador, depending on the species. Some individual Canada Geese continue as far north as Greenland.

On March 22, 2011, in a field in Walpole, I spotted a Canada Goose that sported a yellow neck collar inscribed with the letters GJN. I sent this information to the U.S. Fish and Wildlife Service at www.reportband.gov; several

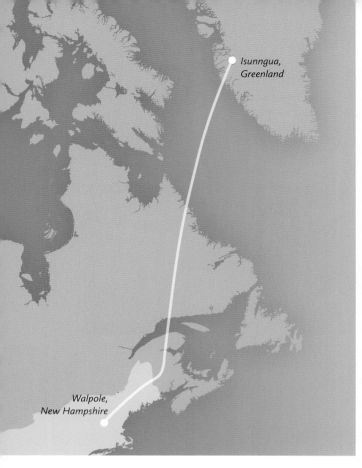
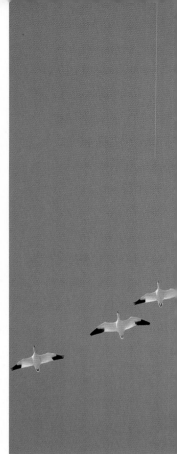

Likely track of Canada Goose GJN between Walpole, New Hampshire, and Isunngua, Greenland.

months later, I received word from a professor at the University of Aarhus in Denmark. His team had banded the bird in western Greenland on July 17, 2008. It is one thing to understand in the abstract that Canada Geese breed in Greenland, but another thing entirely to see a goose in a Walpole field, then discover that it had been born 3,500 miles away, across two time zones and three countries.

Peak time for waterfowl runs from mid-March through early April, earlier when the winter is mild, later when it is severe.

SHOREBIRDS AND TERNS The Connecticut River Valley is probably the best place in New Hampshire to find Black Tern in spring, and the best area for Common Tern away from the coast. Common Terns spend the winter in

Snow Geese above Walpole, March 22, 2011.
Eric Masterson

the Caribbean and along the coast of South America; in summer they nest primarily in coastal areas of North America. Inland nesting is less common, but there are a few breeding sites in Vermont, Maine, and New York. Inland-breeding terns use the river as a highway to their final destinations. Where each individual is headed is anyone's guess, unless you get lucky and find a banded bird—as I did on May 18, 2011. I reported band number 1322-09499 to the U.S. Fish and Wildlife Service and a few days later received an e-mail informing me that the bird, a Common Tern, had originally been banded as a chick on July 11, 2008, 6 miles west of Massena. The location, in St. Lawrence County, New York, is a relatively modest 194 miles northwest of Hinsdale "as the crow flies." (It's a bit longer as the tern flies, though not the 293-mile route recommended by MapQuest.)

Caspian Tern is becoming a more regular occurrence, with 4 birds seen in May 2012. Arctic Tern has been recorded twice here in spring. This species is one of the world's great long-distance migrants, wintering in the Antarctic and breeding as far north as northern Greenland. Mid-May is the peak time for all species of terns in the river valley. During inclement weather, there is an excellent chance of finding Black or Common Terns between Hinsdale and Charlestown, especially at Hinsdale Setbacks, Retreat Meadows, or Herrick's Cove. Spofford Lake also draws many of the same species and has an excellent record of hosting Black Tern, Common Tern, and Bonaparte's Gull in spring.

Shorebirds migrate north during the same period as the terns, and can be brought to ground by the same weather conditions, making for a potentially excellent day in the field. At least 27 species of shorebird have been recorded along the Connecticut River in Vermont and New Hampshire, including such regional rarities as Upland Sandpiper, Hudsonian Godwit, Marbled Godwit, Ruff, Ruddy Turnstone, Sanderling, White-rumped Sandpiper, Purple Sandpiper, Stilt Sandpiper, Buff-breasted Sandpiper, Wilson's Phalarope, Red-necked Phalarope, and Red Phalarope.

Water level can affect shorebird occurrence, although terns pay it no heed. When the river is low, Herrick's Cove and the cove just north of Bellow's Falls (both in Vermont) provide excellent habitat. Retreat Meadows in Brattleboro, Vermont, also requires low water to offer the best shorebird habitat. When the river is high during bad weather, birds are likely to lay over in one of the many stubble fields that line the riverbanks. They also will rest on pieces of driftwood.

OTHER SPECIES Peak time for the Rough-legged Hawk is the same as that for waterfowl: from mid-March through early April. A close cousin of the more common Red-tailed Hawk, Rough-legged Hawk breeds in the far northern tundra zone and winters across the northern United States. They are relatively common in coastal areas of Massachusetts, especially the Parker River National Wildlife Refuge on Plum Island, but remain uncommon in New Hampshire.

Warbler migration peaks in May. Though they do not have an aquatic lifestyle like waterfowl or shorebirds, they do use the river as a migration corridor. Herrick's Cove and the rail trail in Hinsdale are excellent spots to observe spring warbler migration.

Black Tern and Common Tern along the Connecticut
River, Hinsdale, May 18, 2011. *Eric Masterson*

Short-billed Dowitcher at Herrick's Cove on the Connecticut
River, May 24, 2011. *Eric Masterson*

Dunlin resting on a piece of driftwood, Hinsdale, October 20, 2011. *Eric Masterson*

FALL MIGRATION

In late summer, Great Egrets—which breed as close as Massachusetts—bring a touch of the tropics to the region. In fall, this species engages in a behavior known as post-breeding dispersal, whereby both young and adult birds, released from the territorial bonds of nesting, move away from the nesting area once the young have fledged. This provides the birds with an opportunity to explore new feeding and nesting areas for future colonization. You might find an egret in your local beaver marsh, but the Connecticut River proper is the best bet, where they can be observed wading knee-deep in pickerelweed, searching out fish and amphibians alike.

Look for southbound shorebirds beginning in mid-July. They will occur in the same places described in the section on spring migration. Herrick's Cove, on the Vermont side, is one of the best spots for shorebirds along this stretch of river; in recognition of its value to migrating and breeding birds, it has been named an Important Bird Area (IBA).

Shorebirds can be viewed from Herrick's Cove park itself, although I prefer to observe the flats from a nearby bluff. Pull off to the side of Route 5 just south of the intersection with Route 103 and walk out to the bluff overlooking the river. This will give you an unobstructed view of the whole area, though a telescope is needed here.

There is another good site for shorebirds just south of Herrick's Cove. Go south on Route 5 for 2 miles, then turn left into the parking lot of the Joy Wah Chinese restaurant. There will be a variable amount of good shorebird habitat—depending on the water level—viewable from the parking lot. This area is also known as Albee's Cove.

The lagoons at the Charlestown Wastewater Treatment Plant in New Hampshire are worth checking, especially if the river is high. Shorebirds can be difficult to spot along the pond edges but, if you look closely during August and September, you should be able to find a few Least Sandpipers, in addition to the more common Killdeer and Spotted Sandpiper. Black-bellied Plover,

Pectoral Sandpiper, Red-necked Phalarope, and Red Phalarope also have been seen here in fall.

Although most agricultural fields are still under corn during the fall shorebird migration, any field where the corn has been cut will provide suitable habitat, especially for later migrants like American Golden-Plover and Pectoral Sandpiper. Look especially for the ponds that form after heavy rains. A cornfield in Westminster Station, Vermont, held a large mixed flock of shorebirds in the fall of 2011, including Semipalmated Sandpiper, White-rumped Sandpiper, Pectoral Sandpiper, and a single Stilt Sandpiper, an extremely rare bird in the interior of New England.

Hinsdale to Brattleboro

The area from Hinsdale, New Hampshire, to Brattleboro, Vermont, includes Vernon Dam, Hinsdale Setbacks, and Wantastiquet Mountain Natural Area (all in New Hampshire), and Brattleboro Retreat Meadows in Vermont.

VERNON DAM AND HINSDALE SETBACKS

This area offers a combination of excellent birding and easy walking along an old rail bed. The trails are well maintained and usually dry. Depending on where you park (at the boat launch, Hinsdale High School, or the end of River Road), the walk to the dam can take up to 45 minutes at a leisurely pace. The birding is excellent along the way. From spring through summer, area specialties include Blue-gray Gnatcatcher, Yellow-throated Vireo, and Orchard Oriole. The last is most easily found in the trees around the bluffs overlooking Lake Wantastiquet (the name for the body of water above the dam).

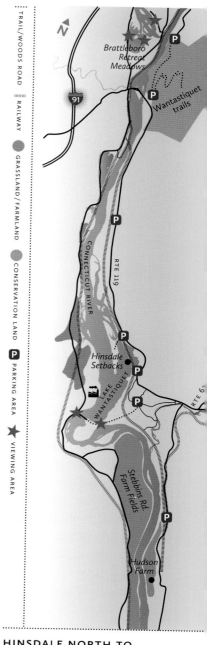

HINSDALE NORTH TO BRATTLEBORO, VERMONT

Bald Eagle carrying nesting material, Vernon Dam,
March 21, 2011. *Eric Masterson*

The bluffs are also excellent sites to scan for waterfowl during winter and
spring, especially at dusk, when the birds fly in from fields off Stebbins Road
in Vermont. A pair of bald eagles has bred nearby for several years and they
are usually seen perched in one of the trees lining the river.

The rail trail continues north and south of Hinsdale Setbacks for several
miles. For a great one-way walk, leave a car at the boat launch and another
at the gas station about 3 miles north on Route 119. You also can walk south
of the boat launch for a similar distance; the trail ends at a gravel parking
lot off Route 63.

In addition to the species mentioned previously, Red-bellied Woodpeckers are common at this site, and Rough-winged Swallows often breed in
the stone embankment near the boat launch. Eastern Screech-Owl also is
reliably encountered here at night, though usually only by call. In fact, this
is one of the more reliable places to hear them in New Hampshire, outside
the coastal plain.

At the north end of Hinsdale Setbacks, a side trail leads into the cattail
marsh opposite the Vermont Yankee nuclear power plant. This is an excellent

Rough-winged Swallow, Hinsdale Setbacks, April 26, 2010.
Eric Masterson

spot for a variety of birds, including Virginia Rail, Willow Flycatcher, and Marsh Wren. Ospreys have bred on the high-voltage pylons, and Peregrine Falcons can often be seen perched on the towers or on the smokestack on the opposite side of the river.

About 3.5 miles south of Hinsdale along Route 63, just before a sharp curve in the road, you reach Hudson Farm on the right (west) side of the road. This is an excellent spot for birding in September and October. Dickcissel is a regular here in fall, and Grasshopper Sparrow also has occurred, with large numbers of the more common species.

WANTASTIQUET MOUNTAIN NATURAL AREA

This is one of two sites in New Hampshire where Cerulean Warbler still occurs regularly. (The other is Pawtuckaway State Park in Nottingham and Raymond.) The trailhead is at the end of Mountain Road, which is off Route 119 immediately north of Walmart but before the bridge. A gentle 1.7-mile trail leads to the top of Wantastiquet Mountain in a series of switchbacks. The Cerulean Warblers have traditionally been found within the first half-mile. Also watch and listen for Prairie Warbler and Eastern Towhee under the power lines, and Dark-eyed Junco toward the summit of the mountain.

Do *not* use sound recordings to lure Cerulean Warblers. They are declining nationally and extremely rare in New Hampshire.

BRATTLEBORO RETREAT MEADOWS

This site includes an expanse of shallow water, with varying amounts of exposed mud, at the confluence of the West River and the Connecticut River. The area is excellent for waterfowl during spring, less so in fall, and occasionally holds birds into the winter when the weather is mild. Cackling Goose is usually recorded once or twice annually.

Brattleboro Retreat Meadows also is one of the best spots in the Connecticut River Valley for shorebirds. Semipalmated Plover, Killdeer, Spotted Sandpiper, Solitary Sandpiper, Greater Yellowlegs, Lesser Yellowlegs, Semipalmated Sandpiper, and Least Sandpiper are all regularly observed, with Black-bellied Plover and Dunlin occuring less commonly.

Black Vultures have been seen several times, particularly in spring. During winter, the surrounding fields, as well as the islands in the middle of the river, often host Northern Shrike. Just north of the boat launch on Vermont's Route 30, a gated access road leads to the Brattleboro Wastewater Treatment Plant. The trail along the southern perimeter of the treatment plant is a good area for warblers and sparrows in fall. Nelson's Sparrow has been recorded here several times.

Best viewing of the meadows is by scope from the marina off Route 9 and Route 5, just north of the bridge, or from the boat launch on Route 30, which runs along the western edge of the meadows.

Westmoreland to Walpole

The area from Westmoreland to Walpole includes Westmoreland Chickering Farm, Walpole Chickering Farm, and Malnati Farm.

WESTMORELAND CHICKERING FARM

There are two Chickering farms, both excellent for birding. The Westmoreland farm is located on the west side of Route 63, three-quarters of a mile north of the junction with River Road. You can park along the edge of Chickering Road, a dirt road that borders the southern edge of the large cornfield.

The best birding is in fall, when the weedy edges and ditches are a magnet for sparrows. Dickcissel has been an annual visitor here in recent years, and "Ipswich" Savannah Sparrow and Nelson's Sparrow also have been recorded. The fields are excellent for Horned Lark and American Pipit during migration and occasionally through the winter, when they may be joined by Snow Bunting and Lapland Longspur.

The Connecticut River Valley is a good location for Rough-legged Hawk, especially the fields between Westmoreland Chickering Farm and the junction with Route 12. I have most often seen them hunting in the fields immediately north of Goodrums Crossing in late winter and early spring.

WALPOLE CHICKERING FARM

Walpole Chickering Farm provides habitat for the same species as the Westmoreland farm. It tends to be better for waterfowl, especially at its southern end, which often floods in spring. In addition to the common ducks and geese, Eurasian Wigeon has occurred here, one of the only state records for this species away from Great Bay.

North of Walpole Chickering Farm, also on River Road, is Boggy Meadow Farm. This is an excellent spot in winter for Horned Lark and Snow Bunting. During the winter of 2010–11, a flock of 1,000 Snow Buntings frequented the area.

MALNATI FARM

This Walpole farm is one of the best spots along the Connecticut River for waterfowl in spring. The creek that runs through the farm often floods at this time, creating excellent habitat for dabbling ducks, especially Wood Ducks, which

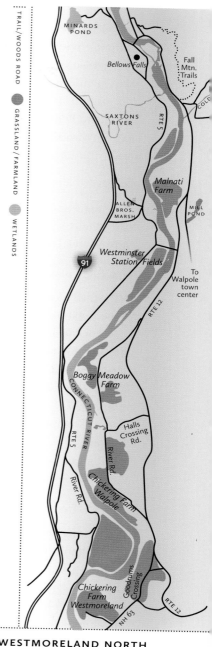

WESTMORELAND NORTH TO WALPOLE

can occur in abundance in late March. A greater diversity of geese has been recorded here than at any New Hampshire site other than Moore Fields in Durham: at least five species, including Pink-footed Goose, Greater White-fronted Goose, and Cackling Goose. Glossy Ibis—perhaps as rare as the aforementioned geese in this part of New Hampshire—has been observed here as well.

Malnati Farm is also one of the more reliable spots, during migration, for Eastern Meadowlark.

Bellows Falls to Charlestown

The area from Bellows Falls, Vermont, north to Charlestown includes Minards Pond, Albee's Cove, Herrick's Cove, Great Meadows, and Charlestown Wastewater Treatment Plant.

MINARDS POND

Waterfowl viewing along the New Hampshire stretch of the Connecticut River is chiefly a spring phenomenon. I suspect this is due in part to hunting pressure—which forces waterfowl to continue south in hopes of finding safer refuge. Minards Pond, just north of Bellows Falls on the Vermont side, is one of the few spots worth checking for waterfowl in the fall. Because the area is closed to hunting, large numbers of waterfowl sometimes collect on the reservoir, including both diving ducks and dabblers. Greater White-fronted Goose, Northern Shoveler, and Ruddy Duck all have been recorded there. To reach Minards Pond, continue north of Bellows Falls along Route 5 for about a half-mile, until you reach Pond Road on the left. Minards Pond is at the end of Pond Road. Best light is in the morning.

ALBEE'S COVE

Continuing north on Route 5, past the junction with Pond Road, you will see a restaurant on your right named Joy Wah. The restaurant's parking area overlooks Albee's Cove, a good spot for diving ducks. During spring and fall, any exposed mud at the mouth of the cove is worth checking for shorebirds. Species seen here include Sanderling and White-rumped Sandpiper, both uncommon in the Connecticut River Valley.

HERRICK'S COVE

Herrick's Cove is ranked as an Important Bird Area, a formal designation that is part of a global effort to save critical habitat for birds. North of Albee's Cove, on the Vermont side, it is one of the best spots on the river for a wide variety of species. If a bird occurs elsewhere on the river, then it can occur here too. There are three main ways to approach the area (four if you have a canoe).

View the cove from the Vermont side. Continue north on Route 5 from Albee's Cove and pull off to the side of the road just before Route 5 joins Route 103. This is an excellent spot from which to scan Herrick's Cove with a scope. The extra elevation (compared to the other two spots) allows you to see parts of the cove that are otherwise hidden from view.

Turn into Herrick's Cove Road and bird the area by foot. The parkland setting makes it an excellent spot to find migrant warblers and other passerines in spring and fall. Yellow-throated Vireo and Orchard Oriole breed here. The extensive cattail marsh supports a good diversity of marshbirds, including Virginia Rail, Sora, and Marsh Wren. Least Bittern, Snowy Egret, and Little Blue Heron have also occurred here. There is a trail that leads from the end of the road to a point that overlooks the cove. You can see most of the cove from here, but any shorebirds using the south mudflats will be obscured from view.

View the cove from the New Hampshire side. On Route 12, about 2.5 miles north of the bridge to Bellows Falls, there is a pull off on the

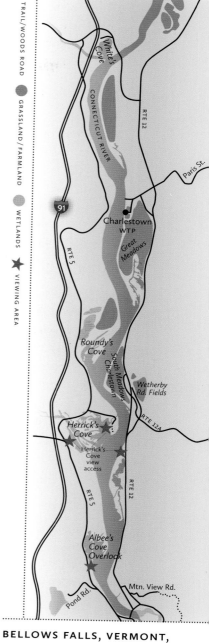

BELLOWS FALLS, VERMONT, NORTH TO CHARLESTOWN

American Kestrel, Great Meadows, Charlestown,
April 9, 2011. *Eric Masterson*

west side of the road. Walk to the edge of the field to set up your scope. Shorebirds, terns, and other birds can be viewed on the mudflats, especially during morning light.

GREAT MEADOWS, CHARLESTOWN

If I had to choose the top three sites along the Connecticut River, I would pick Hinsdale Setbacks, Herrick's Cove, and Great Meadows, with apologies to fans of Retreat Meadows in Brattleboro. Great Meadows is a large farm that includes a habitat type rare in the region: pasture. Spring flooding can make this area especially appealing to waterfowl. Along with Herrick's Cove, it is probably the best spot in the region for the less common dabbling ducks, including Gadwall, American Wigeon, Blue-winged Teal, Northern Shoveler, Northern Pintail, and Green-winged Teal. It is not unusual for more than a hundred Green-winged Teal to crowd the ponds at the south end of the fields during early April. The Eurasian race of Green-winged Teal, called Common Teal, has occurred here several times.

This area is also one of the two best spots for Rough-legged Hawk in the valley (Goodrums Crossing in Westmoreland is the other). Look for this species in late March and early April when birds migrate north en route to their tundra breeding grounds. Great Meadows is an excellent site for American Kestrel during migration as well.

Access to this site is limited, as it is bounded by Route 12 on the east and there is no room for a car to pull to the side of the road. The best strategy is to park at the north end of the field, then walk south along the road with care. There are several spots where you can set up a scope. *Do not park in the driveway of the house at the southern end of the field.* This is private property.

You also can bird this area by walking the trail that runs south from the Charlestown Wastewater Treatment Plant along the Connecticut River. It is a quieter, safer, and more scenic route, although the waterfowl habitat in Great Meadows is not easily visible from this vantage. However, birds often commute between the fields and the river, and I have seen Greater White-fronted Geese from this trail.

CHARLESTOWN WASTEWATER TREATMENT PLANT

Though not the state's best treatment plant for birding, it is still worth visiting, especially in spring and fall. The site is just north of Great Meadows. All three phalaropes have been recorded here, in addition to Black-bellied

Plover, both species of yellowlegs, Pectoral Sandpiper, and Black Tern. A public trail follows the Connecticut River south from the treatment plant.

OTHER SITES

Other good sites along this stretch of river valley include South Meadows and the adjacent fields on Wetherby Road in New Hampshire, as well as Roundy's Cove and White's Cove in Vermont. As you might expect, the numbers of birds using these areas depend both on rainfall and the height of the river.

Fall Mountain, in northern Walpole, is accessed by trails from the end of Mountain View Road. The area is worth checking for Cerulean and Worm-eating Warblers, though neither has been recorded here.

Lebanon to Lyme

The area between Lebanon and Lyme, New Hampshire, includes Wilder Dam, Boston Lot Lake, the Ompompanoosuc River Flats, and Mascoma Lake.

WILDER DAM AND BOSTON LOT LAKE

This is a good site for waterfowl during fall migration. Access is via Passumpsic Avenue and Wilder Dam Road from the Vermont side, or from the parking lot of the TransCanada offices on the New Hampshire side. East Wilder Road offers a somewhat obscured view of the northern part of the impoundment, where ducks tend to congregate in spring. Ring-necked Duck, Greater Scaup, Lesser Scaup, Common Goldeneye, and Red-breasted Merganser are recorded annually, along with the more common species. Scoters are observed in fall, especially in late October. Bald Eagles are frequently seen perched in the larger pines overlooking the area.

A trail to Boston Lot Lake, another good spot for waterfowl in spring and fall, begins at the parking area at the south end of Wilder Dam Reservoir.

OMPOMPANOOSUC RIVER FLATS

Although the Connecticut River south of Charlestown seems to be more productive for waterfowl and shorebirds, there is some excellent habitat in the Upper Valley area, especially at the confluence of the Ompompanoosuc and the Connecticut Rivers, known as the Ompompanoosuc River Flats or "Pompy" Flats. The site is on the Vermont side, a short drive north of White

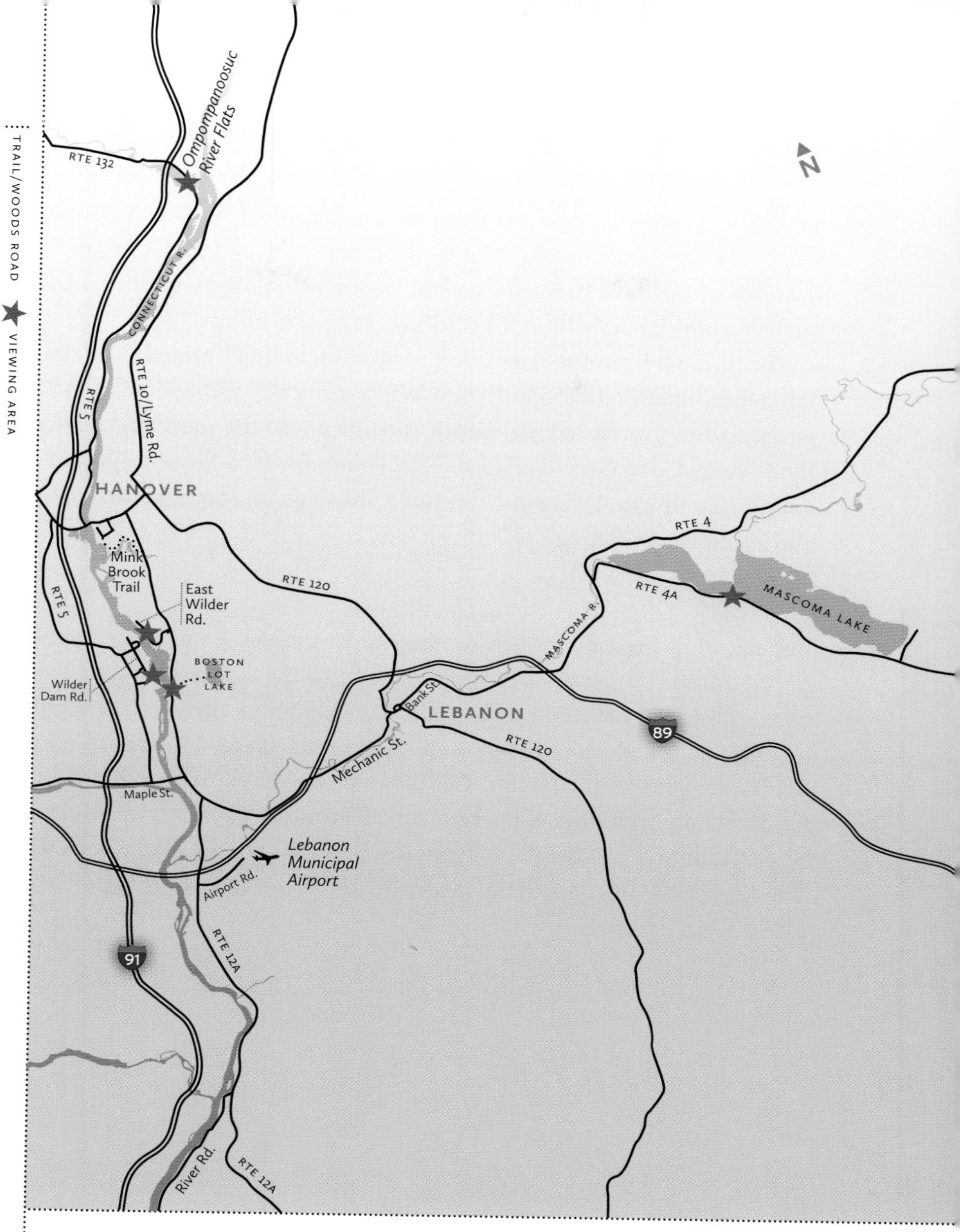

N

RTE 132

Ompompanoosuc River Flats

CONNECTICUT R.

RTE 10/Lyme Rd.

RTE 5

HANOVER

Mink Brook Trail

East Wilder Rd.

RTE 120

Wilder Dam Rd.

BOSTON LOT LAKE

Maple St.

Bank St.

Mechanic St.

LEBANON

RTE 120

RTE 5

RTE 4

RTE 4A

MASCOMA LAKE

MASCOMA R.

89

Lebanon Municipal Airport

Airport Rd.

RTE 12A

91

River Rd.

RTE 12A

CONNECTICUT RIVER VALLEY FROM LEBANON TO LYME

River Junction along Route 5. The water level depends both on precipitation and on regulated outflows from Wilder Dam. TransCanada has a hotline that provides daily updates on the water level at the dam (see Web Resources).

The flats are best viewed with a scope from an old road that leads off Route 5. South of the flats, there are several lagoons along the Connecticut River that also offer good habitat for waterfowl and shorebirds.

The bird list from the flats is impressive, including Tundra Swan, Glossy Ibis, Hudsonian Godwit, Sanderling, White-rumped Sandpiper, Baird's Sandpiper, and Buff-breasted Sandpiper, in addition to the more regularly seen Blue-winged and Green-winged Teal, Semipalmated Plover, Spotted and Solitary Sandpiper, Lesser and Greater Yellowlegs, and Semipalmated, Least, and Pectoral Sandpiper.

MASCOMA LAKE

Because of its location in the Connecticut River flyway, this lake is excellent for migrant waterbirds, as is Spofford Lake to the south. The area was exceptionally well covered by Pam Hunt from 1989 to 2000, and its bird list includes all the expected species, plus rarities such as Red-throated Loon, Black-crowned Night-Heron, Canvasback, Baird's Sandpiper, Little Gull, Iceland Gull, Lesser Black-backed Gull, Glaucous Gull, Common Tern, and Black Tern. Access is primarily from Route 4A, on the lake's southern shore. The northeast side of the lake is heavily developed and there is no viewing access from the road.

3 | Southwestern Highlands

Greater Keene Area

The Greater Keene region includes Green Wagon Farm, Jonathan Daniels Trail, Robin Hood Park, Krif Road, Keene State College Wildlife Management Area, Dillant-Hopkins Airport, Surry Mountain Lake, and Spofford Lake.

GREEN WAGON FARM

This is a good site close to downtown Keene for migrants and birds of open fields. Northern Shrike, Horned Lark, and Snow Bunting are seen here most winters, and there is good scrub habitat for sparrows during migration.

JONATHAN DANIELS TRAIL

Named for Jonathan Daniels, the civil rights leader and Keene native, the trail begins at the junction of Island Street and West Street, then winds north along the Ashuelot River for a little more than a mile, where it joins the Appel Way Trail (not shown). You can exit quickly onto Court Street by taking a right, or turn left and continue on the Appel Way Trail to Wheelock Park, though this section is not as scenic.

ROBIN HOOD PARK

This park includes almost 300 acres of forested conservation land with a trail that loops around a small pond. Here you can find many of the breeding species expected of a southern New Hampshire woodland.

KRIF ROAD AND KEENE STATE COLLEGE
WILDLIFE MANAGEMENT AREA

This is an excellent site, very close to downtown Keene, with a wide variety of habitats. The road ends at some cornfields that offer excellent habitat for shorebirds and waterfowl in spring. Green-winged Teal is a regular here

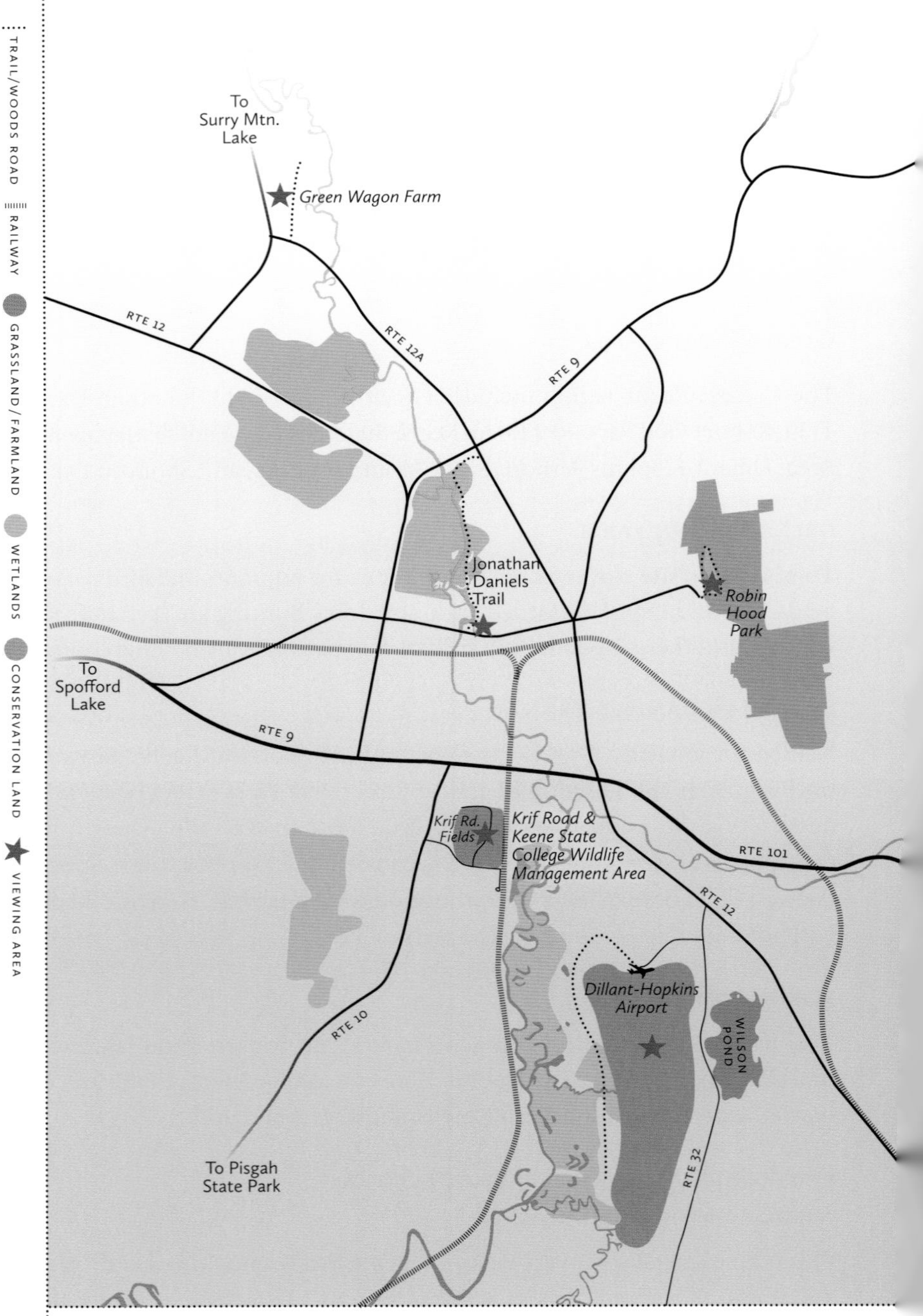
TRAIL/WOODS ROAD
RAILWAY
GRASSLAND/FARMLAND
WETLANDS
CONSERVATION LAND
VIEWING AREA
To
Surry Mtn.
Lake
Green Wagon Farm
RTE 12
RTE 12A
RTE 9
Jonathan
Daniels
Trail
Robin
Hood
Park
To
Spofford
Lake
RTE 9
Krif Rd.
Fields
Krif Road &
Keene State
College Wildlife
Management Area
RTE 101
RTE 12
Dillant-Hopkins
Airport
WILSON
POND
RTE 10
RTE 32
To Pisgah
State Park

KEENE AREA

from March onward. A Common Teal (the Eurasian race of Green-winged Teal) was seen here in the spring of 2007. Spotted and Solitary Sandpiper, Greater Yellowlegs, Least Sandpiper, and Wilson's Snipe occur in May, and are occasionally joined by Lesser Yellowlegs and Dunlin. The birds are usually in the flooded southerly section of the last field before the rail trail.

The gate at the end of Krif Road is sometimes closed to traffic but pedestrians are welcome to pass through. A short walk takes you around the Keene State College athletic fields. This is a good site from spring through fall. Listen for Alder Flycatcher in the Ashuelot Floodplain just past the rail trail. The scrubby habitat under the adjacent power line is excellent for migrant warblers and sparrows; a trail conveniently follows the power line south. By wandering between this location and the Krif Road cornfields in May, an excellent diversity of species can be seen in just a couple of hours.

DILLANT-HOPKINS AIRPORT

New Hampshire's airfields are the last refuge of our rarer grassland birds, and Dillant-Hopkins Airport (aka Keene Airport) in Swanzey is as good as any. American Kestrel, Vesper Sparrow, Grasshopper Sparrow, and Eastern Meadowlark are uncommon in New Hampshire but all probably breed here. Go early in the morning in late May or early June, when the birds are in song. View access is from Route 32 and Airport Road. The grassland specialists such as Grasshopper Sparrow and Eastern Meadowlark can sometimes be seen teed up on weed stalks, or sitting atop one of the directional markers that line the runways. Field and Vesper Sparrows will most likely be found along the edge of the grassland in the scrubby areas. Look also for Brown Thrasher, Prairie Warbler, and Eastern Towhee in this area. On weekends, Airport Road is sometimes gated beyond the terminal, but the walk is a worthwhile 3-mile roundtrip.

SURRY MOUNTAIN LAKE

Surry Mountain Lake is a state park located 6 miles north of Keene on Route 12A. Although it is a bit farther from the Connecticut River than the excellent Spofford Lake, the river valley's influence can still be felt here. There is a marsh at the north end that is reliable for American Bittern in spring and summer and Great Egret in fall. The shallows around the lake's edge, especially bordering this marsh, are worth checking in spring and fall for shorebirds. Watch for Bald Eagles, which breed nearby.

Spofford Lake is one of the most productive lakes for birding in the entire state. I admit I am somewhat biased, as I have birded this area for years, but it is consistently good for Black Tern, Common Tern, and Bonaparte's Gull in spring, and waterfowl in fall. With coverage of the lake on a par with that of Mascoma Lake in the 1990s, it is likely that rarer birds will continue to be recorded. Access is from Route 63 along the western shore, and from Route 9A along the southern shore. Terns and gulls usually occur in the western half of the lake, just north of the island, where they often perch on rocks or buoys.

Monadnock Region

The Monadnock Region includes the Pack Monadnock Raptor Observatory, the Monadnock Highlands, Mud Pond, Tolman Pond, and Howe Reservoir.

PACK MONADNOCK RAPTOR OBSERVATORY

Raptor migration is one of the most fascinating events on the natural history calendar. In New Hampshire, the drama spans three months: September to early November. It peaks quickly, however, due to the early movement of Broad-winged Hawks.

Much of a Broad-winged Hawk's diet consists of cold-blooded animals, including snakes and frogs. With the onset of cooler autumn weather, these creatures become less active, then eventually disappear beneath the forest floor or find refuge at the bottom of ponds. Denied a large part of its diet, the Broad-winged Hawk, or "broadie" as the species is colloquially known, has no option but to leave for warmer climes and is one of the first hawks to head south. They do this in spectacular fashion. The hawks gather on columns of warm air called thermals, which rise out of the sun-baked landscape like natural elevators. Birds crowd together in a dense swirling mass called a kettle, rising upward until the thermal begins to dissipate. They use the altitude gained to glide south to the next thermal, where the process starts over. This technique allows the birds to expend as little energy as possible in their travels, which can range as far south as Brazil.

Many hawks are secretive and difficult to count during the breeding season. Traditional census methods, such as the Patuxent Wildlife Research Center's Breeding Bird Survey, have proven unsuitable for detecting their presence; this is especially true for forest dwellers like Broad-winged Hawk, Red-shouldered Hawk, Sharp-shinned Hawk, Cooper's Hawk, and Northern Goshawk. These species are most easily observed during fall migration, when they follow established and time-tested routes that provide the updrafts and thermals they need to ride south. Biologists across the nation count them from known sites along favored pathways, documenting population increases in some species—notably Merlin, Cooper's Hawk, Osprey, Peregrine Falcon, and Bald Eagle—and decreases in others, such as American Kestrel. These data help wildlife managers make informed management decisions for the different species.

Pack Monadnock is the only staffed raptor observatory in New Hampshire. The site has received complete coverage in September and October since 2005, during which time 9,985 raptors on average have been counted each season, with a low of 6,963 birds in 2005 and a high of 14,256 in 2011. These figures are hugely influenced by the annual numbers of Broad-winged Hawks, which usually account for about 70 percent of the total. Sharp-shinned Hawks are consistently the second most common hawk, with about 1,200 per year. Eleven other species are included in the count, from Golden

Flock of 34 Bonaparte's Gulls with 1 Black Tern, Spofford Lake, May 14, 2010. *Eric Masterson*

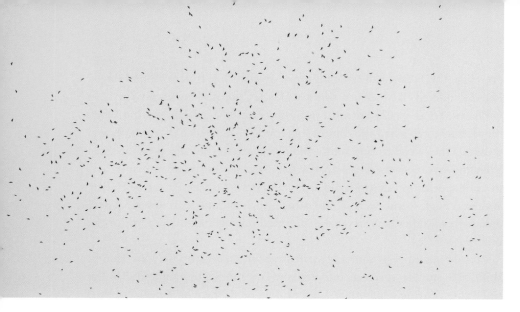

A massive kettle of more than 900 Broad-winged Hawks over my house in Hancock, September 18, 2011. *Eric Masterson*

Eagle (an average of 7 birds per season) to Red-tailed Hawk (an average of 325 birds per season).

The decision facing birders each September is when to skip work to try to witness the big day. There are two factors to consider: date and weather. Data clearly show that Broad-winged Hawk migration in New Hampshire peaks during the third quarter of September. The bell curve is centered on September 18 and, since 2005, two-thirds of the birds have passed the observatory between September 16 and 19. These are the days to keep open on your calendar.

As this window of time approaches, it is important to watch the weather. The best flights come on calm clear days or when winds are light and out of the north. If these conditions follow a run of poor weather, then so much the better, as birds may be backed up to the north. A combination of the right conditions at the right time doesn't occur often but, when it does, the results can be the stuff of legend.

Pack Monadnock Raptor Observatory is located in Miller State Park on the border of Peterborough and Temple. Take the auto road to the top of Pack Monadnock, then follow the trail to the observatory, about 100 yards northeast of the summit. It is open daily from September 1 to October 31, with a small fee payable at the entrance ($4.00 in 2011).

If you can't make it to Pack Monadnock at all, don't fret. I took the picture opposite from my backyard in Hancock. During mid- to late September, hawks will be migrating overhead no matter where you are.

Other good hawkwatching sites in the Monadnock region include Pitcher Mountain in Stoddard and Crotched Mountain in Greenfield, both of which are a short 10-minute hike from the road.

THE MONADNOCK HIGHLANDS

Pine Siskin, Red Crossbill, and White-winged Crossbill can sometimes be found in spruce-fir forest on the higher peaks, especially in winter. Swainson's Thrush used to breed on Mount Monadnock but has not been found in recent years, although reports from North Pack suggest this northerly species might still be hanging on in the area.

Big Flights of Broad-winged Hawks on Pack Monadnock

Date	Number of Hawks
September 14, 2004	1,235
September 18, 2005	1,687
September 11, 2006	3,044
September 13, 2007	1,352
September 16, 2007	2,676
September 17, 2007	2,480
September 11, 2008	1,448
September 18, 2008	2,424
September 16, 2009	2,042
September 18, 2010	3,328
September 19, 2010	1,727
September 17, 2011	3,544
September 18, 2011	5,208
September 12, 2012	2,401
September 17, 2012	2,556
September 20, 2012	1,266

American Bittern in Colburn Meadow, New Boston, April 6, 2009. *Eric Masterson*

MUD POND

As a birding destination, Mud Pond should rank with the more distinguished Cascade Marsh in Sutton. It is an excellent wetland complex, located just southeast of the junction of Route 101 and Route 127 in Dublin. Mud Pond hosts both American Bittern and Virginia Rail. I have no doubt that Sora also occurs, and would not be too surprised if King Rail or Least Bittern were to occasionally occur here as well. The site is best accessed by canoe.

TOLMAN POND

This small nondescript pond in Nelson hosts a large number of Ring-necked Ducks in fall, while other nearby and similar ponds do not (perhaps a suitable thesis topic for a graduate student). The pond is in the heart of the Harris Center for Conservation Education's Super Sanctuary.

Several public trails leading from the Harris Center access the highlands on Mount Skatutakee above Lake Nubanusit. These woodlands are rich in wildlife, including some highland specialists like Purple Finch and Evening Grosbeak.

HOWE RESERVOIR

In late fall, after the water level is lowered, Common Mergansers—and occasionally Bald Eagles—put on a great show on Howe Reservoir. (Lower water levels concentrate the fish on which these species feed.) Counts of 200 Common Mergansers are not uncommon.

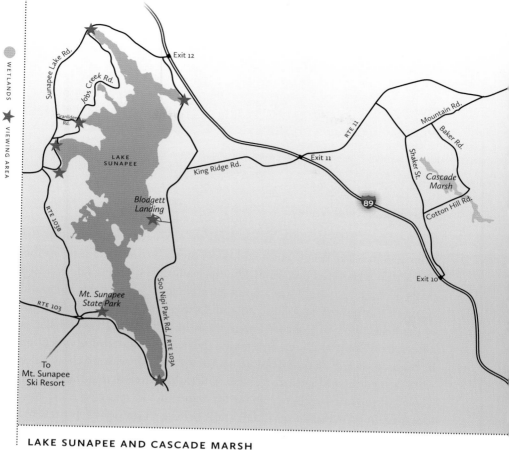

LAKE SUNAPEE AND CASCADE MARSH

Lake Sunapee Region

Lake Sunapee, like the state's other large lakes, is perhaps best considered as a stopover site for migrant and storm-blown waterbirds in spring and fall. The map identifies some productive access points. It's possible that Sunapee is visited by some of the more uncommon species during migration, but birding records for this lake suffer from a lack of coverage.

Cascade Marsh in Sutton is accessible only by canoe but is well worth the effort. A reliable place for marshbirds such as American Bittern, Virginia Rail, and Sora, Cascade Marsh also has a reputation for hosting rarer species, including several records of King Rail and Least Bittern. Canoe access is from Cotton Hill Road.

Merrimack River Valley

The Merrimack River Valley is not quite as productive for birding as the Connecticut River Valley, but it still ranks highly, especially during spring. The action is centered on farm fields, especially during spring floods, when pools of standing water form among the stubble. The best fields are found between Canterbury and Concord and, farther south, in Litchfield. Most of the fields north of Concord are on the west side of the river and can be accessed off Route 3. The exceptions are the fields in Canterbury, which can be reached via Exit 18 on Interstate 93. For a variety of reasons, these fields were farmed for sod until 2012, after which they were planted with corn. They still provide excellent habitat for waterfowl in spring, but are now less appealing for shorebirds in fall. (Buff-breasted Sandpiper has occurred here multiple times.) A trail bisects the eastern end of the field and leads to a second, more southerly field that often has standing water in spring and should be checked for waterfowl and shorebirds.

All of the species that occur in the Connecticut River Valley have the potential to occur along the Merrimack, though when they do show up, they tend to appear in lower numbers. This is especially true of the rarer species. Greater White-fronted Goose and Cackling Goose are seldom recorded, although they are annually seen along the Connecticut. This pattern is likely to be repeated with Pink-footed Goose and Barnacle Goose, which are showing signs of becoming more frequent in the Connecticut River Valley but have yet to show up along the Merrimack. Snow Goose, American Wigeon, Blue-winged Teal, Northern Pintail, and Green-winged Teal usually occur in small numbers every spring.

THE BIG BEND

This is the most notable of the Merrimack sites, and can be accessed from River Road in Boscawen. The best strategy is to bring a scope and walk the old railroad tracks to the west of the field. It is important to be quiet and to move slowly, as waterfowl can be extremely wary. This is the best location in the area for scarce ducks like Gadwall, American Wigeon, and Northern Pintail.

SEWALLS FALLS

The fast section of the Merrimack River at Sewalls Falls rarely freezes. This makes it the best spot in the Concord area to find Common Goldeneye, and occasionally the rarer Barrow's Goldeneye, during winter. Sewalls Falls is at the end of Second Street, which intersects Sewalls Falls Road.

OTHER SITES

There are several other productive fields in the Concord area, including Horseshoe Pond, the Post Office fields, and the fields off West Portsmouth Street. South of Manchester, the fields in Litchfield are right along Route 3A. McQuesten Farm and Wilson Farm are both excellent. Access is by permission.

MERRIMACK RIVER VALLEY FROM CONCORD TO CANTERBURY

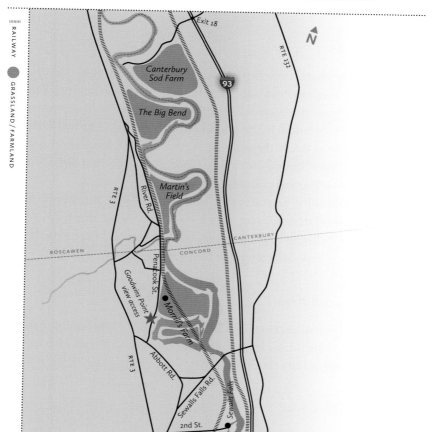

Greater White-fronted Goose with Canada Geese, Meaderboro Road, Farmington, March 9, 2012. *Scott Young*

Sandhill Crane over Moore Fields, Durham, April 17, 2011. *Len Medlock*

All of these fields offer excellent habitat for grassland specialists, including Horned Lark, American Pipit, Lapland Longspur, and Snow Bunting. You can expect to encounter these species in both spring and fall, although longspur is by far the least common of the four in New Hampshire. Horned Lark and Snow Bunting may occur through the winter in small numbers. Look for sparrows and other seedeaters in fall, especially in the Post Office fields, where weeds have grown up around the high-voltage pylons.

A Sandhill Crane has been stopping briefly in the West Portsmouth fields during spring migration for several years in a row. Given this species' longevity, and its fidelity to migration routes, it can reasonably be expected to occur here again, especially as cranes are increasing in the region.

Greater Concord Area

The Greater Concord area includes Turkey Pond, Silk Farm Wildlife Sanctuary, Penacook Lake, Carter Hill Raptor Observatory, Concord Airport, and Birch Street Community Gardens.

TURKEY POND AND SILK FARM WILDLIFE SANCTUARY

Turkey Pond's chief significance is that its birdlife has been documented more thoroughly—and for a longer period of time—than perhaps anywhere else in New Hampshire except Lake Umbagog. A great deal of the surrounding land is owned by St. Paul's School, while New Hampshire Audubon's statewide headquarters and Silk Farm Sanctuary sit on the eastern shore. A procession of ornithologists—including Frances Abbott, Charles Goodhue, Francis Beach White, and Tudor Richards—have recorded a history of the area's birdlife, and that tradition continues to this day. Not surprisingly, the birdlist for the Concord region itself is impressive, numbering more than 275 species. Most of these have been seen at Turkey Pond, including some truly remarkable events. On May 22, 1972 (a calm day), a flock of 16 Black-legged Kittiwakes and 1 Forster's Tern visited the pond.

Concord birder Rob Woodward has conducted a regular census of the birdlife of Turkey Pond for almost a decade. The following table lists the area's ten most common birds in June and December, by order of abundance, based on Rob's data.

Common Birds of Turkey Pond in Order of Abundance

June	December
Veery	Black-capped Chickadee
Common Yellowthroat	Rock Pigeon
Black-capped Chickadee	White-breasted Nuthatch
Red-winged Blackbird	American Goldfinch
Red-eyed Vireo	Blue Jay
American Robin	Tufted Titmouse
Ovenbird	American Robin
Cedar Waxwing	American Crow
Barn Swallow	Hairy Woodpecker
Song Sparrow	Brown Creeper

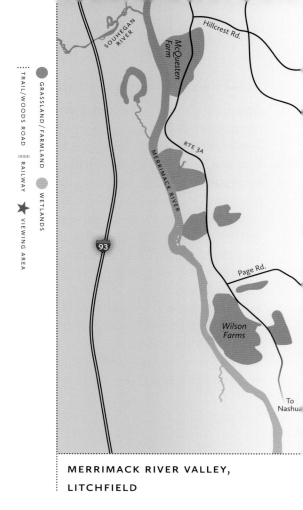

GRASSLAND / FARMLAND ● WETLANDS ●

MERRIMACK RIVER VALLEY, LITCHFIELD

Rob also started an annual Common Nighthawk watch in downtown Concord. Now rare breeders in New Hampshire, Common Nighthawks pass quickly through the state during their fall migration, a strategy not unlike the Broad-winged Hawk's. The peak period in which to see this curious bird includes the last week of August and the first week of September. (Despite its name, this bird is not a hawk but a close relative of the Whip-poor-will.)

Prior to the city's development, much of the area known as Concord Heights provided suitable habitat for this species, where it bred in pine barrens. Recently, a very few have been found nesting in developed areas in Concord, such as construction yards. New Hampshire Audubon is now working to encourage them to nest on flat rooftops that have been prepared with a special gravel substrate, a strategy that has shown promise in other areas.

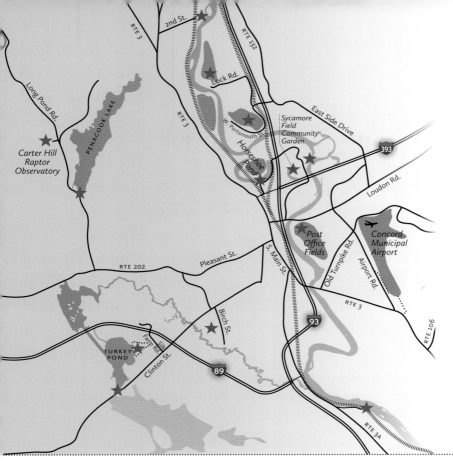

CONCORD AND
SURROUNDING REGION

Apart from the land birds that can be seen throughout the year from the trails on New Hampshire Audubon's Silk Farm Sanctuary, Turkey Pond also is worth checking for waterfowl in spring and fall. Diving ducks like Ring-necked Duck and Lesser Scaup are possible in spring. They tend to occur in the northeastern section of the southern pond (the northern pond is called Little Turkey Pond), and are best observed from the Audubon trails that lead to the shore. Wood Duck and Hooded Mergansers are more common and breed locally.

PENACOOK LAKE

This site deserves mention for the significant waterfowl roost that occurs here in late fall. The waterfowl gather each evening on the lake, when hundreds

Common Nighthawk, East Concord, May 30, 2009.
Eric Masterson

fly in at dusk from surrounding streams and rivers. This continues until the lake freezes. A scope is necessary to view the roost from the southern end of the lake near the junction of Long Pond Road and Lake View Drive.

CARTER HILL RAPTOR OBSERVATORY

About a mile past the junction of Long Pond Road and Lake View Drive, a road on the left leads up to Carter Hill Orchard. New Hampshire Audubon volunteers conduct a raptor observatory on this site during September and October. There is an elevated platform that offers commanding views to the north. Though the site has been in operation for less time than Pack Monadnock, it has had some impressive days. On September 18, 2011, for example, 7,212 Broad-winged Hawks passed by—the highest single-day count of hawks in New Hampshire.

CONCORD AIRPORT

This is a reliable site for all of the state's grassland species except Upland Sandpiper. The most productive way to bird the area is from Airport Road, which flanks the western side of the airfield. There are several areas to pull in and park, and a trail leads alongside the airport boundary fence. Eastern Towhee, Field Sparrow, and Vesper Sparrow often occur in the scrub adja-

Prairie Warbler, Goffstown, May 8, 2009.
Eric Masterson

cent to the fence. One must scan the grassland inside to find Grasshopper Sparrow and Eastern Meadowlark, both of which nest here. Also watch for American Kestrel, Brown Thrasher, and Prairie Warbler, the last especially from the southern access point off Route 3.

BIRCH STREET COMMUNITY GARDENS

This site is one of the largest community gardens in the state and, thanks to the diverse and weed-tolerant practices of the gardeners, it has become an excellent fall location for seed-eating birds. Rarities including Clay-colored Sparrow, Lark Sparrow, Blue Grosbeak, and Dickcissel have occurred in recent years, and it is a reliable site for good numbers of the scarcer sparrows, especially Lincoln's Sparrow and White-crowned Sparrow.

Another large garden, Sycamore Field Community Garden, is located north of Route 393 and can be accessed from College Drive. It has not yet attracted the attention of birders, but should be worth checking in the fall.

Greater Manchester Area

The Greater Manchester area includes Dorrs Pond, Lake Massabesic, and the Massabesic Audubon Center.

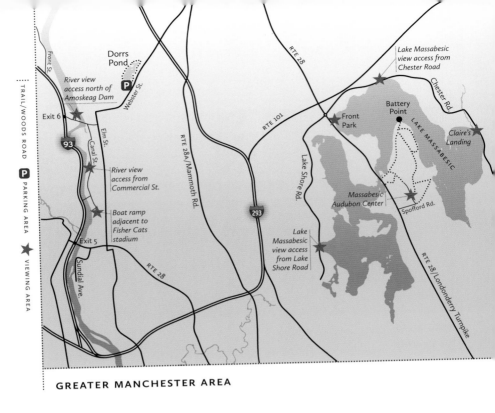

GREATER MANCHESTER AREA

DORRS POND

During the nineteenth century, Dorrs Pond supplied ice to the Manchester market. Today it supplies Manchester's residents and wildlife with 100 acres of sanctuary from the bustling activity of New Hampshire's largest metropolitan area. The pond and surrounding forest are home to most of the expected denizens of a southern New Hampshire oak–white pine forest, including Brown Creeper. Waterfowl occasionally include scarcer species like Northern Pintail.

The boat ramp adjacent to Fisher Cats stadium is a good location in winter for Common Goldeneye. Barrow's Goldeneye, Great Cormorant, Iceland Gull, and Glaucous Gull have all been seen along this stretch of the Merrimack River several times. The view of the river from behind the mill buildings on Commercial Street provides another good opportunity to see both species of goldeneye during winter. During the fall, the river north of Amoskeag Dam hosts diving ducks and, occasionally, scoters.

LAKE MASSABESIC

Lake Massabesic has not been well covered by birders. This is somewhat surprising, given its proximity to a major metropolitan area. Some of the lake's more unusual records include 625 Ruddy Ducks on December 18, 1997; 635 Ruddy Ducks on December 18, 1999; and rare inland records of Forster's Tern on August 25, 2010, and Leach's Storm-Petrel on October 30, 2012.

Diving ducks are regular visitors in the fall, including all three scoters, Long-tailed Duck, Bufflehead, and Common Goldeneye. Other migrants that regularly appear on the lake are Pied-billed Grebe, Horned Grebe, and Red-necked Grebe. A large number of gulls—including Ring-billed, Herring, and Great Black-backed Gulls—use the lake as a roost site; their numbers build in the fall. Counts in excess of 500 birds are not uncommon. Bonaparte's Gull is an occasional fall migrant, and Iceland Gull, Lesser Black-backed Gull, and Glaucous Gull also are likely possibilities.

There are three main access points from which to view the lake; a scope is essential at all of them. Front Park off Route 28, near the traffic circle, is a good spot to watch the gulls come in to bathe and roost in the evening. Fish Crow is occasional at this site. The same stretch of lake also can be viewed from Chester Road. Clair's Landing, south of Auburn, provides views of the eastern expanse of the lake. I have seen large flocks of Black Scoter in this section, and this is where the Forster's Tern occurred. The western portion of the lake is best viewed from Lake Shore Road. All three areas can be equally productive, and if one site has good birds on a particular day, the other sites should be checked as well.

During the fall, it can be worthwhile to check the muddy edges of the lake along Chester Road for shorebirds.

MASSABESIC AUDUBON CENTER

Managed by New Hampshire Audubon, the center provides access to several miles of trails that wind through the Audubon bird sanctuary and the adjacent land (owned by Manchester Water Works). Eastern Bluebirds and other grassland birds are common in the open fields. The trails that lead through the forest to Battery Point provide opportunities to observe Osprey and Bald Eagle, and several pairs of Common Loon nest around the lake.

Forster's Tern, Lake Massabesic, August 25, 2010.
Eric Masterson

Greater Nashua Area

The Greater Nashua area includes Greeley Park, Mine Falls Park, Fields Grove Park, Four Hills Landfill, and Southwest Park.

GREELEY PARK

Greeley Park contains a community garden and offers good fall birding for sparrows and warblers close to Nashua city center. It is located on the east side of Concord Street, 1 mile north of the junction with Amherst Street.

To access a rail trail that runs parallel to the Merrimack River, drive 0.3 miles north of the park and take a right on Hills Ferry Road. A large field just east of the rail trail provides good habitat for grassland and scrub species.

MINE FALLS PARK

The west end of Mine Falls Park was the site of a lead mine. Main access is from Whipple Street (0.3 miles east of Route 3, off Hollis Street) or Coliseum Avenue (0.3 miles west of Route 3, off Broad Street). Though located in a

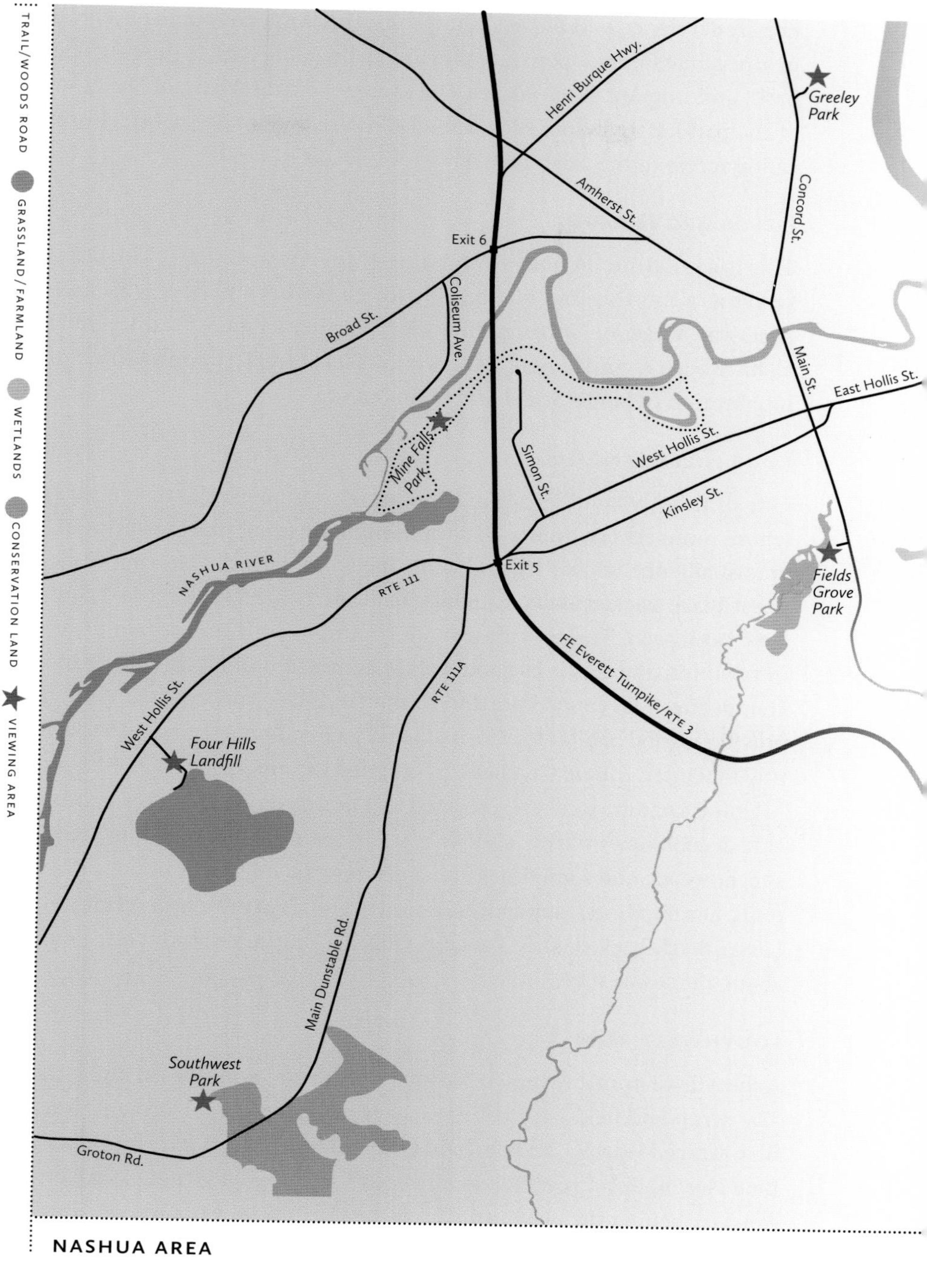

TRAIL/WOODS ROAD
GRASSLAND/FARMLAND
WETLANDS
CONSERVATION LAND
VIEWING AREA
Henri Burque Hwy.
Greeley Park
Amherst St.
Concord St.
Exit 6
Coliseum Ave.
Broad St.
Main St.
East Hollis St.
West Hollis St.
Mine Falls Park
Simon St.
Kinsley St.
NASHUA RIVER
Exit 5
Fields Grove Park
RTE 111
FE Everett Turnpike/RTE 3
RTE 111A
West Hollis St.
Four Hills Landfill
Main Dunstable Rd.
Southwest Park
Groton Rd.

NASHUA AREA

heavily developed part of New Hampshire, this is a good spot to observe birds of forest, marsh, and open water, including breeding Osprey (just outside the park) and migrant Ring-necked Ducks (on the oxbow lake at the east end of the park). Boat launches in Mine Falls Park and on Broad Street provide canoe access to the Nashua River.

FIELDS GROVE PARK

This is a good site in both winter and spring for waterfowl. The park also serves as a roosting and bathing site for gulls from the Four Hills Landfill. American Wigeon, Northern Shoveler, Northern Pintail, and Iceland Gull all have been recorded here. Access is via Field Street, 0.7 miles south of the intersection of Hollis Street and Main Street.

FOUR HILLS LANDFILL

One of the few landfills left in the state, this is an excellent spot for gulls, whose numbers can approach a thousand individuals during winter. There are usually one or two Iceland Gulls mixed in with the Herring Gulls and Great Black-backed Gulls; Laughing Gull and Lesser Black-backed Gull also have been seen. Turkey Vultures are common, with one or two persisting into winter, and this is as good a place as any to find Black Vulture in New Hampshire. The capped portion of the landfill is now covered with grass, providing good habitat for Horned Lark, Lapland Longspur, and Snow Bunting in winter. A Blue Grosbeak frequented the area during late May 2012.

Unfortunately, access is restricted and no convenient vantage points provide decent views of the landfill. You can scan the birds circling above the site, however, and sometimes find gulls roosting on nearby ponds or factory roofs. During winter, any concentration of gulls is worth checking for Iceland, Lesser Black-backed, and Glaucous Gull. The entrance road is off Route 111, about 2 miles west of Route 3.

SOUTHWEST PARK

A short drive from downtown Nashua, Southwest Park is a great bird location. The scrub and field edge habitat makes it a good bet for Brown Thrasher, Blue-winged Warbler, and Orchard Oriole. Rare sightings have included Little Blue Heron, Fish Crow, Yellow-breasted Chat, and Mourning Warbler. You can park behind the playing fields on the north side of Route 111A, opposite Gregg Road (about 3.2 miles south of the junction with Route 111).

Iceland Gull, Jeffreys Ledge, December 11, 2011.
Eric Masterson

Amherst Area

The Amherst area includes Ponemah Bog and the Nichols Road pumpkin fields.

PONEMAH BOG

New Hampshire Audubon owns this wildlife sanctuary, situated just north of Route 101A in a heavily developed part of the state, between Milford and Nashua. Ponemah may be more interesting for its plant life than its birds: it features a small kettle hole bog and pond that are circumnavigated by a boardwalk. Insectivorous sundew and pitcher plants grow alongside black spruce and tamarack in the nutrient-poor soil of the bog, with upland forest occupying the remainder of the 75-acre site. Its birds include common resident species like White-breasted Nuthatch and Tufted Titmouse. During summer, the distinctive call of the Eastern Kingbird is a familiar sound near the bog, while the equally distinctive calls of Eastern Wood-Pewee and Great Crested Flycatcher emanate from the surrounding canopy forest. Ruffed Grouse, Whip-poor-will and Eastern Towhee were once more frequent, but these species have become rarer as development has increasingly isolated

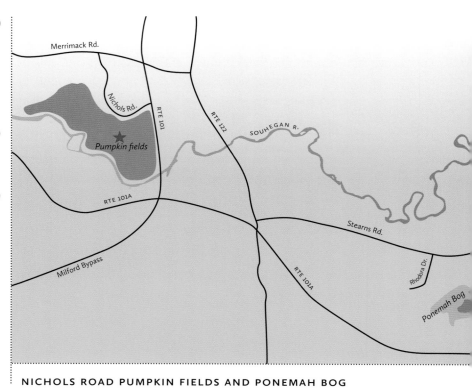

NICHOLS ROAD PUMPKIN FIELDS AND PONEMAH BOG

the bog. This is especially true of Whip-poor-will, which is declining across New Hampshire.

In August and September, Spotted, Solitary, and Least Sandpipers stop off on their way south to feed along the edge of the pond. Access to the trails is from the end of Rhodora Drive.

NICHOLS ROAD PUMPKIN FIELDS

The weedy edges of these pumpkin fields are full of sparrows from September to late October. It is possible to spot more than 10 species of sparrow in a day. Dickcissel is likely an annual occurrence, and the habitat seems promising for other rarities, including Connecticut Warbler and Blue Grosbeak, though neither has yet been recorded here. From fall through winter, look for Horned Lark, American Pipit, and Snow Buntings.

The fields are privately owned and access is by permission only. Nichols Road is a dead end, accessible only from Merrimack Road.

Greater Kingston Area

The Greater Kingston area includes Powwow Pond in Kingston, Brookside Wildlife Sanctuary in South Hampton, and Bodwell Farm in East Kingston.

POWWOW POND

This shallow, warm water pond on the Powwow River in Kingston is the state capital for Ring-necked Duck. Peak numbers can sometimes exceed 300 individuals in late March. It also is one of the better locations in the state for Ruddy Duck and American Coot, both of which tend to occur more frequently in the fall—from mid-October through December. Much rarer—but more likely here than elsewhere in New Hampshire, with the exception of Great Bay—are Canvasback and Redhead.

Access to Powwow Pond can be difficult. The Bakie Conservation Easement, on the pond's north side, is open to the public, and there are several locations from which to launch a canoe.

POWWOW POND

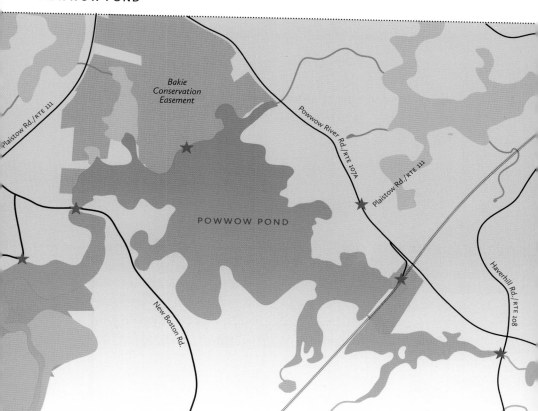

BROOKSIDE WILDLIFE SANCTUARY

Brookside and the adjacent Crosby Conservation Land create an almost 150-acre tract of mixed oak and pine forest near the Massachusetts border, close to the ocean. It is a fine birding location, with hiking trails. The typical birds of a southern New Hampshire forest are occasionally joined by species that are scarce along the coast, including Red-breasted Nuthatch and Winter Wren. Acadian Flycatcher and Worm-eating Warbler also have occurred here, emphasizing the diversity of birds possible in this preserve. A large rookery of Great Blue Herons is visible from Woodman Road. Their nests are easily seen in the tops of the dead snags in the middle of the beaver swamp. Great Horned Owl and Osprey have both bred here in recent years, reusing old heron nests. Other birds to watch for include Wood Duck, Green Heron, and Red-shouldered Hawk.

To reach Brookside from Route 150 in South Hampton, go west on Highland Road. After 0.6 miles, turn left (south) on Woodman Road. After 0.4 miles, you will reach the trailhead and parking lot on the right (west) side of the road.

BODWELL FARM

This farm in East Kingston is a roadside birding site. It is located on Route 108, 2.4 miles south of the junction with Route 150, or 0.9 miles north of the

BROOKSIDE WILDLIFE SANCTUARY   BODWELL FARM

P PARKING AREA

★ VIEWING AREA

TRAIL/WOODS ROAD

WETLANDS

CONSERVATION LAND

junction with Route 107. A creek runs through the pasture on the east side of the road. It usually floods during spring thaw, creating ideal habitat for geese, dabbling ducks, and—occasionally—Glossy Ibis. About 170 acres of the farm is under a conservation easement held by the Rockingham County Conservation District.

Rochester

The Rochester area includes the Rochester Wastewater Treatment Plant, Turnkey Landfill, Pickering Ponds, Strafford County Farm, and Dover Cassily Community Garden.

ROCHESTER WASTEWATER TREATMENT PLANT AND TURNKEY LANDFILL

This is the rare gull capital of New Hampshire and perhaps New England, although new management practices to discourage gulls at the adjacent Turnkey Landfill have severely impacted its value to birders. In the past, thousands of gulls would commute the short distance from the landfill to the sewage treatment plant, where they would rest and bathe. The site has produced an outstanding list of rarities through the years, including the first record of Glaucous-winged Gull for the eastern United States, the first record of Slaty-backed Gull for New England, and the first New Hampshire record of Thayer's Gull. Two of the state's six records of Franklin's Gull are from this site, and it used to be the best spot in the state for Iceland Gull, Lesser Black-backed Gull, and Glaucous Gull—all of which could be found here in numbers. The future use of this site by gulls will depend on management of the adjacent landfill.

However, Rochester Wastewater Treatment Plant would still rank as a birding hotspot even without gulls. The roster of unusual birds that have occurred here is too long to list, and includes such oddities as King Eider, Eared Grebe, and American Oystercatcher. The lagoons are good spots for waterfowl and shorebirds in fall, and their use of this habitat is not affected by management practices at the landfill. Scarce waterfowl species occur annually, including Gadwall, Blue-winged Teal, Northern Shoveler, Northern Pintail, and Ruddy Duck, while American Black Duck and Mallard are a constant feature of the settling ponds. The common peeps also are annual visitors, and even the less common species are found here on a surprisingly regular basis. At least 26 species of shorebirds have been recorded.

TRAIL/WOODS ROAD

GRASSLAND/FARMLAND

WETLANDS

P PARKING AREA

★ VIEWING AREA

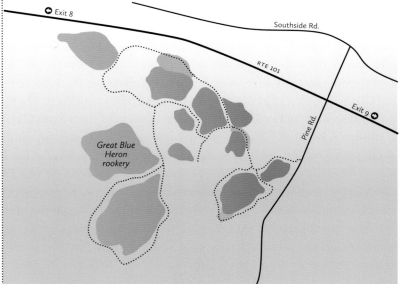

RTE 125

★ Rochester
Wastewater
Treatment
Plant

P Parking for Pickering Ponds

Spaulding Turnpike/RTE 16

★ Turnkey
Landfill

Rochester Neck Rd.

COCHECO RIVER

Pickering Rd.

Strafford
County
Farm ★

County Farm Rd.

Exit 9

Indian Brook Dr.

Dover
Cassily
Community
Garden

6th

Tolend Rd.

Whittier

4th ★

ROCHESTER AREA

Exit 8

Southside Rd.

RTE 101

Pine Rd.

Exit 9

Great Blue
Heron
rookery

BRENTWOOD MITIGATION AREA

Trails are especially wet where they cross swamp / marsh.

The gates of the plant are open Monday through Friday, from 9:00 a.m. to 3:00 p.m., and closed on weekends. You must park in front of the office building and check in with the staff before birding. Do not block the roads, do not drive on the dikes, and make sure you depart before 2:45 p.m. so that plant personnel do not have to ask you to leave.

PICKERING PONDS

Two miles of trails begin from the parking lot at Pickering Ponds, which is located just east of the wastewater treatment plant off Pickering Road. The trail that leads from the north end of the parking lot circumnavigates two settling ponds. Large numbers of gulls can be found resting and bathing here, especially at the first pond, though this again depends on management practices at the adjacent Turnkey Landfill.

Pickering Ponds is one of a handful of nesting sites in the state for Pied-billed Grebe, and it is also a good site for waterfowl and American Coot in fall. Black-crowned Night-Heron, Clay-colored Sparrow, and Blue Grosbeak also have been recorded here.

To reach the Pickering Ponds parking lot from the south, take Exit 9 off the Spaulding Turnpike in Dover and turn left at the end of the exit ramp. After 0.5 miles, turn right at the traffic light onto Sixth Street and follow it north toward Gonic. The name of the road will change from Sixth Street to Pickering Road. After 4 miles, a paved access road on your left leads to the trailhead. The trails are open seven days a week, during daylight hours.

STRAFFORD COUNTY FARM

The farm includes about 200 acres of grassland, less than 7 miles from downtown Dover as the crow flies. Not surprisingly, the area is a hotspot for birds of open country (including crows) in both winter and summer. Northern Shrikes are regularly recorded from November through March, while American Kestrels are a common sight during spring migration—providing little respite for the small birds and mammals that are preyed upon by both species. The wooded banks of the Cocheco River, which borders the farmland to the south, are home to Yellow-throated Vireo and occasionally Orchard Oriole. Eastern Bluebird and Bobolink are regularly observed in the fields during summer, and Eastern Meadowlarks are occasional visitors. The Forest Society holds a conservation easement on the land, which is open to public access.

DOVER CASSILY COMMUNITY GARDEN

This garden is a great spot if you have an hour or two to spare, especially during fall. The 3-acre site is close to downtown Dover and offers access to a mile-long trail along the Cocheco River.

Other Areas

Other areas include Brentwood Mitigation Area, Derry Wastewater Treatment Plant, and Pawtuckaway State Park.

BRENTWOOD MITIGATION AREA

Also known as Deer Hill Wildlife Management Area, Brentwood was recently designated a regionally significant site for Pied-billed Grebe. Its main feature is a series of ponds created when gravel was extracted during the construction of Route 101 during the 1990s. As many as 7 pairs of Pied-billed Grebes have bred on the ponds, making this the largest colony in New Hampshire.

A network of trails winds through the area, but they are not maintained, frequently flooded, and can be overgrown during the summer. Knee-high boots and appropriate clothing are recommended.

Pied-billed Grebes may be found on any of the ponds, and a visit during spring is recommended, when grebes perform remarkable courtship displays. One of the westernmost ponds has a Great Blue Heron rookery, and Green Heron also breed in the area. The entire site is excellent for birds of scrub and early successional forest, including Brown Thrasher, Cedar Waxwing, Blue-winged Warbler, Prairie Warbler, Eastern Towhee, Field Sparrow, and Indigo Bunting. Other birds to watch for include Wood Duck, Hooded Merganser, Belted Kingfisher, and Orchard Oriole during summer, and various waterfowl species during migration.

Sharp-shinned Hawk, Cooper's Hawk, Red-shouldered Hawk, Broad-winged Hawk, and Red-tailed Hawk are all regularly observed during the summer. Several points along the trails provide decent vistas, where you might be amply rewarded for a few minutes scanning.

From Route 101 take Exit 8, then drive 0.3 miles to Route 27. Turn right and go 1.1 miles to Pine Road. Go south on Pine Road for 0.4 miles, passing under Route 101. The entrance and parking area is on your right, just after Seacoast Mills Building Supply.

DERRY WASTEWATER TREATMENT PLANT

This is one of the few treatment plants in the state which still has open lagoons; these offer good birding from fall through spring. As at most such sites, look out for waterfowl, shorebirds, gulls, terns, swallows, and all ground-foraging passerines, such as pipits, buntings, and sparrows. Interesting records from the plant include Gadwall, Northern Shoveler, Greater and Lesser Scaup, Ruddy Duck, Semipalmated Plover, Solitary Sandpiper, Greater and Lesser Yellowlegs, Pectoral Sandpiper, Wilson's Phalarope, Red-necked Phalarope, Bonaparte's Gull, Laughing Gull, Iceland Gull, Glaucous Gull, Fish Crow, and the Ipswich race of Savannah Sparrow.

Take Exit 4 off Route 93. Drive east on Nashua Road / West Broadway (Route 102) for almost a mile, then take a right on Fordway Extension and continue for a half mile. Turn right on Transfer Station Road and continue to the end. Prior to birding the site, visitors must check in at the plant office (Building 43) for permission.

PAWTUCKAWAY STATE PARK

This 5,500-acre forest in Nottingham is located about 20 minutes from Route 101 (take Exit 5). The southeastern New Hampshire setting makes it one of the state's very best places to find birds that are at—or just beyond—the northern limit of their range. Included in this list are Acadian Flycatcher, Cerulean Warbler, and Worm-eating Warbler. Pawtuckaway State Park was

DERRY WASTEWATER TREATMENT PLANT

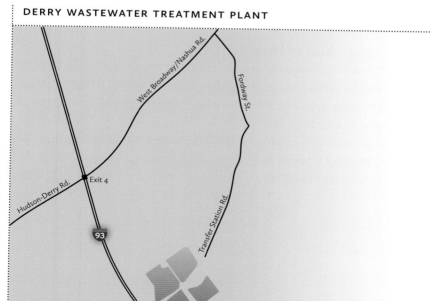

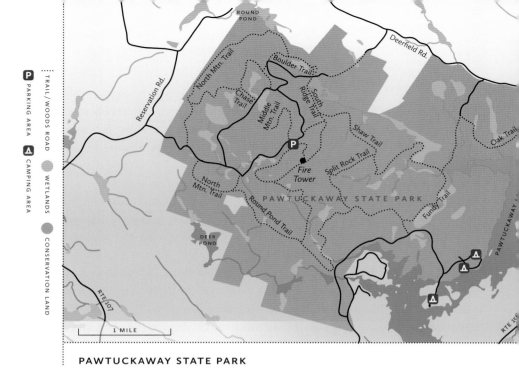

P PARKING AREA

TRAIL/WOODS ROAD

WETLANDS

CAMPING AREA

CONSERVATION LAND

ROUND
POND

Deerfield Rd.

Reservation Rd.

Boulder Trail

North Mtn. Trail

Chase
Trail

Middle
Mtn. Trail

South
Ridge Trail

Shaw Trail

Oak Trail

Split Rock Trail

Fire
Tower

North
Mtn. Trail

PAWTUCKAWAY STATE PARK

Round Pond Trail

Fundy Trail

PAWTUCKAWAY L

DEER
POND

RTE 107

RTE 156

1 MILE

PAWTUCKAWAY STATE PARK

the state's lone outpost for Cerulean Warbler for many years (they have been rediscovered recently at Wantastiquet Mountain Natural Area in Hinsdale), and they are most regularly seen and heard along the trail to the fire tower. Please put the welfare of these rare birds ahead of your desire to see them and do *not* play recordings. Kentucky Warbler also has been observed in the park.

Other less common birds to be found here include Yellow-billed Cuckoo, Yellow-throated Vireo, Blue-gray Gnatcatcher, and Canada Warbler. Louisiana Waterthrush occurs along the many brooks throughout the park. The fire tower trail is good for all these species.

Pawtuckaway is also one of the best places in southeastern New Hampshire to find some species more typical of the Monadnock Highlands and northern New Hampshire, including Yellow-bellied Sapsucker, Winter Wren, and Evening Grosbeak.

The large power-line cut that crosses Reservation Road is an excellent spot for Prairie Warbler, Eastern Towhee, Field Sparrow, and Indigo Bunting. The wide panorama also makes this a good spot for finding vultures and hawks.

5 The Coast and Ocean

I live in the Monadnock Region, a quiet, bucolic retreat in southwestern New Hampshire where traffic is light and parking is free, but it's not the coast. There are no substitutes for the sight of the horizon line, the smell of seaweed, or the sounds of a dock. Although I have affirmed, in previous chapters, the potential of the state's interior to occasionally host coastal birds (especially during spring), there also is no substitute for the state's 20-mile coastline and its diversity and quantity of birds. Any birding visit to this region will be enhanced by a telescope, especially if you are looking for waterfowl on the ocean or shorebirds in Hampton Marsh.

Coast

The coastal area includes Hampton Marsh, Hampton Estuary, Hampton Beach State Park, Bicentennial Park, Plaice Cove, Meadow Pond, Henry's Pool, Little River Saltmarsh, Runnymede Farm, Little Boars Head, Philbrick Pond, Eel Pond, Rye Harbor State Park, Foss Beach, Odiorne Point, the Urban Forestry Center, New Castle, and Portsmouth.

The following sites are listed in order from south to north, but the visitor should plan a route by tide and, in summer, by traffic. For example, Hampton Estuary is best on a falling tide, usually 2 to 3 hours after high tide, though this interval can be longer after especially high tides.

During summer and early fall, traffic along Route 1A can be appalling; it is worth checking online for local events prior to your visit. If you are going on a pelagic cruise or whalewatch, allow plenty of time to get to the marina.

Parking is metered at many spots along Route 1A and is strictly and regularly enforced during the season. If you are parked illegally, then you will get a ticket. In 2011, metered parking cost $1.50 per hour, with four-hour tokens available for $5 at change machines. These machines can be found at the

Red-throated Loon, North Hampton, January 7, 2012. This species is relatively common off New Hampshire's coast during winter. *Len Medlock*

parking lot south of the Hampton Seashell complex, and in the restrooms on Ross Avenue, North Beach, Jenness Beach, and North Hampton State Beach.

Most whalewatching companies offer discount coupons on their Web sites (see Web Resources). All operators sell water and snacks, but you will have to provide more substantial provisions yourself.

HAMPTON MARSH

This extensive saltmarsh forms part of the Great Marsh ecosystem, which stretches south to Plum Island and Essex Harbor in Massachusetts. Hampton Marsh itself is about 5,000 acres of saltmarsh and estuary extending around Hampton Harbor.

The marsh formed in the lee of Hampton's dune systems as salt-meadow cordgrass colonized sediments. It is drained by an extensive network of ditches, in addition to tidal creeks. The ditches were dug in the eighteenth and early nineteenth centuries to increase the production of salt hay and to

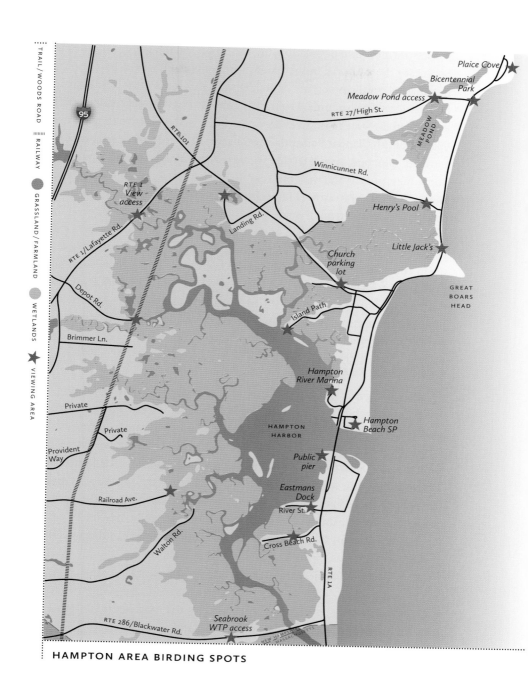

95

Plaice Cove

Bicentennial Park

Meadow Pond access

RTE 27/High St.

MEADOW POND

Winnicunnet Rd.

RTE 1 View access

Henry's Pool

Landing Rd.

Little Jack's

RTE 1/Lafayette Rd.

Church parking lot

GREAT BOARS HEAD

Depot Rd.

Island Path

Brimmer Ln.

Hampton River Marina

Private

Hampton Beach SP

Private

HAMPTON HARBOR

Provident Way

Public pier

Railroad Ave.

Eastmans Dock

River St.

Walton Rd.

Cross Beach Rd.

RTE 1A

RTE 286/Blackwater Rd.

Seabrook WTP access

NEW HAMPSHIRE
MASSACHUSETTS

HAMPTON AREA BIRDING SPOTS

reduce the mosquito population, but the ecological integrity of the area is the poorer for these efforts. Immediately north of Great Boars Head, the original marsh is relatively intact; not coincidentally, this is the most productive area for classic saltmarsh birds. From early June through August, this is the best location in the state to find Seaside Sparrow, as well as Saltmarsh and Nelson's Sparrow. Both Clapper Rail and King Rail also have been recorded here during summer. The best access to this section of the marsh is from a parking lot immediately north and west of Great Boars Head, directly opposite the south end of the seawall fronting Hampton's North Beach. Little Jack's Restaurant currently operates from this lot.

A canoe allows unmatched access to the entire marsh ecosystem via the network of tidal creeks and channels. It is surprising how quiet it can get when you paddle into the middle of the marsh, where the hustle and bustle of Hampton Beach and Route 1A is replaced by the calls of Willets and Common Terns, both of which breed here. During the warmer seasons, insect repellent (or netting) is an absolute necessity. Walking out into the marsh is not recommended, as this can disturb nesting birds.

HAMPTON ESTUARY

The estuary drains Hampton Marsh and is an excellent spot year round for a variety of shorebirds, gulls, and terns. A public fishing pier off Route 1A, just south of the drawbridge, allows an excellent view of the area. During a falling tide, the south side of the harbor, just north of River Street, is exposed first. This area can be viewed from a pier and boat launch beside Eastman's Docks. The receding tide then exposes the clam flats directly opposite the fishing pier; check these flats with a telescope or binoculars. This is the best area in the state for Whimbrel and Hudsonian and Marbled Godwits. In winter, it is not unusual for Glaucous and Iceland Gulls to linger in the area, often roosting on the roof of the Yankee Fisherman's Co-op.

Other worthwhile viewing sites include the following:

Cross Beach Road at high tide, just north of the road, there is often a gull roost that may include Glaucous or Iceland Gull

Hampton River Marina continue through the marina, which is located on the north side of the drawbridge, to the end of the gravel driveway; shorebirds roost on the far bank of the saltmarsh during high tide

Great Egret, Rye, April 14, 2009. Great and Snowy Egrets are common sights during summer throughout New Hampshire's saltmarshes, especially at Hampton Marsh.
Eric Masterson

Island Path Road from fall through spring, scan the marsh from the end of the road for Rough-legged Hawk, Snowy Owl, and Short-eared Owl

Landing Road this provides a view of Landing Road Marsh, which is an excellent spot for shorebirds, especially on a falling tide

Route 1 Access this pull-off on the east side of Route 1, less than a mile south of Route 101, overlooks a saltpan that provides a high-tide roost for shorebirds

Depot Road provides access to a rail trail from which you can scan the marsh in evening, with the sun at your back

Railroad Avenue from the end of Railroad Avenue, a 5-minute walk will take you to a wooded island surrounded by saltmarsh; this is a good spot for fall migrants and, in winter, for owls, with the rare possibility of Long-eared Owl

Seabrook Wastewater Treatment Plant this plant does not have open lagoons and hence is not a good site for waterfowl, gulls, or shorebirds, but the woodland south of the plant sometimes holds late migrants and occasional wintering warblers; the site has produced several winter records of Pine Warbler along with a Hooded Warbler.

THE COAST AND OCEAN

Snowy Owl, Hampton Beach, January 9, 2012. New Hampshire's coast—especially the marshes and dunes of Hampton—is the best place in the state to search for Snowy and Short-eared Owls in winter. *Jason Lambert.*

HAMPTON BEACH STATE PARK

This park, located just north of the drawbridge, offers good birding during fall and winter, when there is relatively little traffic. During August and September, large flocks of peeps roost in the park during high tide. Species can include Western Sandpiper and White-rumped Sandpiper among the more common Semipalmated Plover, Sanderling, and Semipalmated Sandpiper. Do *not* disturb the roosting shorebirds, which are in the midst of migration and need to conserve their energy. Hampton Beach and Seabrook Beach, either side of the harbor, are the only two sites in New Hampshire where Piping Plovers still nest. Look for them from April onward. As soon as the plovers lay their eggs, New Hampshire Fish and Game creates exclusion zones around the nests and places wire cages over the incubating birds. The mesh is large enough for the birds to pass through but not big enough for cats, foxes, and other predators.

The park's grassy expanse is one of the better locations along the seacoast to see Horned Lark, Lapland Longspur, and Snow Bunting, and its dune system is the best location in the state to find the Ipswich race of Savannah Sparrow. The outflow of Hampton Harbor, especially toward the end of the breakwater, is worth checking for Bonaparte's Gulls and terns in summer and fall.

From April through December, charter boats return to the harbor's docks around 4:30 or 5:00 p.m. If the fishing has been good, the deckhands often are still cleaning the catch as the boats enter the harbor. I have seen Black-legged Kittiwake, Great Shearwater, and even Northern Fulmar enticed all the way to the harbor walls in this way.

During summer and early fall, there is a $15 charge to enter Hampton Beach State Park.

BICENTENNIAL PARK AND PLAICE COVE

Bicentennial Park is located at the north end of North Beach, just across from the junction of Route 1A and High Street (Route 27). The sheltered cove just north of the park is an excellent place to find Bonaparte's Gulls; you also should scan any flock for Little Gull or Black-headed Gull.

Seaweed accumulates on the beach north of the park and at adjacent Plaice Cove. This attracts shorebirds, which feed on the invertebrates that thrive in the rotting mass. In mid-August 2011, for example, Plaice Cove featured an extraordinary collection of almost 20 species of shorebirds, including American Golden-Plover, Western Sandpiper, White-rumped Sandpiper, Baird's Sandpiper, Pectoral Sandpiper, Buff-breasted Sandpiper, and the state's sixth record of Curlew Sandpiper.

Piping Plover, Hampton Beach State Park, April 10, 2011. *Len Medlock*

MEADOW POND

This site can be accessed from Route 27, which runs west from Route 1A, opposite Bicentennial Park. A quarter-mile from Route 1A, there is a pull-off on the left. Follow a short path through the reeds to the north end of Meadow Pond. Approach the pond quietly, as the birds here are easily spooked. Though hemmed in on all sides by development, the brackish lagoon hosts large flocks of Greater and Lesser Yellowlegs during migration, and is a good spot for Short-billed Dowitcher. Stilt Sandpiper occurs most years and this is one of the better locations in the state for the rare Long-billed Dowitcher. It also is an excellent spot for migrating waterfowl, especially in spring, when several hundred Green-winged Teal can linger from late March through early May. An occasional Common Teal (the Eurasian subspecies of Green-winged Teal) can be found among their ranks. The pond drains at its south end, through a creek that passes under Winnacunnet Road (Route 101E) then empties into Hampton Marsh at Henry's Pool.

HENRY'S POOL

This small expanse of mudflat, about 100 yards west of Route 1A on Winnacunnet Road (Route 101E), is best visited midway between high tide and low tide. It often holds good numbers of peeps, both Greater and Lesser Yellowlegs, and Short-billed Dowitcher.

LITTLE RIVER SALTMARSH

The ecological integrity of this marsh had been seriously compromised by an undersized culvert that restricted the flow of saltwater into the system, allowing freshwater species like phragmites and purple loosestrife to invade. Larger culverts were installed during the past decade, restoring the flow of seawater under Route 1A. Little River Saltmarsh is now a New Hampshire Audubon Sanctuary and provides excellent shorebird habitat. It is one of the best spots in the state to see Stilt Sandpiper, although access is difficult. The best saltpans are at the south end of the marsh. They can be reached on foot from Route 1A at low tide; the walk takes at least 30 minutes each way. Knee-high boots are advisable.

RUNNYMEDE FARM

This horse farm on Atlantic Avenue, just west of Little River Saltmarsh, is a good spot for Glossy Ibis and flocks of geese during spring and fall.

MAINE

New Hampshire Ave.
Spaulding Turnpike
Market St.
Prescott Park
NORTH MILL POND
SOUTH MILL POND
Fort Constitution
Portsmouth International Airport at Pease
Grafton Rd.
RTE 33
95
Middle Rd.
South St.
Sagamore Ave.
Wentworth Coolidge
Fort Stark
Wooden Bridge
Ocean Rd.
Odiorne Point
Urban Forestry Center
Elwyn Rd.
Sagamore Rd.
Brackett Rd.
Marsh Rd.
Lafayette Rd. / RTE 1
Lang Rd.
Wallis Rd.
Wallis Sands SP
Long John Rd.
Washington Rd.
Locke Rd.
Foss Beach
West Rd.
Central Rd.
RTE 1A / Ocean Rd.
Rye Harbor SP
North Rd.
South Rd.
Love Ln.
Mill Rd.
Sea Rd.
Jennes Beach & Eel Pond
RYE LEDGES
PHILBRICK POND
Runnymede Farm
Atlantic Ave. / RTE 111
Little Boars Head
Little River Saltmarsh
Plaice Cove

COASTAL BIRDING SPOTS FROM
NORTH HAMPTON TO PORTSMOUTH

Caspian Tern at Eel Pond in Rye, April 28, 2011.
Len Medlock

LITTLE BOARS HEAD

This bluff at the eastern end of Atlantic Avenue (Route 111) is probably the state's best spot for conducting a seawatch during storm conditions (ideally, winds of at least 30 knots out of the southeast quadrant). There is a pullout directly across from the junction with Route 1A. The height is perfect, and the location allows you to watch from the shelter of a vehicle. That said, New Hampshire's coastline is at the western edge of the Gulf of Maine; there are far superior locations for seawatching in neighboring Massachusetts.

PHILBRICK POND

Located on the west side of Route 1A, this pond is a good spot for both Great and Snowy Egrets. Tricolored Heron also has occurred here.

EEL POND

One of the few freshwater ponds along the coast, Eel Pond has a relatively poor record for birds considering its location. In spring and fall, however, it is

Little Gull, Rye, August 1, 2010.
Jason Lambert

a good spot for waterfowl, especially diving ducks, including Ring-necked Duck, Lesser Scaup, Bufflehead, Common Goldeneye, and Ruddy Duck. Also look for American Coot in fall and, more rarely, Common Gallinule (formerly Common Moorhen).

A freshwater creek drains Eel Pond, entering the sea through a culvert under Route 1A. This is an excellent spot for gulls, which gather to preen and bathe in the creek. It is one of the better places along the coast to find the scarce and rare gulls, including Black-headed Gull, Laughing Gull, Iceland Gull, Lesser Black-backed Gull, and Glaucous Gull. Rare terns also have been seen here, including Caspian Tern and Royal Tern. The adjacent beach is an excellent spot for Sanderling in winter.

RYE HARBOR STATE PARK

Worth checking for migrants in spring and fall, Rye Harbor occasionally hosts interesting species of waterfowl and alcids. For example, King Eider, Harlequin Duck, and Common Murre have all occurred within the harbor walls. The park is one of the more easterly points on the coast, thus offering a good vantage point for seawatching. During ideal winds, however, the location offers little shelter and leaves the birder exposed to the elements.

FOSS BEACH

This beach lies directly north of Rye Harbor State Park. As at Plaice Cove, seaweed accumulates here, especially at the two ends of the beach. During fall, these areas are excellent spots to search for the more unusual shorebirds, including Baird's Sandpiper and Buff-breasted Sandpiper. Numbers of Bonaparte's Gulls build here during the fall, with an occasional Black-headed Gull or Little Gull hiding in their midst.

ODIORNE POINT

This is the best spot on the mainland coast for migrant passerines. There is a pull-off on the east side of Route 1A, just south of the state park. You can leave your car here and walk into the park via a shingle beach. The cove on the south side of the park is an excellent spot during fall for the rarer southern migrants, including White-eyed Vireo and Yellow-breasted Chat. Several rarities have been recorded in this area, including the state's first Fork-tailed Flycatcher and third Bell's Vireo. There is an extensive woodland north of the Seacoast Science Center, much of it impenetrable to humans and thus providing excellent cover for birds. It is accessed by a well-developed trail system, any part of which is as good as the next. The trail that follows the shingle beach has a good track record of holding late migrants, which are attracted to the warmth of the morning sun as well as the insects living among the rocks and accumulated seaweed. A Cape May Warbler survived the 2011–12 winter by holing up at this location.

There is a small freshwater marsh at the north end of the park which often hosts Virginia Rail and Sora. Continue walking past the marsh to the point for a view of Little Harbor, a good spot for Bufflehead and Bonaparte's Gull.

If you continue on Route 1A north, you will cross a bridge (formerly known as the "Wooden Bridge"). On the left (south) side of the bridge, there is a good mudflat for shorebirds on a falling tide. This section of saltmarsh also has a good track record for Short-eared Owl.

URBAN FORESTRY CENTER

Located just off Route 1, the center offers self-guided trails through forest, saltmarsh, and a tidal creek. The land is owned by the state and managed by the New Hampshire Division of Forest and Lands. This is a good birding site year round. The forest includes red pine and blue spruce plantations in addition to the native northern hardwood forest and mixed deciduous forest. This diverse mix offers habitat to a wide range of species including more common birds like Downy and Hairy Woodpecker, Black-capped Chickadee, and White-breasted Nuthatch, as well as scarcer species like Red-breasted Nuthatch and Purple Finch, especially during migration. Egrets are a common sight during summer, while shorebirds, especially Greater and Lesser Yellowlegs, occur in the creeks during fall.

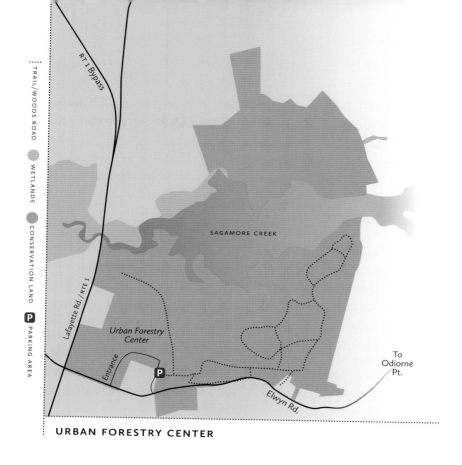

TRAIL/WOODS ROAD

WETLANDS

CONSERVATION LAND

P PARKING AREA

RT 1 Bypass

SAGAMORE CREEK

Lafayette Rd. / RTE 1

Urban Forestry
Center

Entrance

P

To
Odiorne
Pt.

Elwyn Rd.

URBAN FORESTRY CENTER

NEW CASTLE

Route 1B through New Castle offers several access points—including Fort Constitution, Great Island Common, and Fort Stark—from which to scan the Piscataqua Estuary and the ocean for waterfowl, gulls, terns, alcids, and other species. The list of good birds seen from this stretch of road is long, including New Hampshire's first Western Reef-Heron, which frequented the area during fall 2006. Bonaparte's Gulls are especially numerous in the mouth of the river, and this is one of the better locations to find Black-headed Gull and Little Gull. Fort Constitution is a particularly good spot from which to scan for gulls; a scope is necessary, however, since the birds are often on the north (Maine) shore. All areas are good for alcids. Razorbill is the most likely, but Dovekie, Common Murre, and Thick-billed Murre have all been recorded more than once. These species are more likely to be encountered here during rough weather, especially when winds are out of the east or south.

There are several productive birding sites close to downtown Portsmouth. South and North Mill Ponds are good locations for waterfowl during migration; in winter, they often host one or two holdouts—such as Northern Shoveler or Northern Pintail—that would otherwise be absent from the state. North Mill Pond also often hosts a significant roost of gulls in winter. Iceland Gull, Glaucous Gull, and Lesser Black-backed Gull, though uncommon, should not be unexpected.

Prescott Park offers good views of Portsmouth Harbor, a good site for winter gulls and occasional alcids.

Peregrine Falcons have bred in the city for several years, most recently nesting on the substructure of the main bridge that carries Interstate 95.

Wentworth Coolidge Mansion is one of the better locations along the coast for Northern Saw-whet Owl. They are unlikely to breed here, but are regularly observed during migration and even in winter. Eastern Screech-Owls also have been recorded in the area, which is worth checking year round. Breeding birds include Pine Warbler and Eastern Wood-Pewee. The mansion is located on Little Harbor Road off Sagamore Avenue (Route 1A).

Peregrine Falcon, Rye, March 5, 2011. Although use of the pesticide DDT had eliminated this falcon from the eastern United States by the 1950s, the species returned to New Hampshire in the early 1980s. Today, the state is home to almost 20 pairs of this charismatic bird. *Jason Lambert*

Great Bay and Durham Area

The Great Bay and Durham area includes Sunset Farm, Chapman's Landing, Portsmouth International Airport at Pease, Great Bay National Wildlife Refuge, Exeter Wastewater Treatment Plant, Bellamy River Wildlife Sanctuary, Foss Farm, Surry Lane Marsh, Moore Fields, Gonet Road, and Longmarsh Road.

Great Bay is a large tidal estuary that encompasses more than 10,000 acres, across two counties and nine towns. Several rivers, including the Bellamy, Lamprey, Oyster, Squamscott, and Winnicut, drain into Great Bay, which empties into the Piscataqua River in Dover. The mix of habitats also includes saltmarsh and mudflat.

Great Bay National Wildlife Refuge covers more than 1,000 acres on the northeast side of the bay. Efforts to protect additional shoreline and the surrounding upland have resulted in several thousand more acres being conserved.

The area is one of the very best spots for birding in New Hampshire from fall through spring, highlighted by an extraordinary diversity and abundance of waterfowl. During winter, both Canada Geese and American Black Duck occur in numbers not found elsewhere in the state. Greater Scaup can be hard to find anyplace else in New Hampshire, yet occur in huge rafts in Great Bay, often numbering in excess of a thousand birds. The following peak waterfowl counts during the past 20 years illustrate just how important the bay is for waterfowl.

Great Bay is by far the best place in New Hampshire to see several of the rarer species of ducks, including Eurasian Wigeon, Canvasback, and Red-

Peak Great Bay Waterfowl Counts during the Past 20 Years

Date	Number and Species
February 28, 1998	3,056 Greater Scaup
October 24, 1998	303 American Wigeon
January 8, 2000	251 Bufflehead
April 4, 2001	374 Common Goldeneye
November 1, 2005	463 Ruddy Duck
October 9, 2010	4,186 Canada Goose
November 15, 2010	1,753 American Black Duck

Scarce to Rare Species Found in Great Bay

Date	Number and Species
February 22, 1990	21 Canvasback
November 14, 1998	5 Eurasian Wigeon
December 18, 2004	13 Gadwall
November 1, 2005	6 Redhead

head. However, apart from a few records of Greater White-fronted Goose, the rarer geese tend not to be seen here, which is curious given the large number of Canada Geese that occur from fall through spring. The above list shows several of Great Bay's high counts for species that are scarce to rare elsewhere in New Hampshire.

Bald Eagles are another feature of the bay, which is a winter stronghold for the species. Although eagles can be spotted from any access point by scanning the trees at the water's edge, Adams Point in Durham is an especially good place to spot them in winter. The birds roost on an island just south of the point, sometimes rewarding evening birders with views of several birds coming in at once.

A small colony of Common Terns breeds on Hen Island, which was of greater significance prior to the restoration of the tern colony on White and Seavey Islands. Several thousand acres of conservation land along the shore support a healthy community of field and forest birds, including Eastern Screech-Owl and Orchard Oriole, both of which can be hard to find elsewhere in New Hampshire. Great Horned Owl, Barred Owl, and Northern Saw-whet Owl also are found in the area.

SUNSET FARM

This site in Greenland is excellent for waterfowl viewing in winter—except during late afternoon and evening, when the sun is low in the western sky. The majority of the Eurasian Wigeon in New Hampshire are seen from Sunset Farm. Canvasback and Redhead also occur here; these tend to assort with the raft of Greater Scaup. A telescope is necessary.

Great Bay Farm—on the eastern side of Newington Road, directly opposite the entrance to Sunset Farm—is worth checking for unusual sparrows and blackbirds. The entire area provides good habitat for Rough-legged Hawk and Northern Shrike in winter, and Glossy Ibis in spring.

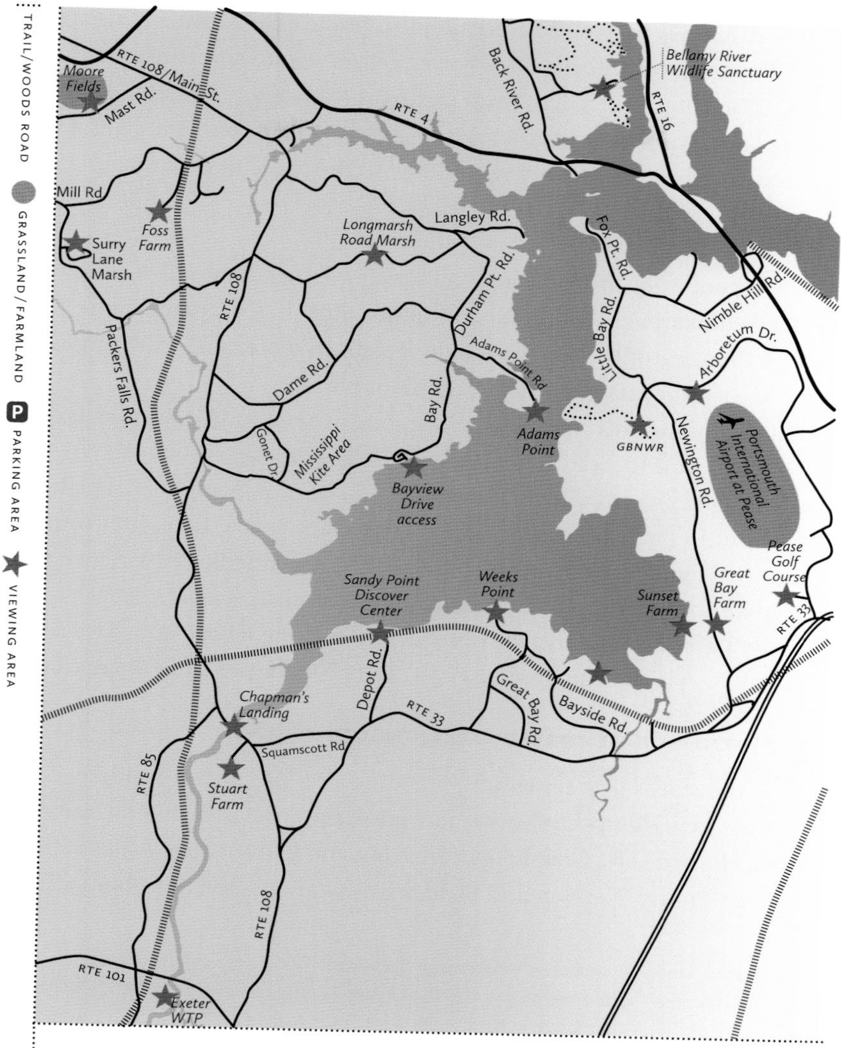

TRAIL/WOODS ROAD

GRASSLAND/FARMLAND

P PARKING AREA

★ VIEWING AREA

RTE 108/Main St.

Moore Fields

Mast Rd.

RTE 4

Back River Rd.

Bellamy River Wildlife Sanctuary

RTE 16

Mill Rd

Surry Lane Marsh

Foss Farm

RTE 108

Packers Falls Rd.

Longmarsh Road Marsh

Langley Rd.

Fox Pt. Rd.

Nimble Hill Rd.

Durham Pt. Rd.

Little Bay Rd.

Arboretum Dr.

Dame Rd.

Gonet Dr.

Bay Rd.

Adams Point Rd.

Adams Point

GBNWR

Newington Rd.

Portsmouth International Airport at Pease

Mississippi Kite Area

Bayview Drive access

Sandy Point Discover Center

Weeks Point

Sunset Farm

Great Bay Farm

Pease Golf Course

RTE 33

Chapman's Landing

Depot Rd.

RTE 33

Great Bay Rd.

Bayside Rd.

RTE 85

Squamscott Rd.

Stuart Farm

RTE 108

RTE 101

Exeter WTP

THE BEST BIRDING LOCATIONS
IN THE GREAT BAY AREA

Sunset Farm is under a conservation easement that allows public access. From Route 33, turn north onto Portsmouth Avenue and continue for 0.7 miles to Newington Road, then go north on Newington Road for 0.7 miles. Sunset Farm will be on your left and Great Bay Farm on your right. It is a quarter-mile walk from Newington Road to the shore of Great Bay.

CHAPMAN'S LANDING

This is a good spot in spring and fall for shorebirds, especially Greater and Lesser Yellowlegs and Pectoral Sandpiper. Ruff has occurred twice here; though there are only 10 records of this Eurasian species in New Hampshire, it could easily occur again, as the habitat is perfect.

Saltmarsh Sparrow and Nelson's Sparrow breed in the saltmarsh grass and should be expected from late May. Easier to hear than see, Virginia Rail is usually present during summer. A pair of Osprey nests on a platform farther out in the marsh and visible through binoculars. Look for Common Merganser, Hooded Merganser, Great Blue Heron, and Belted Kingfisher on the Squamscott River in spring, fall, and occasionally winter.

Chapman's Landing has plenty of room for parking, a boat launch for access to Great Bay via the Squamscott River, and restrooms during the season.

PORTSMOUTH INTERNATIONAL AIRPORT AT PEASE

This is the state's sole remaining breeding site for Upland Sandpiper, and also hosts New Hampshire's other rare grassland species, including American Kestrel, Horned Lark, Grasshopper Sparrow, and Eastern Meadowlark. Brown Thrasher, Prairie Warbler, and Field Sparrow are relatively common in the

Buff-breasted Sandpiper at Exeter Wastewater Treatment Plant, September 12, 2010. The Great Bay area—including the grasslands of Pease Airport—is one of the better locations to spot this species, which is rare in New Hampshire. *Jason Lambert*

scrub and field-edge habitat here. Clay-colored Sparrow has been seen during summer in recent years, although breeding has not yet been confirmed.

This is one of the better locations in the state to find Buff-breasted Sandpiper in fall. American Golden-Plover and Whimbrel are occasional visitors.

To bird this area, take Exit 1 off Route 16 (the Spaulding Turnpike) and turn onto Pease Boulevard heading into Pease International Tradeport. Continue for 0.6 miles, through a stoplight, then turn right after the stop sign, onto Arboretum Drive. Follow the road around the northwest side of the airport for 2.3 miles until you reach the end of the runway. Park on the side of the road and walk to the fence overlooking the runway. Upland Sandpiper can usually be seen foraging in the grassy median areas between the runways, from May through August; a telescope is usually required. American Kestrel, Horned Lark, Brown Thrasher, Vesper and Grasshopper Sparrows, and Eastern Meadowlark also can be seen from here.

To check the southern end of the airfield, turn left at the stop sign where Pease Boulevard intersects Arboretum Drive. Follow the signs for Interstate 95, turning right after about 0.6 miles. Follow the road along the edge of the airfield to Pease Golf Course, on your right. This is another good spot for the previously mentioned species, as well as Buff-breasted Sandpiper in fall.

GREAT BAY NATIONAL WILDLIFE REFUGE

The refuge has two public trails: the Ferry Way Trail and the Peverly Pond Trail. The remainder of the refuge is closed to unauthorized entry. The trails wind through a diversity of habitats, including scrub, shrub, field, forest, and pond. Peverly Pond is occasionally good for waterfowl during migration. Ferry Way Trail begins across the road from the visitor center and leads through woods and past beaver ponds to the shore of Great Bay, directly opposite Adams Point. This area is worth checking for waterfowl and Bald Eagles fall through spring.

Both trails offer good birding for a wide variety of common species and some less common ones, including American Kestrel, Brown Thrasher, and Field Sparrow. Expect any of the warblers or sparrows during migration.

To reach the refuge parking lot, take Exit 1 off Route 16 (the Spaulding Turnpike) and turn onto Pease Boulevard heading into Pease International Tradeport. Continue for 0.6 miles, through a stoplight, then turn right at the stop sign onto Arboretum Drive. Follow the refuge signs for 3 miles around the northwest side of the airport. Bathrooms are available in season.

This sewage treatment plant has an excellent birding pedigree. Its list of rarities is perhaps not quite as outstanding as that of the Rochester Wastewater Treatment Plant, as there is no nearby landfill. Instead, the birding here is influenced by Great Bay, which is just a few miles downstream along the Squamscott River. The site boasts New Hampshire's only record of Mew Gull. Other remarkable sightings include Piping Plover and Bell's Vireo. Rarities aside, the plant's lagoons are excellent locations for waterfowl and shorebirds. Both dabbling and diving ducks frequent the ponds during migration and most of the waterfowl species that have been recorded in New Hampshire have been seen here. American Wigeon, Blue-winged Teal, Northern Shoveler, Ring-necked Duck, Greater Scaup, Lesser Scaup, and Ruddy Duck are all annual visitors. The diving ducks often linger through the winter, including relatively large numbers of Lesser Scaup in recent years.

Marsh Wren is a common breeder in the reed beds bordering the river. During late summer and fall, the ponds are magnets for swallows, and it is not uncommon to find Northern Rough-winged Swallow, Tree Swallow, Bank Swallow, Barn Swallow, and Cliff Swallow flying above the ponds in giant mixed-species flocks. There is a fine freshwater reed bed just downstream of the plant on the opposite side of Route 101 which likely hosts Virginia Rail, Sora, and possibly Least Bittern during summer. This is an enjoyable paddle from Chapman's Landing (it should take less than an hour against the slow current).

The southwest pond has filled in with sediment and supports a large reed bed surrounding a small lagoon. It suffers less disturbance than the three main ponds and is worth checking for dabbling ducks, herons, rails, and gallinules. The reeds support a large roost of blackbirds and grackles during the fall, including a count of 300 Rusty Blackbirds in 2009.

The whole area is worth checking for rarer sparrows and other seed-eaters, including Lapland Longspur and Snow Bunting, in the fall. During August and September, shorebirds feed along the edges of the ponds or along the berms. Careful scrutiny is required as they blend in against the background and can be easily overlooked.

Because the trails at Exeter Wastewater Treatment Plant afford a 360-degree view of the sky, this also is an excellent location to check for raptors, especially as the day warms and thermals begin to develop. Black Vulture and Golden Eagle have both been recorded here.

Black Vulture, Newmarket, February 18, 2011. This species is an increasingly frequent visitor to southern New Hampshire in spring and fall, with occasional winter sightings. *Len Medlock*

About a half mile south along Newfields Road (Route 85), a left turn will put you on the Swasey Parkway, which follows the river before rejoining Route 85 in Exeter. There is usually a large flock of Ring-billed Gulls present, fall through spring, and this flock is worth checking for something more interesting. (The Mew Gull observed at the treatment plant was first seen here.) Powder House Pond, directly across the river from Swasey Parkway, also is worth checking for waterbirds. A Purple Gallinule was seen here in October 2000, and the surrounding parkland is good habitat for Orchard Oriole. Cliff Swallows can be seen catching insects over the river in summer; these birds nest under the eaves of the apartment buildings just south of Powder House Pond.

BELLAMY RIVER WILDLIFE SANCTUARY AND
BELLAMY RIVER WILDLIFE MANAGEMENT AREA

These two sites are managed by New Hampshire Audubon and New Hampshire Fish and Game, respectively. Together they form an approximately 400-acre expanse of abandoned farmland and a haven for the state-endangered New England Cottontail Rabbit. Several trails lead through the area,

THE COAST AND OCEAN

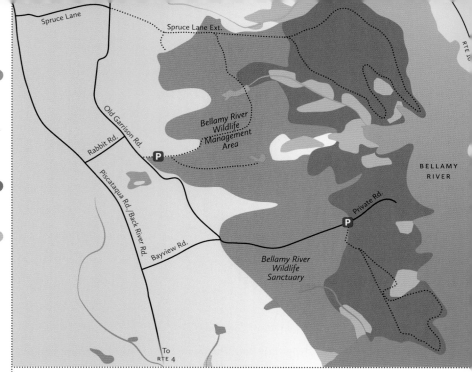

Spruce Lane

Spruce Lane Ext.

RTE 10

Old Garrison Rd.

Rabbit Rd.

Bellamy River
Wildlife
Management
Area

**BELLAMY
RIVER**

Piscataqua Rd./Back River Rd.

Private Rd.

Bayview Rd.

Bellamy River
Wildlife
Sanctuary

To
RTE 4

**BELLAMY RIVER WILDLIFE MANAGEMENT
AREA AND WILDLIFE SANCTUARY**

which is one of the best spots in the state for birds of field edges, including the uncommon Brown Thrasher, Blue-winged Warbler, and Orchard Oriole. Brewster's Warbler, a hybrid of the Golden-winged and Blue-winged Warblers, has been recorded here several times. The scrubby areas support a healthy population of Willow Flycatcher, and the surrounding forest is as good as any in the state for both Yellow-billed Cuckoo and Black-billed Cuckoo. More common field-edge birds include Gray Catbird, Chestnut-sided Warbler, and Indigo Bunting. Bobolinks breed in the fields, though these are being allowed to revert to scrub, while the mixed oak and pine woodlands host Eastern Wood-Pewee, Great Crested Flycatcher, and Scarlet Tanager. Green Heron and occasionally Black-crowned Night-Heron occur in the ponds and along the shore of the Bellamy River.

To reach the Bellamy River Wildlife Sanctuary, follow Route 4 east for 2.5 miles after the junction with Route 108, then turn onto Back River Road. Continue 0.8 miles, then turn right onto Bayview Road. At the end of Bayview Road, bear left onto a gravel road and continue through the field to the parking area.

To reach Bellamy River Wildlife Management Area from Back River Road, continue north for 1.2 miles after leaving Route 4, then turn right onto Rabbit Road. Follow Rabbit Road for 0.1 mile and turn right onto Old Garrison Road. After another 0.1 mile, turn left onto a dirt road and continue to the parking area.

FOSS FARM

This is one of the better locations in southeast New Hampshire for birds of field and forest. It boasts a variety of habitats, including mixed deciduous forest, fields, and marsh. Reliable species include several with a southern influence, such as Red-shouldered Hawk, Red-bellied Woodpecker, Yellow-throated Vireo, Blue-Gray Gnatcatcher, and Blue-winged Warbler. Occasional rarities have included Sedge Wren and Golden-winged Warbler. Access is from a walking trail that starts from Mill Road, immediately west of the railroad.

SURRY LANE MARSH

This is a productive marsh, especially for some of the more difficult to find marshbirds like American Bittern and Least Bittern. Access is via Mill Road from Durham or Packers Falls Road from Newmarket.

MOORE FIELDS

These large agricultural fields are best in spring or fall, when they offer habitat for migrant shorebirds and waterfowl (better in spring). Five species of geese have been recorded here, including Greater White-fronted Goose, Cackling Goose, and New Hampshire's first record of Ross's Goose. The scarcer dabbling ducks—including Gadwall, American Wigeon, and Northern Pintail—are occasionally observed among the more common spring migrants like Wood Duck, American Black Duck, and Green-winged Teal.

The fields also are good for raptors during migration, partly due to the habitat and partly because of the commanding view of the sky from Route 155A, which borders the fields' southern edge. One needs a good panorama to enable good hawkwatching.

The list of shorebirds that have occurred here is impressive. At least 20 species have been recorded, including Upland Sandpiper, Baird's Sandpiper, and Buff-breasted Sandpiper, along with rare inland occurrences of Sanderling, White-rumped Sandpiper, and Stilt Sandpiper. As with other inland shorebird sites, appropriate weather conditions are essential to produce good results (see "When to Find Good Birds").

Because the fields are bordered by scrub and forest, a good variety of sparrows and warblers have been recorded here as well, especially during fall migration.

GONET ROAD

This leafy residential suburban neighborhood, located in Newmarket, has been the state's most reliable site for Mississippi Kite since the remarkable discovery of a nesting pair in 2008. At the time, the pair represented the first nesting record for this species in New England. They have returned to the

Mississippi Kite, Newmarket, June 19, 2008. This represents the first nesting record in New England for this species—one of New Hampshire's most remarkable ornithological events. *Jason Lambert*

Newmarket area every year since then. In addition to Gonet Road, the birds have been seen from Wadleigh Falls Road and in the Bay Road area.

LONGMARSH ROAD

Longmarsh Road runs through a heavily conserved part of Durham, ending at a marsh about 1.5 miles from Route 108. This area is the center of nearly 600 contiguous acres of conservation land, and the forest has an abundance of birds to match. It is especially good for Red-bellied Woodpecker, an increasingly common species throughout southern New Hampshire. The presence of several beaver swamps adds Wood Duck, Hooded Merganser, Great Blue Heron, Osprey, and Virginia Rail to the list of possibilities. There is no vehicle access from the west side through to Durham Point Road, but a walking trail connects both ends of Longmarsh Road, with additional side trails leading off the main trail.

The Isles of Shoals

The Isles of Shoals group comprises nine islands spread between New Hampshire (Star, Seavey, White, and Lunging [aka Londoners]) and Maine (Appledore, Smuttynose, Duck, Cedar, and Malaga). All are of interest to birders, but it is only possible to access Appledore, Star and, with difficulty, White and Seavey. A boat tour of the islands can be rewarding from spring through summer. Black Guillemot breeds most years on Appledore (and on White Island in 2012); one or more often can be found in the sheltered cove formed by Appledore, Smuttynose, and Star Islands, known as Gosport Harbor.

The tern colony on White and Seavey Islands is easily viewed by boat. Roseate Terns can be picked out from the masses of Common Terns by their calls and, for experienced observers, by their paler upperparts and stiffer, snappier flight style. Arctic Terns usually number fewer than 10 pairs and can be hard to distinguish from the Common Terns; in recent years, a pair has nested on the shingle beach among discarded lobster pots.

APPLEDORE ISLAND

The island has hosted a bird-banding laboratory during spring and fall since the 1970s; the lab's primary purpose is to study the migration and stopover ecology of Nearctic-Neotropical migrants. In 2009, the lab banded its 100,000th bird—a Gray Catbird—and banding recaptures have occurred all

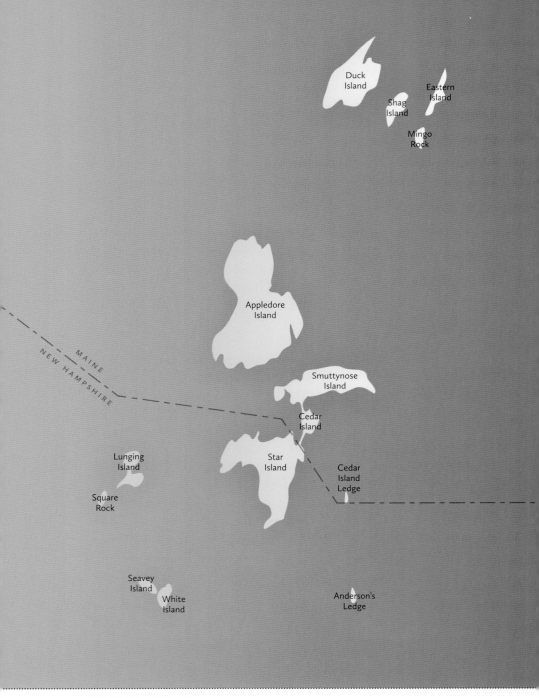

Duck
Island

Shag
Island

Eastern
Island

Mingo
Rock

Appledore
Island

MAINE
NEW HAMPSHIRE

Smuttynose
Island

Cedar
Island

Lunging
Island

Star
Island

Cedar
Island
Ledge

Square
Rock

Seavey
Island

White
Island

Anderson's
Ledge

ISLES OF SHOALS

along the Eastern Seaboard. A Northern Waterthrush banded on Appledore on August 23, 1992, was captured and released in Venezuela's Henri Pittier National Park on October 22, 1994.

Access to the island is available only through the Shoals Marine Laboratory (www.sml.cornell.edu). Star Island offers equally outstanding birding and is much more accessible to the public.

STAR ISLAND

About 30 species of warblers spend the summer months in New Hampshire. Many are beautifully colored and patterned but, for the most part, these birds are small and shy. They often lurk high in the forest canopy or deep in swampy wetlands, proving frustratingly elusive to the untrained eye. By the time these birds reach New Hampshire in the spring, many are at the end of a long, arduous trek from Central or South America. Of the millions that stream north across the continent, some inevitably get disoriented and discover themselves over the ocean. These birds must find land before they run out of energy and perish. Islands function like magnets for birds caught in such situations. Lighthouses increase the local attraction for disoriented birds, guiding them to safety during darkness or fog.

Star Island is a small, 46-acre island only 45 minutes by boat from mainland New Hampshire. It is a wonderful place to find a highly concentrated variety of birds in spring. The island has few trees, its cover consisting mostly of low scrub and shrubs, so most birds are observed at eye level. As these birds often are preoccupied with finding food, they pay little attention to people and offer astoundingly close views. Simply put, the opportunities to witness birds that are otherwise difficult to observe are terrific. The same is true in fall, although many of the species are in duller plumage at that time.

The island is owned by the Star Island Corporation (www.starisland.org), which charges a nominal fee for day visitors. Daily ferry service is available from June through August and on weekends only beginning in September (www.uncleoscar.com). Access outside these months is by charter only.

WHITE ISLAND AND SEAVEY ISLAND

White Island and Seavey Island, each about 4 acres of mostly bare granite, are the sites of a tern restoration project, one of the most successful conservation initiatives in the history of the state.

Like all ground-nesting birds, terns are vulnerable to predation by a vari-

Mourning Warbler, Star Island, May 24, 2010. The wonder of birding on Star Island is partly attributable to the fact that otherwise difficult-to-see birds can be studied at close range. This species, though quite common in northern New Hampshire, is ordinarily very shy and can be extremely hard to spot. *Jim Hully*

Arctic Tern, White and Seavey Islands, June 6, 2008. *Eric Masterson*

ety of wild and feral animals, including cats, raccoons, and opossums. They tend to fare much better on offshore islands—where the range of potential predators is smaller than on the mainland. White and Seavey had historically supported a tern colony, but the birds were driven off by Herring Gulls and Great Black-backed Gulls, both of which increased dramatically in New Hampshire over the past century. Because these gulls are large, aggressive, and do not migrate, they are able to commandeer the island's real estate before the migratory terns return from the tropics in May.

Beginning in 1997, New Hampshire Audubon biologists, led by Diane DeLuca, deployed wooden tern decoys on the islands and installed a sound system that broadcast tern vocalizations. At the same time, the biologists discouraged gulls from nesting. Six pairs of common terns nested in 1997 and raised six young. Their numbers grew almost exponentially after that, peaking at about 2500 pairs. The tern colony, which now includes a small number of Arctic Terns and federally listed Roseate Terns, has become the largest in the Gulf of Maine.

The two islands are connected by a shingle beach during low tide. The bulk of the terns nest on Seavey Island, where the habitat is more suitable, but birds have also begun to nest on White Island. Although there are no scheduled landings at the moment, the islands are state-owned and open to the public, with restrictions during nesting season. Several boats visit during summer but do not land, and excellent views of the terns can be obtained from the water. Arctic Terns are hard to differentiate from Common Terns, but a pair often nests on the shingle beach. Roseate Terns are a little bit easier to identify, and often nest on the edge of the colony.

Two operators offer daily trips to the tern colony during summer, as part of their tours of the Isles of Shoals. The *Uncle Oscar* (www.uncleoscar.com) departs from Rye Harbor, while the *Thomas Laighton* (www.islesofshoals.com) leaves from Portsmouth. For visitors interested strictly in the terns, the *Uncle Oscar* offers a superior experience.

Ocean

Any guide to the birds of New Hampshire would be incomplete without reference to those species that occur in the Gulf of Maine, just off the coast. Beneath the surface is a complex underwater topography, featuring the glacial moraines of Jeffreys Ledge and an underwater mountain known as Cashes

Ledge. Although you can't see them from the surface, these features profoundly affect the fertility of the ocean by redistributing nutrients upwards through the water column. During August and September, birds are drawn to the waters above these areas like filings to a magnet. Whales and dolphins are not uncommon either. In fact, Jeffreys Ledge offers an experience comparable to that of nearby Stellwagen Bank, which is consistently rated as one of the top ten places in the world for whalewatching.

Along with the familiar gulls and terns, pelagic bird species like Northern Fulmar, shearwaters, storm-petrels, phalaropes, Black-legged Kittiwake, Sabine's Gull, jaegers, and alcids can be encountered at these offshore sites. These ocean wanderers are rarely seen from land.

JEFFREYS LEDGE

A 2-hour boat ride from the coast, Jeffreys Ledge is easily visited during the summer and early fall, when several whalewatching companies operate out of New Hampshire's Rye Harbor and Hampton Harbor, as well as Newburyport and Gloucester in Massachusetts. The boats prioritize whales, but whales and seabirds often feed on the same resources. If you are fortunate enough to have access to private transport, the area of Jeffreys Ledge northwest to Old Scantum is often a productive spot, frequented by alcids in winter. A series of westward extensions off the northern tip of Jeffreys Ledge—known as the Fingers—also can be productive.

Eastman's (www.eastmansdocks.com) is the only New Hampshire company that operates into November and December and thus offers the only scheduled opportunities to go offshore during the best months for alcids, Northern Fulmar, and Black-legged Kittiwake. The trips are intended for anglers, but they welcome birders too. As all the fishing is done from the lower deck, birders have the upper deck to themselves. More importantly, the bait and chum used during fishing can attract large numbers of seabirds to the boat.

PLATTS BANK, FIPPENNIES LEDGE, AND CASHES LEDGE

Farther offshore (and requiring a long day in the field), Platts Bank, Fippennies Ledge, and Cashes Ledge are all excellent sites. The latter two are especially noteworthy for being the most reliable places to see Leach's Storm-Petrel, a bird which is rarely seen over Jeffreys Ledge and is even rarer close to shore.

These sites also offer a higher likelihood of jaegers, Sabine's Gull, and other

Cory's Shearwater,
Jeffreys Ledge, September
12, 2011. *Len Medlock*

Leach's Storm-Petrel (at far right) with Wilson's Storm-Petrels,
Fippennies Ledge, August 18, 2009. *Eric Masterson*

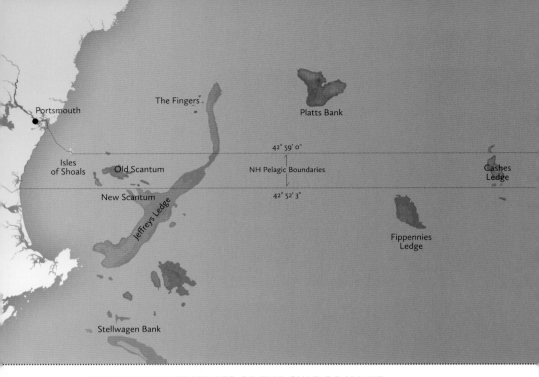

UNDERWATER FEATURES OF THE GULF OF MAINE
WITHIN REACH OF NEW HAMPSHIRE PORTS

rare pelagic species than Jeffreys Ledge. The Yankee Fleet (www.yankeefleet .com), based in Gloucester, is the only operator to offer regularly scheduled trips to Cashes Ledge. Like Eastman's trips, these are primarily for fishing, but offer excellent birding as well. Eastman's sometimes runs one trip to Cashes or Fippennies Ledge in late summer (inquire by phone at 603-474-3461). Note that a trip to Cashes or Fippennies Ledge requires a minimum 130-mile roundtrip. Expect to be on the boat for at least 16 hours. Some other New Hampshire operators are listed here:

www.algauron.com Al Gauron's fleet operates out of Hampton, with whale-watch cruises offered in July and August.

www.atlanticwhalewatch.com This company offers charter fishing and whalewatching aboard the *Atlantic Queen* out of Rye Harbor, from June through September.

www.granitestatewhalewatch.com The *Granite State* departs from Rye Harbor on whalewatching trips from June through September.

WINTER BIRDING

Alcids are the stars of Jeffreys Ledge during the winter. Six species occur in New Hampshire: Dovekie, Common Murre, Thick-billed Murre, Razorbill, Black Guillemot, and Atlantic Puffin. In many ways, they are the Northern Hemisphere's penguins, a group with which they share many traits. Like penguins, alcids walk upright and are dark above and white below, to help the birds escape detection from airborne and submarine predators. Also like penguins, they use their wings to "fly" underwater, unlike most other diving birds, which use their feet. These shared characteristics are a classic case of convergent evolution, a process by which distantly related life forms evolve similar body plans in order to accomplish similar tasks.

Black Guillemot occasionally breeds on one or more islands in the Isles of Shoals. Atlantic Puffin populations are increasing at breeding sites in Maine

Atlantic Puffin, Jeffreys Ledge, February 13, 2010. You can expect to find one or two of these birds on any trip to Jeffreys Ledge between November and April. *Len Medlock*

and this bird is becoming a more frequent sight in New Hampshire waters during spring and early summer. Otherwise they are a winter phenomenon in New Hampshire. Of the six species, only Black Guillemot and Razorbill are seen from the mainland coast with any regularity. The other four species are largely confined to the Jeffreys Ledge area.

Unfortunately, the low-pressure systems that dominate New England's weather during winter usually produce strong winds. For this reason, it can be extremely difficult to get offshore, as scheduled birding trips more often than not fall victim to weather cancellations. To compound the problem, fewer companies operate during winter. Eastman's, in Hampton, usually has a boat in the water until mid-December to cater to the recreational fishing community. They will take birders too. If the weather is good, their trips provide a perfectly good substitute for a chartered birding trip. The fishing activity provides a constant supply of chum and, as all anglers cast from the lower deck, the upper deck is left free for birders.

The birds tend to be unevenly distributed across Jeffreys Ledge, and you should not be disappointed if you do not meet with instant success. The New Scantum area and the Fingers at the north end of the ledge typically are excellent, but birds can occur anywhere, especially at depths of 300 feet or less. Data on bird abundance are sparse due to the infrequent nature of visits

Northern Fulmar, Jeffreys Ledge, November 27, 2011.
Eric Masterson

Red-necked Phalarope, Jeffreys Ledge, September 11, 2008.
Rarely seen from land in New Hampshire, this shorebird is commonly
observed during whalewatches in fall. *Len Medlock*

to the area, but it is likely that numbers peak during early November and late February or early March, when birds are migrating south in fall and north in spring. Dovekie, Common Murre, and Razorbill are relatively common, though abundance varies from year to year. Most trips during winter will produce at least one Atlantic Puffin, with Thick-billed Murre the least common species. Northern Fulmar and Black-legged Kittiwake are easily found.

A NOTE ON WHALEWATCHING

To tell the truth, it can be difficult to focus on birds when the largest animals on the planet are vying for your attention. In summer and early fall, Jeffreys Ledge offers close encounters with several species of whales, including Minke, Fin, Humpback and, less commonly, Sei and Northern Right Whales. This last species is one of the rarest animals in the world, with only a few hundred left in existence. Because they migrate through the Gulf of Maine, however, on the way to their winter quarters off the Carolinas, it is not uncommon to see one or two later in the fall.

Fin Whales are one of the more commonly seen species on Jeffreys Ledge. They usually show only their back and dorsal fin above water, so one has to imagine the bulk beneath the waves—which can reach 70 feet in length and weigh 260,000 pounds. As these whales feed, Wilson's Storm-Petrels patter the water around them, grabbing scraps that escape the whales' giant maws. The two species are a study in contrast, with the birds weighing in at slightly more than an ounce. Like the whales, however, these birds also trade in the spectacular. In fall, Wilson's Storm-Petrels migrate south to breeding grounds in the Antarctic—a roundtrip of about 20,000 miles.

Great Shearwater, Sooty Shearwater, and Manx Shearwater also are fairly reliable offshore during the summer. Although abundance varies from year to year, Cory's Shearwater has become a more regular sighting in New Hampshire in recent years.

6 The White Mountains and the North Country

New Hampshire from the White Mountains north offers a stark contrast with the rest of the state in many ways. The North Country—also known as the Great North Woods—marks the southern front of a vast belt of boreal forest that stretches across Canada, northern Europe, and Russia. In New Hampshire, this forest provides wildlife habitat not found elsewhere in the state, save for a very few spots in the southwest. Moose are more common in the North Country than elsewhere in New Hampshire, pine marten are found only here, and even lynx are increasingly being spotted in the region.

Similarly, the bird life is very different from that in the southern part of the state. Several species of warbler that breed primarily in Canada extend their range into the northern tip of New Hampshire. Species like Cape May Warbler and Bicknell's Thrush might pass through your southern New Hampshire yard in spring, but their journey won't end until they reach the spruce-fir forest of northern New Hampshire, Maine, and Canada.

The area is also remarkable for its resident specialties, including Gray Jay (aka Canada Jay), Boreal Chickadee, Spruce Grouse, and Black-backed Woodpecker; these species breed nowhere else in New Hampshire. East Inlet, located a few miles from the Canadian border, is an especially good location to spot these birds.

Many of the characteristic birds of the North Country also occur in southern New Hampshire. However, birders will be impressed by how much more common they are in the north. This disparity is especially evident in locations like Pondicherry, where Yellow-bellied Sapsucker, Red-breasted Nuthatch, Winter Wren, Golden-crowned Kinglet, Hermit Thrush, Northern Waterthrush, Nashville Warbler, Northern Parula, Magnolia Warbler, Yellow-rumped Warbler, White-throated Sparrow, Dark-eyed Junco, and Purple Finch are far more common than in the south.

Note that migrants to the very far north of New Hampshire arrive signifi-

Gray Jay, North Country, April 21, 2010. *Jim Hully*

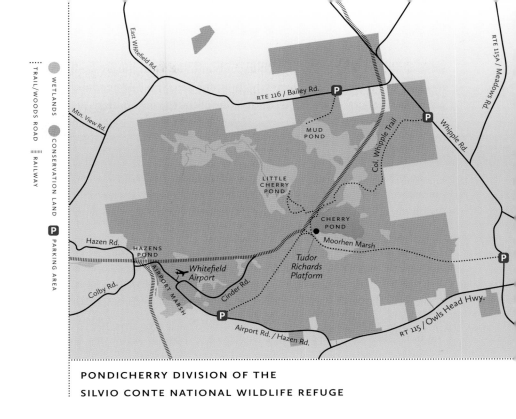

**PONDICHERRY DIVISION OF THE
SILVIO CONTE NATIONAL WILDLIFE REFUGE**

cantly later than they do in southern parts of the state. If you plan on visiting before the beginning of June, for example, you might be disappointed to find that species such as Mourning Warbler have not yet arrived on territory, especially if the weather in May has been poor.

While exploring the area, be aware that it is exceptionally easy to get lost in the vast forest. Do not leave the trail unless you have a map and compass and know how to use them. When planning your trip, remember that the North Country is colder and typically rainier than southern New Hampshire. Even in June, early mornings can be chilly—and the bugs can be fierce.

Pondicherry

Pondicherry, a division of the Silvio Conte National Wildlife Refuge, is one of New Hampshire's great scenic jewels. This spectacular refuge boasts stunning views of the Presidential Range of the White Mountains. The preserve is a mosaic of lowland boreal habitat, including spruce-fir forest and black spruce–tamarack bog. Two pristine ponds at the core of the refuge form the headwaters of the Johns River, which drains into the Connecticut. Pondicherry is a mecca for boreal species and one of the top destinations for birders in New Hampshire and the region. Easily explored by way of a network of walking trails, the refuge hosts 130 species of breeding birds and boasts a birdlist of 238 species in all.

The refuge is a testament to the tireless work of Tudor Richards, who engineered the protection of the first 312 acres while at New Hampshire Audubon, and David Govatski, who has labored tirelessly to build on Tudor's work. Pondicherry is now almost 6,000 acres in size.

Cherry Pond is the larger and more accessible of the two ponds. It can be reached by an excellent, though occasionally wet, 1.5-mile trail that leads directly from a trailhead on Airport Road to Waumbek Junction. Biking is allowed, but motorized traffic is prohibited (except for snowmobiles in winter). The Tudor Richards viewing platform, on the southwest corner of the pond, is accessed by a short trail from Waumbek Junction. This is an excellent vantage point for birding and an apt memorial.

Cherry Pond is an excellent stopover site, especially for fall waterbirds. Most years, all three species of scoter are seen during late October. A floating island is viewable from the railroad that borders the west side of the pond. The island rises and falls with the water level, providing a perfect nesting site for a pair of Common Loons.

Little Cherry Pond is accessed by a trail that begins a quarter-mile north of Waumbek Junction, on the west side of the railroad. On the opposite side of the tracks, the Rampart Path leads along the west shore of Cherry Pond. The views of the Presidential Range from this trail are spectacular; it also is a good place to scan Cherry Pond for waterfowl.

Osprey and Bald Eagle often fish in both Cherry and Little Cherry Ponds, while the black spruce forest that borders Little Cherry Pond is one of the refuge's better locations for boreal specialties, including Black-backed Woodpecker and Palm Warbler, which can be seen and heard along the trail. A pair of Northern Goshawk has bred in this part of the refuge in recent years. Spruce Grouse, Gray Jay, and Boreal Chickadee also occur here, but these species can be easier to find at higher elevations in the White Mountains and farther north in Pittsburg.

The Little Cherry Pond Trail ends at the pond's eastern edge. This is an excellent spot to spend some time listening for birds, including Olive-sided

Flycatcher and Lincoln's Sparrow. A telescope is useful to search the pond for Green-winged Teal and Ring-necked Duck, both of which breed in the refuge. Cape May Warbler and Bay-breasted Warbler also occur here, though the area represents the southern edge of their range in New Hampshire and they too are more easily found farther north.

Upon your return to the main rail trail, listen for Mourning Warbler—especially in forest clearings and thickets. The declining Rusty Blackbird breeds in the refuge's wooded swamps.

Moorhen Marsh, on the east side of Cherry Pond, is an excellent cattail marsh that has traditionally included American Bittern, Virginia Rail, Sora, and Wilson's Snipe among its list of breeding birds. Green-winged Teal frequent the marsh, and both Least Bittern and Long-eared Owl have been recorded. Marsh Wren used to breed here.

Like other airfields in New Hampshire, Whitefield includes a significant area of grassland breeding habitat. The airport hosts several interesting species, most notably a pair of Northern Harriers. Savannah Sparrow, Bobolink, and the declining Eastern Meadowlark also occur here, though rarer grassland specialists like Vesper Sparrow and Grasshopper Sparrow are absent.

Across the road from the airport is a marsh, appropriately called Airport Marsh. It is an excellent site for Hooded Merganser, American Bittern, Virginia Rail, Belted Kingfisher, and Alder Flycatcher during summer. This site also is worth checking during spring and fall storms for shorebirds and rarer migrants, including terns and phalaropes.

Cinder Road, which runs south and east of the airport, overlooks another marsh to the south and occasionally offers glimpses of the airfield to the north. Brown Thrasher and Willow Flycatcher occur in the scrub along the road, and the surrounding area offers good habitat for Merlin and Olive-sided Flycatcher. Whipple Road is one of the better locations in the area to hear Saw-whet Owl and Whip-poor-will.

Fourteen miles south of Pondicherry, Trudeau Road is another excellent stop on your way to or from the North Country. A snowmobile trail that parallels the west side of the road is a great spot for boreal specialties including Black-backed Woodpecker, Yellow-bellied Flycatcher, Boreal Chickadee, Ruby-crowned Kinglet, and Tennessee Warbler. I have even found Black-crowned Night-Heron here. Trudeau Road runs north from Route 3, about five miles from Exit 35 on I93. The trailhead is on the west side of the road a little more than half a mile from the junction with Route 3.

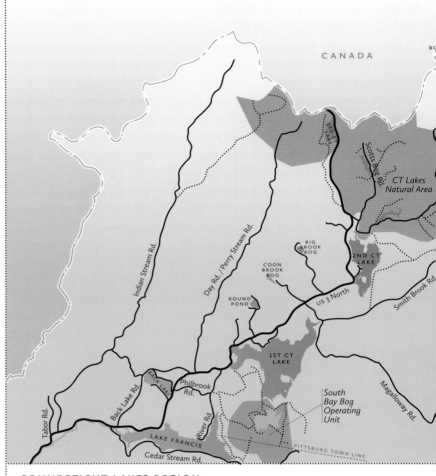

CANADA

3RD CT LAKE

Scotts Bog Rd.

CT Lakes
Natural Area

BIG
BROOK
BOG

2ND CT
LAKE

COON
BROOK
BOG

Indian Stream Rd.

Day Rd. / Perry Stream Rd.

ROUND
POND

US 3 North

Smith Brook Rd

1ST CT
LAKE

Magalloway Rd.

BACK LAKE

Back Lake Rd.

Philbrook
Rd.

River Rd.

South
Bay Bog
Operating
Unit

Tabor Rd.

LAKE FRANCIS

Cedar Stream Rd.

PITTSBURG TOWN LINE

CONNECTICUT LAKES REGION

To visit Pondicherry, take Interstate 93 to Exit 35. Follow Route 3 north until its junction with Route 115, then take Route 115 east for 4 miles and turn left on Airport Road. Continue 1.4 miles on Airport Road. The trailhead for the Pondicherry rail trail will be on your right.

The Connecticut Lakes Region

The Connecticut Lakes region includes Indian Stream Road, Perry Stream Road, Coon Brook Bog, Big Brook Bog, Magalloway Road, Smith Brook Road, Scotts Bog, East Inlet, and the Connecticut Lakes.

Driving north from Concord on Interstate 93, you can reach Franconia Notch in about an hour. It might seem like you have arrived in the North Country, given the feeling of wilderness that comes with the White Mountains and the boreal forest which surrounds you, yet Pittsburg is another two hours north, and the border with Canada almost another hour again. New Hampshire might be a small state, but it is a long one.

The Connecticut Lakes are accessed via Route 3, which continues into Canada as Route 257. It is worth driving north of the border for a few miles to witness the stark change in the countryside. The elevation drops suddenly and the boreal forest gives way to a flat agricultural landscape. The region forms the headwaters of the Connecticut River, New England's longest waterway. A major conservation effort in 2003 protected 171,000 acres of the headwaters, including 146,000 acres that were sold to a timber investment company with restrictions that prevent future development. The remaining 25,000 acres—designated the Connecticut Lakes Natural Area—are to be managed exclusively for wildlife. A 15,000-acre portion of this, east of Route 3 and north of the Second Connecticut Lake, has been preserved as wilderness, where natural regenerative processes are favored in place of active management. The balance—10,000 acres situated south of First Connecticut Lake and east of Lake Francis—is called the South Bay Bog Operating Unit. It will be managed to maintain and enhance a variety of wildlife species and habitats.

The Connecticut Lakes Natural Area is the state's best place to find species that prefer to breed in mature and old-growth boreal forest. This includes Spruce Grouse, Black-backed Woodpecker, American Three-toed Woodpecker, Olive-sided Flycatcher, Gray Jay, Boreal Chickadee, Cape May Warbler, and Bay-breasted Warbler. The working forest, on the other hand, provides excellent habitat for northern specialties that thrive in successional, brushy environments—a common feature of areas that have been recently logged. These species include Mourning Warbler, Fox Sparrow, and Lincoln's Sparrow.

The majority of the best birding spots in this region are in Pittsburg; at 291 square miles, it's the largest township in New England. Many of these sites are accessible only via gated dirt roads; many such remain closed until well after the spring thaw, either to prevent damage or to allow for repairs. East Inlet Road, for example, often doesn't open until late May. Care, caution, and a reliable vehicle are recommended for visiting the area. Logging trucks are frequently encountered on forest roads and have right of way.

You can check on seasonal road closures by visiting the Connecticut Lakes Headwaters Working Forest Recreation Program page on the New Hampshire Division of Parks and Recreation Web site (www.nhstateparks.org).

There is no shortage of accommodation in the area. For some ideas, check out the North Country Chamber of Commerce Web site (www.northcountrychamber.com). If you plan on camping, consider Deer Mountain Campground, 5 minutes south of the Canadian border on the west side of Route 3. It is situated in the best part of the North Country for boreal birds and right in the middle of "Moose Alley." Both American Three-toed Woodpecker and Black-backed Woodpecker have bred in the campground.

INDIAN STREAM ROAD

At 19 miles in length, this is the longest logging road in the region and the most varied in habitat. After leaving Route 3 near Pittsburg, it passes through a variety of habitats, from northern hardwood to spruce-fir forest. Birding is especially good for northern specialties from about mile 5 onward. Look for Olive-sided Flycatcher and Mourning Warbler until about mile 15. Take a left at mile 14.2 to Terrell Pond to check for Black-backed Woodpecker.

PERRY STREAM ROAD

This road also can be accessed from Route 3, about 5 miles north of Pittsburg. Take a left on Day Road, which turns into Perry Stream Road and continues to within a mile of the Canadian border. Black-backed Woodpecker, Olive-sided Flycatcher, Yellow-bellied Flycatcher, Boreal Chickadee, Bay-breasted Warbler, Lincoln's Sparrow, and Rusty Blackbird can be found along this road.

COON BROOK BOG AND BIG BROOK BOG

Both bogs are reliable spots for Ring-necked Duck, which breed in the North Country, and probably Common Goldeneye as well. Coon Brook Road leaves Route 3 opposite Magalloway Road. Go 0.5 miles, stay right at the fork, continue for another 1.25 miles, then take a left to reach the boat launch. Big Brook Road leaves Route 3 another 2.5 miles north of Coon Brook Road.

MAGALLOWAY ROAD AND SMITH BROOK ROAD

These roads provide access to working forest in the Connecticut Lakes Headwaters. This area is less productive for species that prefer mature spruce-fir forest, such as Spruce Grouse, but better for birds that favor recently cut-over forest, such as Mourning Warbler and Lincoln's Sparrow. Multiple logging roads enter the forest from Smith Brook Road and Magalloway Road. The possibilities for exploration seem to increase exponentially, as each new road leads to two more. Many are gated, leaving hiking or biking as your only options for travel.

SCOTTS BOG AND EAST INLET

This area is considered one of the best places in the North Country for birding, and is often the preferred destination of people with limited time. Access is relatively easy along well-maintained logging roads, beginning a half-mile south of Deer Mountain Campground, on the east side of Route 3. The gates usually open in June, allowing you to drive over a small bridge that crosses the headwaters of the Connecticut River. At the T-junction, turn left for Scotts Bog, or right for East Inlet, Boundary Pond, and Rhubarb Pond, which is less than 1 mile from the border.

In recent years, Northern Harrier has bred in a bog on the left side of Scotts Bog Road, about a mile past the junction with East Inlet Road. About 3.5 miles past the junction, you will reach another road that leads down to Scotts Bog itself. This is a good spot for Rusty Blackbird. Check the open water for ducks, especially Green-winged Teal, Ring-necked Duck, and Common Goldeneye. Blue-winged Teal, a rare breeder in the North Country, is an outside possibility. This is an excellent location for Philadelphia Vireo and Wilson's Warbler.

East Inlet Road has slightly better spruce-fir habitat and a better reputation for Spruce Grouse than Scotts Bog Road, although even here this bird can be difficult to find, often requiring several visits for success. The old logging road that runs north from East Inlet Road at mile 3.5 is one of the more productive spots for this species. If this road were to continue (it does not), it would lead to the Norton Pool, a Nature Conservancy preserve encompassing more than 400 acres of virgin, lowland spruce-fir forest, the last of its kind in New Hampshire. This is extremely difficult terrain to navigate, but is likely one of the better spots in the whole region for Spruce Grouse and American Three-toed Woodpecker.

Elsewhere along East Inlet Road, look and listen for Olive-sided Flycatchers perched on dead snags in bogs, especially at Snag Pond at mile 11. Look for Cape May Warbler and the more common Bay-breasted Warbler among the spruce trees, and Philadelphia Vireo in streamside alders and poplars. Tennessee Warblers favor forest openings, especially alongside swamps and tamarack bogs.

East Inlet Road is navigable by car except for the last mile to Rhubarb Pond. It is worth walking this stretch, if only to see the Canadian border, made visible as a cut through the forest on the hills behind the pond. Olive-sided Flycatcher and Mourning Warblers are more common near the pond than elsewhere on East Inlet Road.

Birding by canoe is another enjoyable way to explore the area, especially for waterfowl, Common Loon, and Pied-billed Grebe. There is a boat launch at the dam, located 2 miles along East Inlet Road from Route 3.

THE CONNECTICUT LAKES

Like the state's other large bodies of water, the Connecticut Lakes offer good habitat for migrating waterfowl, grebes, loons, gulls, and occasionally terns. Because birders visit them much less often than the lakes in southern and central New Hampshire, less is known about their use by migrant species, but some intriguing records over the years suggest that they have great potential. Likely suspects during migration include all three species of scoter, Long-tailed Duck, and Horned and Red-necked Grebe. To provide increased water to downstream turbines, Second Connecticut Lake is occasionally drawn down, exposing large areas of muddy lake bottom. If this happens during late August or early September, when shorebirds are migrating, then expect the unexpected. As with other dams operated by TransCanada, you can call a hotline for information on dam releases, although the hotline does not provide the water level for this particular lake. (See Web Resources.)

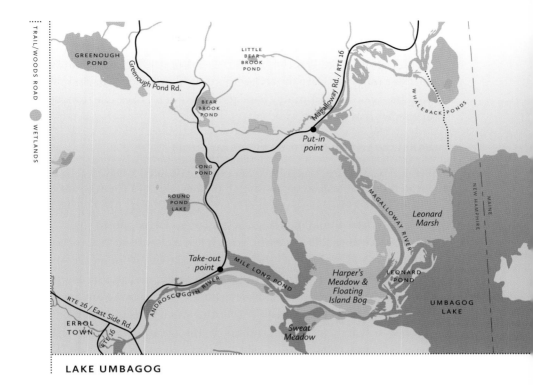

Lake Umbagog

Lake Umbagog area includes Magalloway River, Harpers Meadow, Leonard Pond, Leonard Marsh, Whaleback Ponds, and Pontook Reservoir.

Lake Umbagog is another mandatory stop on your journey to the North Country. The lake is the focal point of the Lake Umbagog National Wildlife Refuge, which conserves more than 25,000 acres of forests, wetlands, lakes, and rivers in New Hampshire and Maine (the state line runs north to south through the refuge). Although most of the typical North Country specialties can be found here, the breeding waterfowl set this place apart from other birding locations in New Hampshire. Several species that are range-restricted or uncommon elsewhere nest here—including Blue-winged Teal, Green-winged Teal, Ring-necked Duck, and Common Goldeneye—along with Wood Duck, American Black Duck, Hooded Merganser, and Common Merganser.

The birdlife of the area has been especially well documented. William

Brewster, a gifted amateur naturalist, conducted fieldwork here from 1871 to 1909.

More than any other place in the North Country, a proper visit to Umbagog demands a canoe. To leave the area without paddling some of its backwaters is to miss a central part of its character. If you don't have one, canoes are available for rent in Errol.

MAGALLOWAY RIVER AND HARPERS MEADOW

The only way to explore this area is by canoe. The downstream access point is located on the Androscoggin River, 1.6 miles north of the town of Errol along Route 16; the upstream access is on the Magalloway River in the Lake Umbagog National Wildlife Refuge, several miles farther north.

It is possible to paddle this entire stretch in a day, putting in at the refuge headquarters and canoeing all the way to the take-out point on the Androscoggin. Shorter trips that begin and end at the same point also are an option, as both the Magalloway and Androscoggin are slow-moving and paddling home against the current is easy. The birding can be fantastic, especially in the backwaters and marshes. In addition to the aforementioned waterfowl, American Bittern, Osprey, Bald Eagle, Northern Harrier, and Wilson's Snipe all breed here, and moose are commonly observed wading in the shallows.

Try to get on the water as early as possible to hear the dawn chorus. Your ears can be more valuable than your eyes for finding and identifying most of the birds you will encounter in the North Country. Common Loons often call at night during the breeding season and are usually quite vocal into the early morning. June is the best time to find Black-backed Woodpeckers, as their noisy young betray their location. You also are likely to encounter family groups of waterfowl in June, especially in backwaters.

The access to Harpers Meadow is about a mile downstream of Leonard Pond on the Androscoggin. Palm Warbler and Lincoln's Sparrow nest here, and the floating bog in the middle of the meadow was designated a National Natural Landmark in 1972. Sweat Meadow has more open water than Harpers Meadow and is usually a productive spot for waterfowl; however, it is sometimes closed due to eagle nesting activity. The entrance to Sweat Meadow is about a quarter-mile upstream from the entrance to Harpers Meadow, on the opposite bank of the river. From either spot it is a short paddle downstream until the river meets Route 16. There is a take-out point on Route 16, as well as a larger boat launch on Mountain Pond Road, on the other side of the river.

LEONARD POND

Leonard Pond, which is actually a series of flooded oxbows, can be a good spot for shorebirds during fall migration when the water is low, with likely species including Semipalmated Sandpiper, Killdeer, Spotted Sandpiper, Solitary Sandpiper, Greater Yellowlegs, Lesser Yellowlegs, Least Sandpiper, and Pectoral Sandpiper. Almost anything is possible, as the refuge boasts an impressive birdlist of 229 species, including 26 types of shorebirds. Florida Power and Light controls the Errol Dam and provides daily water-level reports at 800-557-3569. Black and Common Tern are possible during migration, and potential future nesters.

Bald Eagles disappeared from New Hampshire in 1949 due to the toxic effects of the pesticide DDT; a tree at Leonard Pond was the nesting site of the last pair. In 1989, the first pair of Bald Eagles to return to the state in the post-DDT era nested—amazingly—in the same tree. There are now at least 5 pairs in the refuge. Osprey also have rebounded since the 1972 ban on DDT; they are now common from spring through fall.

LEONARD MARSH

A mile north of Leonard Pond, this is a fantastic site for American Bittern, Virginia Rail, Sora, Wilson's Snipe, and other waterfowl, as well as a good vantage point for checking Lake Umbagog for migrant waterfowl, gulls, and terns. The location also has been mentioned more than once as a possible site for Yellow Rail, an extremely secretive bird that breeds no closer than Quebec's Gaspé Peninsula. Yellow Rail has been recorded only five times in New Hampshire, all during September and October.

WHALEBACK PONDS

A canoe is required to reach these two pristine ponds. Take Route 16 north from Errol for about 5.6 miles until the river begins to veer away from the road. Launch your canoe here and follow the river upstream for about a mile, through a series of sharp turns. There is a small road on the left (Little Berlin Road) that serves some summer cabins and a deep cove on the right with an island. A trail leads southeast from the bank of the river just inside the island. Securely beach your canoe, then follow the trail along a ridge that bisects the two ponds. The pond southwest of the ridge is visible from the trail, but the one on the northeast requires some bushwhacking to reach. Do not attempt to do this without a map and compass! The largest northern white cedar swamp in New Hampshire surrounds the ponds. Spruce Grouse and American Three-toed Woodpecker occasionally occur here, as do the more common Black-backed Woodpecker, Gray Jay, and other northern forest specialists.

PONTOOK RESERVOIR

This reservoir and its impressive wetlands complex are located about 15 miles south of Errol on Route 16. During summer, American Bittern, Virginia Rail, and Sora have been found here with regularity, and it is one of the best sites in the North Country for Marsh Wren. There is a huge winter roost of Common Raven near Pontook, at times in excess of 150 birds. Bald Eagles have nested at Pontook for several years.

The White Mountains

Birding in the White Mountains is a function of elevation, a factor that determines temperature, precipitation, vegetation, and ultimately bird species. I will limit this section to the specialty birds of the Whites, those boreal species that breed only in the spruce-fir forests that dominate this region and much of the North Country. These include Spruce Grouse, American Three-toed Woodpecker, Black-backed Woodpecker, Olive-sided Flycatcher, Yellow-bellied Flycatcher, Philadelphia Vireo, Gray Jay, Boreal Chickadee, Ruby-crowned Kinglet, Bicknell's Thrush, Swainson's Thrush, Tennessee Warbler, Cape May Warbler, Bay-breasted Warbler, Blackpoll Warbler, Lincoln's Sparrow, Rusty Blackbird, and White-winged Crossbill.

The standout bird among these species is the Bicknell's Thrush, which is restricted to a narrow fragmented band running from the Appalachian Mountains in upstate New York through Vermont's Green Mountains, New Hampshire's White Mountains, and the mountains of west and central Maine to parts of New Brunswick, Nova Scotia, and areas of Quebec adjacent to the St. Lawrence River. The entire population is estimated to range from 25,000 to 50,000 individuals, approximately 40 percent of which breed in New Hampshire. Birders from around the globe head to the White Mountains to see this species.

One other bird breeds in the White Mountains and nowhere else in New Hampshire. The American Pipit can be found from June through August on Mount Washington, above the treeline in the tundra zone, including the Alpine Garden.

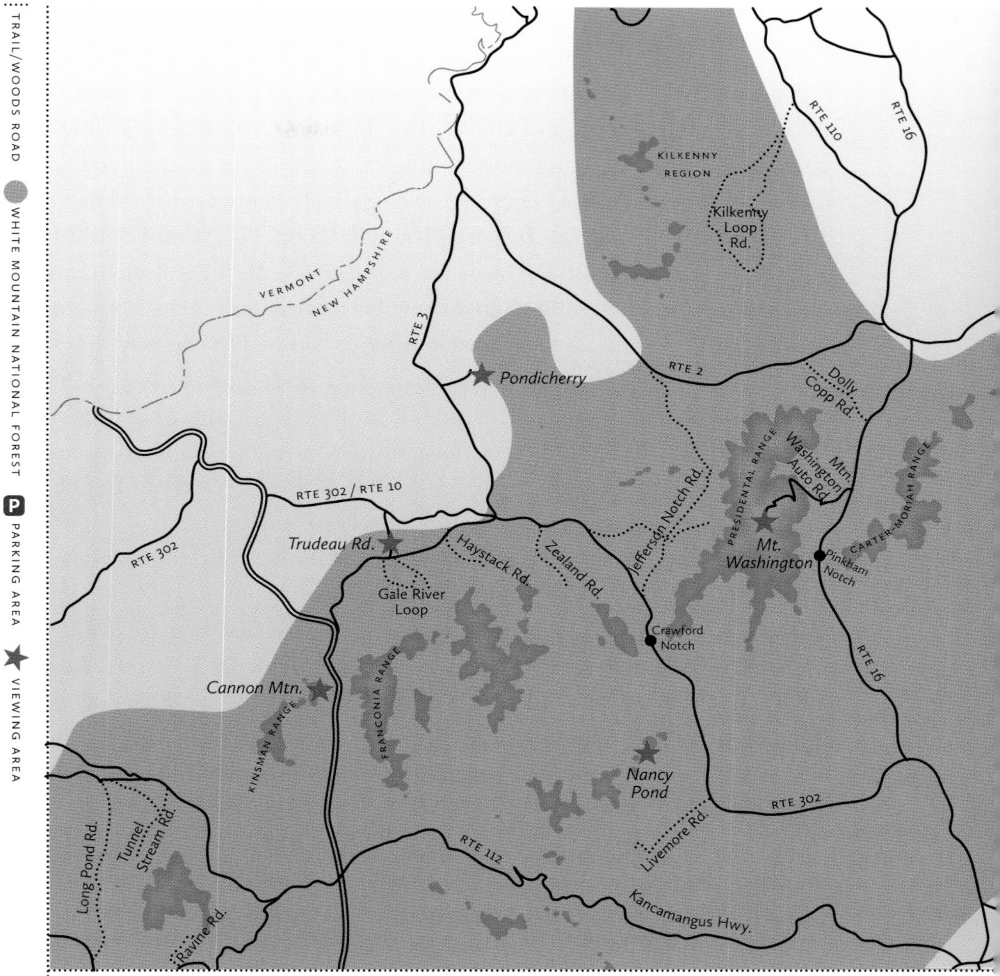

Map legend (left margin):

TRAIL/WOODS ROAD

WHITE MOUNTAIN NATIONAL FOREST

P PARKING AREA

★ VIEWING AREA

Map labels:

KILKENNY REGION

Kilkenny Loop Rd.

RTE 110

RTE 16

VERMONT

NEW HAMPSHIRE

RTE 3

RTE 2

★ Pondicherry

Dolly Copp Rd.

RTE 302 / RTE 10

RTE 302

Trudeau Rd.

Haystack Rd.

Zealand Rd.

Jefferson Notch Rd.

PRESIDENTIAL RANGE

Mtn. Washington / Auto Rd.

Mt. Washington

Pinkham Notch

CARTER-MORIAH RANGE

Gale River Loop

FRANCONIA RANGE

KINSMAN RANGE

Cannon Mtn. ★

Crawford Notch

★ Nancy Pond

RTE 302

RTE 16

Long Pond Rd.

Tunnel Stream Rd.

Ravine Rd.

RTE 112

Livemore Rd.

Kancamangus Hwy.

BIRDING LOCATIONS IN THE WHITE MOUNTAINS

Shaded areas represent elevations above 3,500 feet.

Bicknell's Thrush prefers elevations from 3,500 feet to the treeline. (The shaded areas on the map of the White Mountains represent elevations of 3500 feet or higher. During the breeding season, you are unlikely to find the species outside this range.) There are two relatively easy ways to find Bicknell's Thrush in New Hampshire: by car and by aerial tram. The Mount Washington Auto Road in June, when the birds are in full song, offers the best chance for success. Stop and listen for them at regular intervals after the 3-mile mark. Patience is necessary as they can be difficult to see. On the way down the mountain, patience is particularly essential—stop frequently so your brakes can cool. (The aerial tram to the top of Cannon Mountain, where Bicknell's Thrush also breeds, is the second easy route to these birds. They also occur along the highest points of the Jefferson Notch Road. All other forays to see this species will require at least a moderately strenuous hike!)

You can expect to encounter one or more of Boreal Chickadee, Swainson's Thrush, and Blackpoll Warbler from the Mt. Washington Auto Road, but you will be fortunate to find any of the other boreal species. You are unlikely to see Spruce Grouse by driving the Auto Road. Apart from East Inlet Road in the North Country, the best way to find this species is by hiking one of the many trails in the White Mountains. In this case, the early bird definitely gets the worm. If you set out later, other hikers will have pushed the birds away from the trails, farther into the forest.

Gray Jay is usually an easy find in the White Mountains, especially near popular rest stops, where they often forage for leftovers, hence the nickname "camp robber." Black-backed Woodpeckers are seen by hikers on a fairly regular basis, but the American Three-toed Woodpecker is a real rarity. I have yet to see one in New Hampshire.

NANCY POND TRAIL

As I have been at pains to impress elsewhere in this guide, habitat is the key—when you cross into new habitat, you will likely find new birds. Thus, if your White Mountain hike takes you past bogs and ponds, you can expect to see other species than the birds of the forest. I include this trail out of the hundreds of contenders because it accesses Nancy Pond, Norcross Pond, and the Pemigewasset Wilderness.

This has traditionally been one of the more likely locations to find American Three-toed Woodpecker in New Hampshire. The species is extremely rare in the state, and should not be expected anywhere, but if you wanted to prospect for it, this would be a good spot to start looking because of the high quality of the natural habitat.

The hike to the ponds is moderate for most of its length, with the exception of one quite strenuous section near Nancy Cascades. Because the trail passes through a wide variety of habitats, it is possible to observe many different species, and the view from the ponds will more than make up for any birds you miss.

Expect the roundtrip to Norcross Pond, the farther of the two ponds, to require at least 8 hours.

JEFFERSON NOTCH ROAD

This 18-mile section of road runs along the western flank of the Presidential Range, from Route 302 to Route 2. The south end of the road begins about 0.2 miles north of Crawford Notch, and is called Mount Clinton Road for the first 4 miles. Finding the road from the north is trickier because it is accessed off Valley Road and not Route 2. Jefferson Notch Road rises from 1400 feet to 3,000 feet, is not maintained in winter, and usually not passable until June. If spring floods or snows are especially severe, the road can remain closed for an entire season.

The road reaches its highest elevation in the pass between Mount Jefferson and Mount Dartmouth. This stretch usually produces Bicknell's Thrush, along with Gray Jay and Boreal Chickadee. The entire length of the road is good for most of the boreal specialties of the White Mountains, including Spruce Grouse, Black-backed Woodpecker, Yellow-bellied Flycatcher, Ruby-crowned Kinglet, Swainson's Thrush, Tennessee Warbler, Bay-breasted Warbler, Blackpoll Warbler, Lincoln's Sparrow, Rusty Blackbird, and White-winged Crossbill.

There are other forest roads that venture into the Whites, though none to the extent of Jefferson Notch Road. I have identified some on the map. You should check with the White Mountain National Forest (www.fs.usda.gov/whitemountain) about road closures before setting out.

These roads are a good entry point for those with limited mobility or limited time, but the White Mountains are best experienced on foot, and I encourage you to get out of the car and take to the trails if you are able.

7 The Lakes Region

The larger lakes in the Lakes Region receive relatively little coverage for their size and likely capacity for good birding, thus there is some element of conjecture to what follows. My supposition that the large lakes have the potential to produce good birds is not without foundation. Historical records from Lake Sunapee, Newfound Lake, Lake Winnipesaukee, and Squam Lake include multiple records of scarce and rare species, including Western Grebe, American White Pelican, Sabine's Gull, and all three species of jaeger. Other interesting records include some remarkably high counts of scarce inland waterbirds—for example, 300 Horned Grebes on Lake Winnisquam on December 14, 1957, and 450 Red-necked Grebes on Squam Lake on April 26, 1992—and regularly occurring concentrations of waterfowl from fall through spring, ice conditions permitting. Winnisquam in particular often hosts a relatively large number of Common Goldeneye, with one or more Barrow's Goldeneye. The major lakes also should be productive during harsh spring and fall weather, when they offer safe haven for storm-blown waterbirds, especially unusual gulls and terns.

The Lakes

The vast majority of lake frontage in the region is private property, and access ranges from fair to poor. This is especially true of Squam Lake. The following maps and text identify some of the better access points. A good scope is essential.

SILVER LAKE

This is the second smallest of the lakes covered here. Take Exit 20 off Interstate 93 and follow Routes 11 and 3 north for 2.25 miles. Turn right onto Silver Lake Road, then continue 0.6 miles to the dock. Silver Lake is produc-

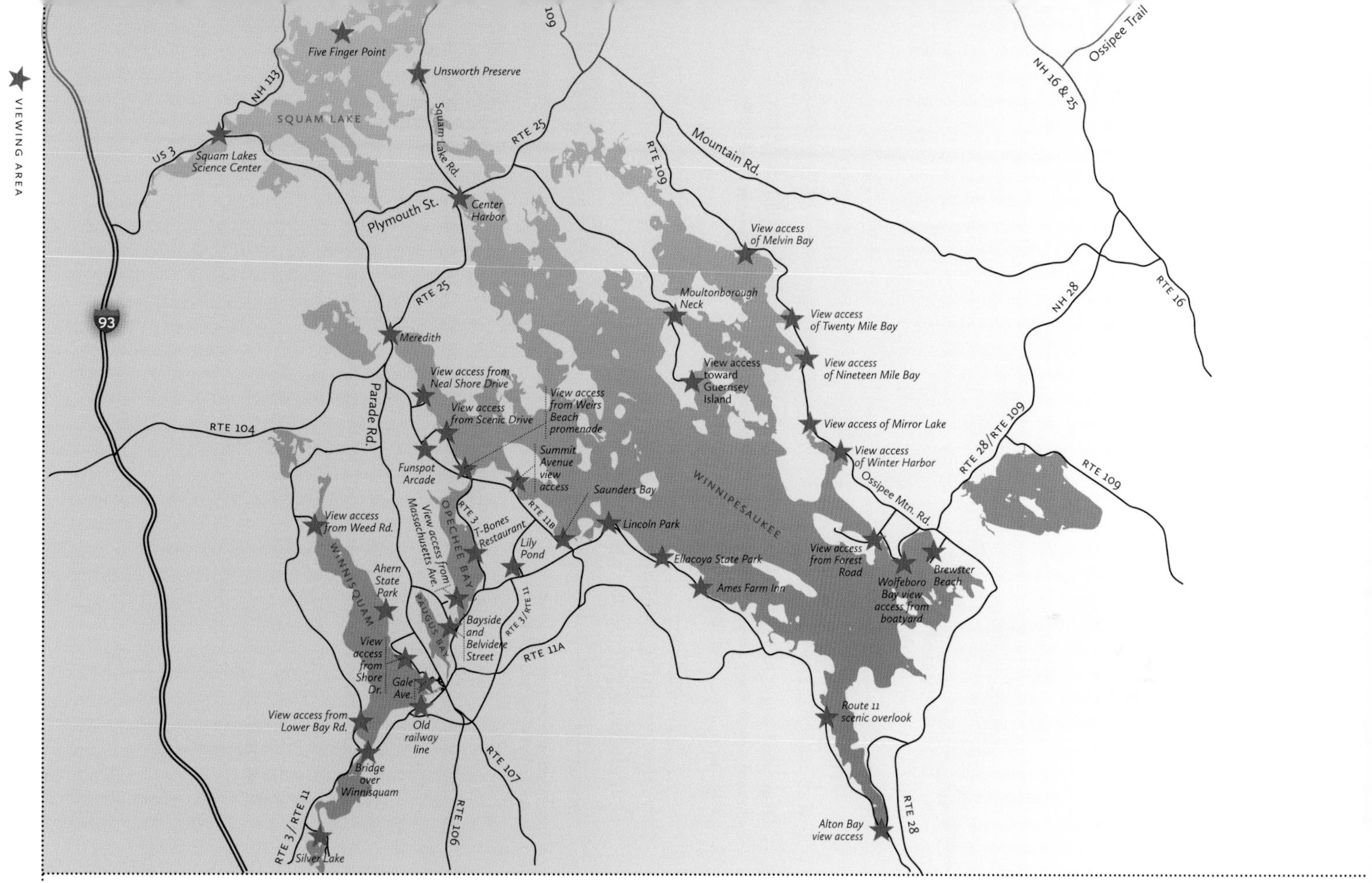

LAKES REGION ACCESS POINTS

★ VIEWING AREA

Ossipee Trail

NH 16 & 25

RTE 16

NH 28

RTE 28 / RTE 109

RTE 109

Ossipee Mtn. Rd.

View access of Melvin Bay

View access of Twenty Mile Bay

View access of Nineteen Mile Bay

View access of Mirror Lake

View access of Winter Harbor

Mountain Rd.

RTE 109

Moultonborough Neck

View access toward Guernsey Island

WINNIPESAUKEE

View access from Forest Road

Brewster Beach

Wolfeboro Bay view access from boatyard

Route 11 scenic overlook

RTE 28

Alton Bay view access

Ellacoya State Park

Ames Farm Inn

Lincoln Park

Saunder Bay

View access from Weirs Beach promenade

Summit Avenue view access

RTE 118

Lily Pond

RTE 3 - Bones Restaurant

Bayside and Belvidere Street

RTE 3 / RTE 11

RTE 11A

RTE 107

RTE 106

109

Unsworth Preserve

RTE 25

Center Harbor

Squam Lake Rd.

RTE 25

Meredith

View access from Neal Shore Drive

View access from Scenic Drive

Funspot Arcade

View access from Massachusetts Ave.

OPECHEE BAY

PAUGUS BAY

Old railway line

Five Finger Point

Plymouth St.

SQUAM LAKE

NH 113

Squam Lakes Science Center

US 3

Parade Rd.

RTE 104

View access from Weed Rd.

Ahern State Park

WINNISQUAM

Gale Ave.

View access from Shore Dr.

Bridge over Winnisquam

View access from Lower Bay Rd.

RTE 3 / RTE 11

Silver Lake

93

Long-tailed Jaeger, Jeffreys Ledge, September 8, 2009. Although many seabirds are rare inland, the Lakes Region has produced records of Sabine's Gull, Black-headed Gull, Long-tailed Jaeger, and Pomarine Jaeger. *Jason Lambert*

tive during spring and fall for diving ducks, including Bufflehead, Common Goldeneye, and Hooded and Common Mergansers. Rarer species to have occurred here include Canvasback, Barrow's Goldeneye, and Iceland Gull.

LAKE WINNISQUAM

The bridge over Winnisquam provides an excellent location from which to scan both north and south. A wide range of species can be seen here in both spring and fall, sometimes including all three scoters as well as Long-tailed Duck, Horned Grebe, and Red-necked Grebe.

The same species can be observed in Winnisquam's southeastern bay from the vantage of an old railway line. Gale Avenue provides another excellent location to scan the southern end of the lake, especially for grebes during fall migration.

Ahern State Park provides access to Winnisquam's northern portion.

OPECHEE BAY

Bayside and Belvidere Street, both located off Elm Street, provide access to the eastern end of Opechee Bay and the impoundment above the dam in Lakeport, the latter an occasional site for Pied-billed Grebe during migration.

Northern Hawk Owl, Center Harbor, January 25, 2009. This northern species is a rare winter visitor to New Hampshire. *Jason Lambert*

LILY POND

This pond in Gilford is one of the more productive waterfowl locations in the Lakes Region and an excellent site for waterfowl during migration, including Ring-necked Duck and Lesser Scaup. Redhead also has been recorded here.

PAUGUS BAY

Route 3 has several establishments with public parking that overlook Paugus Bay, including T-Bones Restaurant, which provides an elevated overlook of the bay's southern end.

LAKE WINNIPESAUKEE

Summit Avenue crosses the narrow strait that separates Governors Island from the mainland. This is a good area to check in fall for migrant waterbirds. A Dovekie was found here many years ago.

Lincoln Park is an elevated spot that provides a wide panorama of the lake and should be one of the best spots on the lake for storm birding. A scope is essential here.

Brewster Beach, off Clark Road, offers the best morning views of Wolfeboro Bay. The boat yard off Sewall Road is better in evening light.

In Meredith, check the tiny island a few hundred feet from the shore for roosting birds, especially cormorants. Farther south along Meredith Bay, the Funspot Arcade hosts an active Purple Martin colony, viewable from Route 3 (Endicott Street).

SQUAM LAKE

Unsworth Preserve, best viewed from Bean Road and Old Harvard Road, is a good location for waterfowl, including Ring-necked Duck in spring and fall.

Five Finger Point consists of more than 70 acres of conservation land off Pinehurst Road, with trails that lead to Squam Lake. Common resident birds include Ruffed Grouse, Pileated Woodpecker, and other birds typical of mixed pine-oak woodland.

Squam Lakes Natural Science Center (www.nhnature.org) offers boat tours during summer to view nesting Common Loon, Osprey, and Bald Eagle.

North Conway Area and Dahl Sanctuary

The Saco River drains the eastern edge of the White Mountains, flows east through North Conway into Maine, and enters the Gulf of Maine just south of Cape Elizabeth. The farm fields along the river floodplain in Conway (Sherman Farm) are excellent birding locations, as are the fields on the Maine side of the border; all are best viewed from Route 113. Birding is most productive in spring, when waterfowl are moving through, including Greater White-fronted Goose, Snow Goose, Gadwall, American Wigeon, Blue-winged Teal, Northern Shoveler, Northern Pintail, and Green-winged Teal. Tundra Swan has been recorded nearby. Upper Kimball Pond is worth checking for diving ducks, especially Ring-necked Duck. Fall migration through the region is comparable with that in other river valleys in the state. New Hampshire's second record of LeConte's Sparrow was found here, and Dickcissel has occurred.

New Hampshire Audubon's Dahl Sanctuary is located off Route 16 on the southern edge of the North Conway strip. The 60-acre sanctuary includes an excellent example of silver maple floodplain forest, some field habitat that Audubon is managing for early successional species, and significant frontage on the Saco River. Look for Red-shouldered Hawks and Barred Owls, as well as Spotted Sandpiper and Belted Kingfisher along the river.

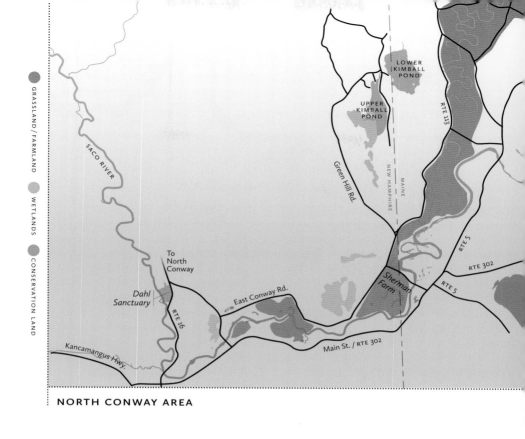

The trailhead to the Dahl Sanctuary is accessed from the parking lot of L.L. Bean, located at the junction of Route 16 and Route 302.

Watts Wildlife Sanctuary

New Hampshire Audubon's Watts Wildlife Sanctuary, in Effingham, is included here largely because of its reliability for northern specialties, especially Olive-sided Flycatcher, a scarce bird of North Country bogs. Most of the sanctuary's 380 acres are too wet to navigate on foot, although a short trail leads along the southern bank of the Ossipee River. The flycatchers are most easily seen from the road, especially Huntress Bridge Road. They like to perch on the tallest snags available, and have a characteristic call likened to "quick, three beers." Other species to watch for during breeding season include Black-billed Cuckoo, Northern Waterthrush, Northern Parula, Palm Warbler, and Lincoln's Sparrow.

THE LAKES REGION

147

TRAIL/WOODS ROAD

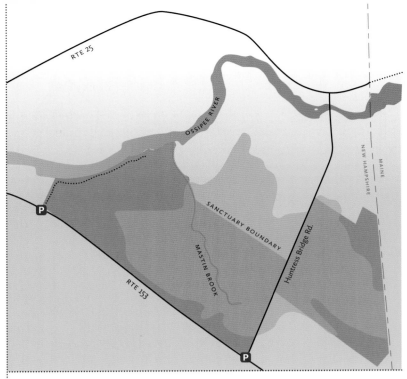

WETLANDS

CONSERVATION LAND

P PARKING AREA

★ VIEWING AREA

RTE 25

OSSIPEE RIVER

SANCTUARY BOUNDARY

MASTIN BROOK

Huntress Bridge Rd.

NEW HAMPSHIRE

MAINE

RTE 153

P

P

P

WATTS WILDLIFE SANCTUARY, EFFINGHAM

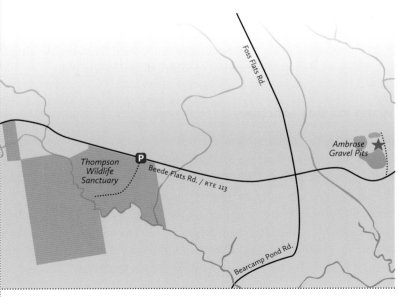

Foss Flats Rd.

Ambrose
Gravel Pits

Thompson
Wildlife
Sanctuary

P

Beede Flats Rd. / RTE 113

Bearcamp Pond Rd.

THOMPSON WILDLIFE SANCTUARY
AND AMBROSE GRAVEL PITS

Thompson Wildlife Sanctuary and Ambrose Gravel Pit

Thompson Wildlife Sanctuary is located on Beede Flats Road (Route 113) in North Sandwich, 2.8 miles west of Route 25. Situated about halfway between the Massachusetts and Canadian borders, the sanctuary's birdlife is similarly bipolar, with a mix of both northern and southern New Hampshire species. Breeding birds include Red-shouldered Hawk, Wilson's Snipe, Alder Flycatcher, Willow Flycatcher, Winter Wren, Scarlet Tanager, and about 15 types of warblers, including scarcer species such as Canada Warbler. Red Crossbill, though rare, is seen here as frequently as anywhere else in the state. Lincoln's Sparrow is suspected of breeding here, and Least Bittern and Sedge Wren have also occurred. The trail system has been reduced by beaver activity and does not cross to the south of Atwood Brook anymore, though New Hampshire Audubon has plans to reopen this section of the sanctuary from Middle Road.

Ambrose Gravel Pit, only 2 miles away, is one the best sites in the Lakes Region for shorebirds during spring weather events. Although the site is private property, birders are welcome to access the reclaimed area near Beede Flats Road. During sufficiently wet springs, the cranberry bog near the entrance has hosted up to 9 species of shorebirds, including Black-bellied Plover, Lesser and Greater Yellowlegs, Solitary Sandpiper, and Short-billed Dowitcher. Do *not* proceed past the first ponds, which are located within a quarter-mile of the highway. The area beyond is an active gravel pit and off limits to birders. Look for Bank Swallow and Cliff Swallow hawking for insects over the ponds, and Vesper Sparrow in the grassy areas, as this bird, though scarce in New Hampshire, is reported to breed here.

The following species are of roughly annual occurrence in New Hampshire or its offshore waters. For the most part, this means that each species is recorded annually. A few species that are irruptive, migrate far off the coast, or are present in small numbers during winter may not be recorded annually, such as Pine Grosbeak, Sabine's Gull, and Pacific Loon.

During winter months, the coastal plain is generally the last refuge of birds that ordinarily leave the state for points south, due to its generally milder weather. For this and other reasons, bird diversity is greatest near the coast at this time.

The charts depict each species breeding status, relative abundance through the year, and conservation status—increasing, stable, or decreasing—when known (mostly from Hunt et al., 2011). When birds thought of as primarily coastal can be seen inland during migration—such as certain waterfowl, shorebirds, gulls, and terns—this also is indicated in the charts.

The bar graphs represent the general arrival times for southern New Hampshire. First arrivals often occur along the southern sections of the Connecticut and Merrimack Rivers a week earlier, while many spring migrants do not arrive in the North Country until two weeks later. I have also included record early and late dates for each species where appropriate.

The four levels of abundance are designed to indicate likelihood of occurrence and should not be compared between species. For example, both Barred Owl and Black-capped Chickadee are well-established breeders in New Hampshire, each with a substantially healthy population in the state, as indicated by their bar graphs. However, a healthy population of chickadees is many times larger than a healthy population of owls.

Note: In the symbols describing frequency or abundance in the species account section, "Common to Abundant" is used for birds observed on most birding trips; "Uncommon to Fairly Common" refers to birds seen on more than half the visits to the appropriate habitat; "Very Uncommon" indicates that the bird is seen on fewer than half the visits to appropriate habitat; and "Rare" is reserved for birds with fewer than ten recorded sightings per year.

Greater White-fronted Goose · *Anser albifrons*

JAN	FEB	MAR	APR	MAY	JUN	JUL	AUG	SEP	OCT	NOV	DEC

Southeast coastal plain and major river valleys, especially the Connecticut River Valley. March 6 early spring date. Birds identified to Greenland race recorded several times.

Snow Goose · *Chen caerulescens*

JAN	FEB	MAR	APR	MAY	JUN	JUL	AUG	SEP	OCT	NOV	DEC

Brant · *Branta bernicla*

JAN	FEB	MAR	APR	MAY	JUN	JUL	AUG	SEP	OCT	NOV	DEC

Mainly coastal. March 2 early spring date. The Brant undertakes one of the longest migrations of any species of waterfowl, from breeding grounds in the Canadian High Arctic to wintering grounds on the mid-Atlantic Coast, passing through New Hampshire spring and fall.

Cackling Goose · *Branta hutchinsii*

JAN	FEB	MAR	APR	MAY	JUN	JUL	AUG	SEP	OCT	NOV	DEC

Southeast coastal plain and major river valleys, especially the Connecticut River Valley. March 6 early spring date.

Canada Goose · *Branta canadensis*

JAN	FEB	MAR	APR	MAY	JUN	JUL	AUG	SEP	OCT	NOV	DEC

Mute Swan · *Cygnus olor*

JAN	FEB	MAR	APR	MAY	JUN	JUL	AUG	SEP	OCT	NOV	DEC

Southern New Hampshire only. Mute Swan was introduced to North America from Eurasia in the mid-nineteenth century, and is now a nuisance species in parts of its North American range, where it is displacing native waterfowl.

Tundra Swan · *Cygnus columbianus*

JAN	FEB	MAR	APR	MAY	JUN	JUL	AUG	SEP	OCT	NOV	DEC

March 2 early spring date.

NONE

RARE

VERY UNCOMMON

UNCOMMON TO FAIRLY COMMON

COMMON TO ABUNDANT

INCREASING

DECREASING

STABLE

IRRUPTIVE

BREEDS IN NH

OCCURS OFFSHORE

INLAND

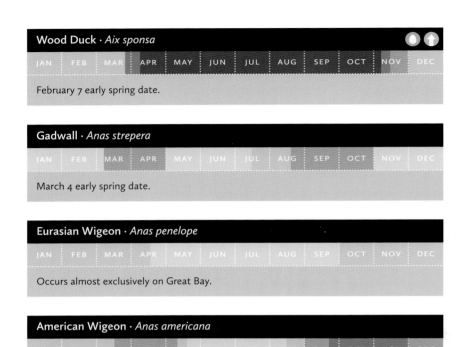

Wood Duck · *Aix sponsa*

JAN	FEB	MAR	APR	MAY	JUN	JUL	AUG	SEP	OCT	NOV	DEC

February 7 early spring date.

Gadwall · *Anas strepera*

JAN	FEB	MAR	APR	MAY	JUN	JUL	AUG	SEP	OCT	NOV	DEC

March 4 early spring date.

Eurasian Wigeon · *Anas penelope*

JAN	FEB	MAR	APR	MAY	JUN	JUL	AUG	SEP	OCT	NOV	DEC

Occurs almost exclusively on Great Bay.

American Wigeon · *Anas americana*

JAN	FEB	MAR	APR	MAY	JUN	JUL	AUG	SEP	OCT	NOV	DEC

August 9 early fall date.

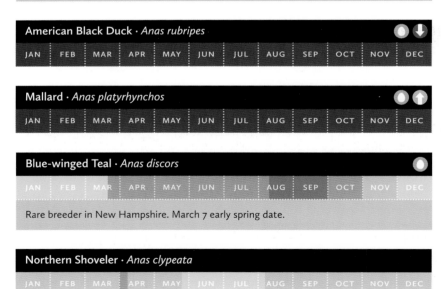

American Black Duck · *Anas rubripes*

JAN	FEB	MAR	APR	MAY	JUN	JUL	AUG	SEP	OCT	NOV	DEC

Mallard · *Anas platyrhynchos*

JAN	FEB	MAR	APR	MAY	JUN	JUL	AUG	SEP	OCT	NOV	DEC

Blue-winged Teal · *Anas discors*

JAN	FEB	MAR	APR	MAY	JUN	JUL	AUG	SEP	OCT	NOV	DEC

Rare breeder in New Hampshire. March 7 early spring date.

Northern Shoveler · *Anas clypeata*

JAN	FEB	MAR	APR	MAY	JUN	JUL	AUG	SEP	OCT	NOV	DEC

Northern Pintail · *Anas acuta*

JAN	FEB	MAR	APR	MAY	JUN	JUL	AUG	SEP	OCT	NOV	DEC

August 18 early fall date.

Green-winged Teal · *Anas crecca*

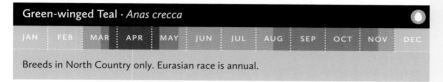

JAN	FEB	MAR	APR	MAY	JUN	JUL	AUG	SEP	OCT	NOV	DEC

Breeds in North Country only. Eurasian race is annual.

Canvasback · *Aythya valisineria*

JAN	FEB	MAR	APR	MAY	JUN	JUL	AUG	SEP	OCT	NOV	DEC

September 21 early fall date.

Redhead · *Aythya americana*

JAN	FEB	MAR	APR	MAY	JUN	JUL	AUG	SEP	OCT	NOV	DEC

March 6 early spring date.

Ring-necked Duck · *Aythya collaris*

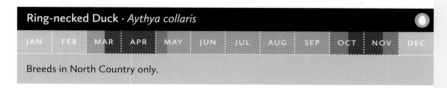

JAN	FEB	MAR	APR	MAY	JUN	JUL	AUG	SEP	OCT	NOV	DEC

Breeds in North Country only.

Greater Scaup · *Aythya marila*

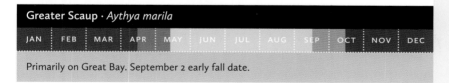

JAN	FEB	MAR	APR	MAY	JUN	JUL	AUG	SEP	OCT	NOV	DEC

Primarily on Great Bay. September 2 early fall date.

Lesser Scaup · *Aythya affinis*

JAN	FEB	MAR	APR	MAY	JUN	JUL	AUG	SEP	OCT	NOV	DEC

August 30 early fall date.

NONE
RARE
VERY UNCOMMON
UNCOMMON TO FAIRLY COMMON
COMMON TO ABUNDANT

INCREASING
DECREASING
STABLE
IRRUPTIVE
BREEDS IN NH
OCCURS OFFSHORE
INLAND

King Eider · *Somateria spectabilis*

JAN	FEB	MAR	APR	MAY	JUN	JUL	AUG	SEP	OCT	NOV	DEC

Coastal (4 inland records).

Common Eider · *Somateria mollissima*

JAN	FEB	MAR	APR	MAY	JUN	JUL	AUG	SEP	OCT	NOV	DEC

Coastal; very rare inland (10 records). Common Eider was greatly reduced in the early part of twentieth century through market hunting, but is now much recovered through protection afforded by the Migratory Bird Convention (1916). Commercial eiderdown collecting in North America is practiced in the St. Lawrence estuary and by a few Inuit communities in the Canadian Arctic. About 120 nests need to be harvested to produce 1 kilogram of eiderdown.

Harlequin Duck · *Histrionicus histrionicus*

JAN	FEB	MAR	APR	MAY	JUN	JUL	AUG	SEP	OCT	NOV	DEC

Coastal; very rare inland (3 records). September 30 early fall date.

Surf Scoter · *Melanitta perspicillata*

JAN	FEB	MAR	APR	MAY	JUN	JUL	AUG	SEP	OCT	NOV	DEC

Mainly coastal and inland in fall. Very rare inland in spring.

White-winged Scoter · *Melanitta fusca*

JAN	FEB	MAR	APR	MAY	JUN	JUL	AUG	SEP	OCT	NOV	DEC

Mainly coastal and inland in fall. Uncommon inland in spring.

Black Scoter · *Melanitta americana*

JAN	FEB	MAR	APR	MAY	JUN	JUL	AUG	SEP	OCT	NOV	DEC

Mainly coastal and inland in fall. Rare inland in spring.

Long-tailed Duck · *Clangula hyemalis*

JAN	FEB	MAR	APR	MAY	JUN	JUL	AUG	SEP	OCT	NOV	DEC

Mainly coastal.

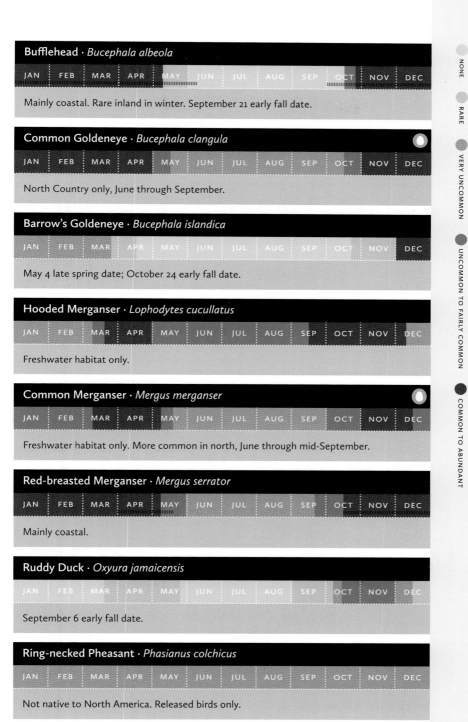

Bufflehead · *Bucephala albeola*

JAN	FEB	MAR	APR	MAY	JUN	JUL	AUG	SEP	OCT	NOV	DEC

Mainly coastal. Rare inland in winter. September 21 early fall date.

Common Goldeneye · *Bucephala clangula*

JAN	FEB	MAR	APR	MAY	JUN	JUL	AUG	SEP	OCT	NOV	DEC

North Country only, June through September.

Barrow's Goldeneye · *Bucephala islandica*

JAN	FEB	MAR	APR	MAY	JUN	JUL	AUG	SEP	OCT	NOV	DEC

May 4 late spring date; October 24 early fall date.

Hooded Merganser · *Lophodytes cucullatus*

JAN	FEB	MAR	APR	MAY	JUN	JUL	AUG	SEP	OCT	NOV	DEC

Freshwater habitat only.

Common Merganser · *Mergus merganser*

JAN	FEB	MAR	APR	MAY	JUN	JUL	AUG	SEP	OCT	NOV	DEC

Freshwater habitat only. More common in north, June through mid-September.

Red-breasted Merganser · *Mergus serrator*

JAN	FEB	MAR	APR	MAY	JUN	JUL	AUG	SEP	OCT	NOV	DEC

Mainly coastal.

Ruddy Duck · *Oxyura jamaicensis*

JAN	FEB	MAR	APR	MAY	JUN	JUL	AUG	SEP	OCT	NOV	DEC

September 6 early fall date.

Ring-necked Pheasant · *Phasianus colchicus*

JAN	FEB	MAR	APR	MAY	JUN	JUL	AUG	SEP	OCT	NOV	DEC

Not native to North America. Released birds only.

NONE
RARE
VERY UNCOMMON
UNCOMMON TO FAIRLY COMMON
COMMON TO ABUNDANT

INCREASING
DECREASING
STABLE
IRRUPTIVE
BREEDS IN NH
OCCURS OFFSHORE
INLAND

BIRDWATCHING IN NEW HAMPSHIRE

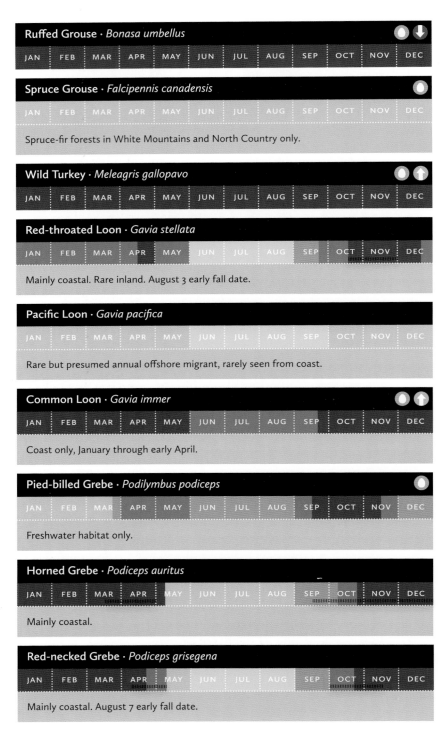

Ruffed Grouse · *Bonasa umbellus*

| JAN | FEB | MAR | APR | MAY | JUN | JUL | AUG | SEP | OCT | NOV | DEC |

Spruce Grouse · *Falcipennis canadensis*

| JAN | FEB | MAR | APR | MAY | JUN | JUL | AUG | SEP | OCT | NOV | DEC |

Spruce-fir forests in White Mountains and North Country only.

Wild Turkey · *Meleagris gallopavo*

| JAN | FEB | MAR | APR | MAY | JUN | JUL | AUG | SEP | OCT | NOV | DEC |

Red-throated Loon · *Gavia stellata*

| JAN | FEB | MAR | APR | MAY | JUN | JUL | AUG | SEP | OCT | NOV | DEC |

Mainly coastal. Rare inland. August 3 early fall date.

Pacific Loon · *Gavia pacifica*

| JAN | FEB | MAR | APR | MAY | JUN | JUL | AUG | SEP | OCT | NOV | DEC |

Rare but presumed annual offshore migrant, rarely seen from coast.

Common Loon · *Gavia immer*

| JAN | FEB | MAR | APR | MAY | JUN | JUL | AUG | SEP | OCT | NOV | DEC |

Coast only, January through early April.

Pied-billed Grebe · *Podilymbus podiceps*

| JAN | FEB | MAR | APR | MAY | JUN | JUL | AUG | SEP | OCT | NOV | DEC |

Freshwater habitat only.

Horned Grebe · *Podiceps auritus*

| JAN | FEB | MAR | APR | MAY | JUN | JUL | AUG | SEP | OCT | NOV | DEC |

Mainly coastal.

Red-necked Grebe · *Podiceps grisegena*

| JAN | FEB | MAR | APR | MAY | JUN | JUL | AUG | SEP | OCT | NOV | DEC |

Mainly coastal. August 7 early fall date.

Northern Fulmar · *Fulmarus glacialis*

JAN	FEB	MAR	APR	MAY	JUN	JUL	AUG	SEP	OCT	NOV	DEC

Ocean, very rarely seen from coast. As New Hampshire data are sparse, graph shows likely abundance levels. Occurs in both color morphs.

Cory's Shearwater · *Calonectris diomedea*

JAN	FEB	MAR	APR	MAY	JUN	JUL	AUG	SEP	OCT	NOV	DEC

Ocean, rarely seen from coast. June 26 early date; October 22 late date.

Great Shearwater · *Puffinus gravis*

JAN	FEB	MAR	APR	MAY	JUN	JUL	AUG	SEP	OCT	NOV	DEC

Ocean, occasionally seen from coast. June 2 early date; December 11 late date.

Sooty Shearwater · *Puffinus griseus*

JAN	FEB	MAR	APR	MAY	JUN	JUL	AUG	SEP	OCT	NOV	DEC

Ocean, rarely seen from coast. May 21 early date; October 24 late date.

Manx Shearwater · *Puffinus puffinus*

JAN	FEB	MAR	APR	MAY	JUN	JUL	AUG	SEP	OCT	NOV	DEC

Ocean, occasionally seen from coast. May 2 early date; October 24 late date. The Manx Shearwater, like many species of seabird, is remarkably long-lived. An individual banded in Wales in 1957, when it was at least 4 years old, was recaptured in 2003. During its 50 years at sea, it is likely to have flown a minimum of 5 million miles.

Wilson's Storm-Petrel · *Oceanites oceanicus*

JAN	FEB	MAR	APR	MAY	JUN	JUL	AUG	SEP	OCT	NOV	DEC

Ocean; 4 inland records, always after storms. May 18 early date; September 27 late date. Wilson's Storm-Petrels are one of the most abundant birds in the world, with an estimated world population of 12 to 30 million individuals. They breed on the Antarctic coastline and sub-Antarctic islands; after nesting, they leave the southern seas before the onset of the austral winter. They migrate north of the equator to spend a second summer over the continental shelves and inshore areas of the world's major oceans, especially the Atlantic. This species and other members of the storm-petrel family have a habit of pattering on the water surface as they forage for plankton and scraps of offal, leading to the impression that they are "walking" on water. The name *petrel* derives from Peter, in reference to the biblical accounts of St. Peter walking on water.

NONE
RARE
VERY UNCOMMON
UNCOMMON TO FAIRLY COMMON
COMMON TO ABUNDANT

INCREASING
DECREASING
STABLE
IRRUPTIVE
BREEDS IN NH
OCCURS OFFSHORE
INLAND

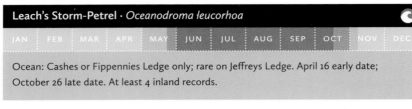

Leach's Storm-Petrel · *Oceanodroma leucorhoa*

JAN	FEB	MAR	APR	MAY	JUN	JUL	AUG	SEP	OCT	NOV	DEC

Ocean: Cashes or Fippennies Ledge only; rare on Jeffreys Ledge. April 16 early date; October 26 late date. At least 4 inland records.

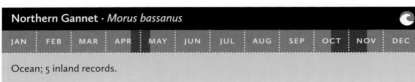

Northern Gannet · *Morus bassanus*

JAN	FEB	MAR	APR	MAY	JUN	JUL	AUG	SEP	OCT	NOV	DEC

Ocean; 5 inland records.

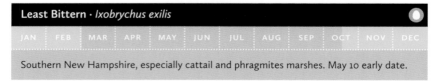

Double-crested Cormorant · *Phalacrocorax auritus*

JAN	FEB	MAR	APR	MAY	JUN	JUL	AUG	SEP	OCT	NOV	DEC

Mainly coastal. March 2 early date. More common inland than Great Cormorant. Double-crested and Great Cormorant are often observed standing with wings spread. Both lack a developed oil gland, common to many species of birds. Consequently they are unable to make their feathers water-repellent and must air-dry them instead.

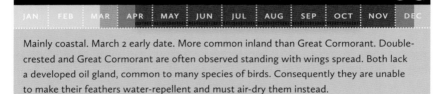

Great Cormorant · *Phalacrocorax carbo*

JAN	FEB	MAR	APR	MAY	JUN	JUL	AUG	SEP	OCT	NOV	DEC

Mainly coastal. Uncommon inland.

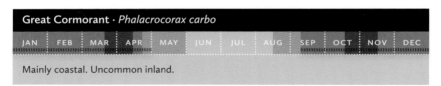

American Bittern · *Botaurus lentiginosus*

JAN	FEB	MAR	APR	MAY	JUN	JUL	AUG	SEP	OCT	NOV	DEC

March 24 early date.

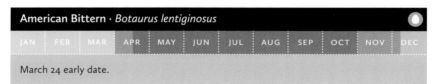

Least Bittern · *Ixobrychus exilis*

JAN	FEB	MAR	APR	MAY	JUN	JUL	AUG	SEP	OCT	NOV	DEC

Southern New Hampshire, especially cattail and phragmites marshes. May 10 early date.

Great Blue Heron · *Ardea herodias*

JAN	FEB	MAR	APR	MAY	JUN	JUL	AUG	SEP	OCT	NOV	DEC

Great Egret · *Ardea alba*

JAN	FEB	MAR	APR	MAY	JUN	JUL	AUG	SEP	OCT	NOV	DEC

Mainly coastal. March 11 early date; November 25 late date. Egrets, including the Great Egret and Snowy Egret, were hunted mercilessly for their plumes, which were used in the millinery trade. Their decline to near extinction in the late 1800s precipitated the Audubon movement, which today uses the Great Egret as its emblem.

Snowy Egret · *Egretta thula*

JAN	FEB	MAR	APR	MAY	JUN	JUL	AUG	SEP	OCT	NOV	DEC

Mainly coastal. March 27 early date; November 16 late date. Much rarer inland than Great Egret.

Little Blue Heron · *Egretta caerulea*

JAN	FEB	MAR	APR	MAY	JUN	JUL	AUG	SEP	OCT	NOV	DEC

Coastal saltmarshes, very rare inland. April 9 early date; November 15 late date.

Tricolored Heron · *Egretta tricolor*

JAN	FEB	MAR	APR	MAY	JUN	JUL	AUG	SEP	OCT	NOV	DEC

Coastal marshes and lagoons; 1 inland record.

Cattle Egret · *Bubulcus ibis*

JAN	FEB	MAR	APR	MAY	JUN	JUL	AUG	SEP	OCT	NOV	DEC

Farmland, pasture fields, mainly southern New Hampshire. Cattle Egret was originally native to parts of Southern Europe, Asia, and Africa. In the late 1800s it began a major expansion of its breeding range, reaching North America in the 1950s.

Green Heron · *Butorides virescens*

JAN	FEB	MAR	APR	MAY	JUN	JUL	AUG	SEP	OCT	NOV	DEC

April 4 early date; November 25 late date.

NONE
RARE
VERY UNCOMMON
UNCOMMON TO FAIRLY COMMON
COMMON TO ABUNDANT

INCREASING
DECREASING
STABLE
IRRUPTIVE
BREEDS IN NH
OCCURS OFFSHORE
INLAND

Black-crowned Night-Heron · *Nycticorax nycticorax*

JAN	FEB	MAR	APR	MAY	JUN	JUL	AUG	SEP	OCT	NOV	DEC

Mainly coastal. March 30 early date.

Yellow-crowned Night-Heron · *Nyctanassa violacea*

JAN	FEB	MAR	APR	MAY	JUN	JUL	AUG	SEP	OCT	NOV	DEC

Mainly coastal.

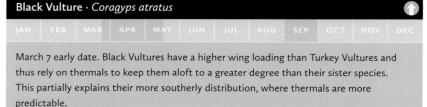

Glossy Ibis · *Plegadis falcinellus*

JAN	FEB	MAR	APR	MAY	JUN	JUL	AUG	SEP	OCT	NOV	DEC

Mainly coastal. March 27 early date; September 22 late date.

Black Vulture · *Coragyps atratus*

JAN	FEB	MAR	APR	MAY	JUN	JUL	AUG	SEP	OCT	NOV	DEC

March 7 early date. Black Vultures have a higher wing loading than Turkey Vultures and thus rely on thermals to keep them aloft to a greater degree than their sister species. This partially explains their more southerly distribution, where thermals are more predictable.

Turkey Vulture · *Cathartes aura*

JAN	FEB	MAR	APR	MAY	JUN	JUL	AUG	SEP	OCT	NOV	DEC

Turkey Vultures have a highly developed sense of smell and can sniff out carrion even when it is hidden beneath the leaf canopy on the forest floor. Black Vultures do not have this ability and often follow Turkey Vultures to food.

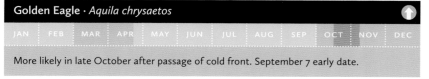

Osprey · *Pandion haliaetus*

JAN	FEB	MAR	APR	MAY	JUN	JUL	AUG	SEP	OCT	NOV	DEC

March 10 early date. Osprey are found on all continents except Antarctica. The Squam Lakes Natural Science Center in Holderness has recently begun to study the migration of New Hampshire birds by attaching satellite transmitters to several individuals.

Golden Eagle · *Aquila chrysaetos*

JAN	FEB	MAR	APR	MAY	JUN	JUL	AUG	SEP	OCT	NOV	DEC

More likely in late October after passage of cold front. September 7 early date.

Mississippi Kite · *Ictinia mississippiensis*

JAN	FEB	MAR	APR	MAY	JUN	JUL	AUG	SEP	OCT	NOV	DEC

Recently discovered breeding in Gonet Road area of Newmarket. May 6 early date; September 9 late date.

Northern Harrier · *Circus cyaneus*

JAN	FEB	MAR	APR	MAY	JUN	JUL	AUG	SEP	OCT	NOV	DEC

Rare breeder in North Country only. Common migrant along river valleys and coast.

Sharp-shinned Hawk · *Accipiter striatus*

JAN	FEB	MAR	APR	MAY	JUN	JUL	AUG	SEP	OCT	NOV	DEC

Cooper's Hawk · *Accipiter cooperii*

JAN	FEB	MAR	APR	MAY	JUN	JUL	AUG	SEP	OCT	NOV	DEC

Northern Goshawk · *Accipiter gentilis*

JAN	FEB	MAR	APR	MAY	JUN	JUL	AUG	SEP	OCT	NOV	DEC

A forest hawk known for its power and aggression. Attila the Hun wore a helmet emblazoned with an image of Northern Goshawk.

Bald Eagle · *Haliaeetus leucocephalus*

JAN	FEB	MAR	APR	MAY	JUN	JUL	AUG	SEP	OCT	NOV	DEC

From 1987 to 2010, the New Hampshire population increased from 0 to 22 territorial pairs. Bald Eagles can live for 20 years or more in the wild.

Red-shouldered Hawk · *Buteo lineatus*

JAN	FEB	MAR	APR	MAY	JUN	JUL	AUG	SEP	OCT	NOV	DEC

Broad-winged Hawk · *Buteo platypterus*

JAN	FEB	MAR	APR	MAY	JUN	JUL	AUG	SEP	OCT	NOV	DEC

During the period from 2003 to 2011, 60 percent of birds counted from the Pack Monadnock Raptor observatory migrated south between September 16 and 19. March 24 early date; November 28 late date.

NONE
RARE
VERY UNCOMMON
UNCOMMON TO FAIRLY COMMON
COMMON TO ABUNDANT

INCREASING
DECREASING
STABLE
IRRUPTIVE
BREEDS IN NH
OCCURS OFFSHORE
INLAND

Red-tailed Hawk · *Buteo jamaicensis*

JAN	FEB	MAR	APR	MAY	JUN	JUL	AUG	SEP	OCT	NOV	DEC

The common roadside hawk in New Hampshire. Rare in north between early November and late March.

Rough-legged Hawk · *Buteo lagopus*

JAN	FEB	MAR	APR	MAY	JUN	JUL	AUG	SEP	OCT	NOV	DEC

Found especially along river valleys and in southeast. June 6 late spring date; September 11 early fall date. Occurs in both color morphs.

Clapper Rail · *Rallus longirostris*

JAN	FEB	MAR	APR	MAY	JUN	JUL	AUG	SEP	OCT	NOV	DEC

Almost exclusively occurs in Hampton Marsh.

Virginia Rail · *Rallus limicola*

JAN	FEB	MAR	APR	MAY	JUN	JUL	AUG	SEP	OCT	NOV	DEC

Sora · *Porzana carolina*

JAN	FEB	MAR	APR	MAY	JUN	JUL	AUG	SEP	OCT	NOV	DEC

Common Gallinule (formerly Common Moorhen) · *Gallinula galeata*

JAN	FEB	MAR	APR	MAY	JUN	JUL	AUG	SEP	OCT	NOV	DEC

Observed breeding in 1960 and 1962. April 18 early date; December 4 late date.

American Coot · *Fulica americana*

JAN	FEB	MAR	APR	MAY	JUN	JUL	AUG	SEP	OCT	NOV	DEC

March 9 early date.

Sandhill Crane · *Grus canadensis*

JAN	FEB	MAR	APR	MAY	JUN	JUL	AUG	SEP	OCT	NOV	DEC

March 4 early date; December 12 late date.

Black-bellied Plover · *Pluvialis squatarola*

JAN	FEB	MAR	APR	MAY	JUN	JUL	AUG	SEP	OCT	NOV	DEC

Mainly coastal. Rare inland along edges of ponds, sandbars, flooded fields. March 27 early date.

American Golden-Plover · *Pluvialis dominica*

JAN	FEB	MAR	APR	MAY	JUN	JUL	AUG	SEP	OCT	NOV	DEC

Found especially with Killdeer in stubble, sod, and farm fields. August 10 early date; November 27 late date. Very rare in spring; only 5 records in the past 50 years. The American Golden-Plover migrates over the western Atlantic from the eastern coast of North America and continues nonstop to the South American mainland. Adult birds leave their Arctic breeding grounds a month before the juveniles, which must find their own way to the grasslands of central and southern South America where they spend the winter.

Semipalmated Plover · *Charadrius semipalmatus*

JAN	FEB	MAR	APR	MAY	JUN	JUL	AUG	SEP	OCT	NOV	DEC

Mainly coastal. Inland habitat as with Black-bellied Plover, but more frequent. May 4 early spring date; July 10 early fall date; December 5 late fall date.

Piping Plover · *Charadrius melodus*

JAN	FEB	MAR	APR	MAY	JUN	JUL	AUG	SEP	OCT	NOV	DEC

Primarily observed at Hampton Beach and Seabrook Beach. March 12 early date; October 24 late date. One inland record.

Killdeer · *Charadrius vociferus*

JAN	FEB	MAR	APR	MAY	JUN	JUL	AUG	SEP	OCT	NOV	DEC

February 17 early date.

American Oystercatcher · *Haematopus palliatus*

JAN	FEB	MAR	APR	MAY	JUN	JUL	AUG	SEP	OCT	NOV	DEC

Coastal; 1 inland record. April 5 early date.

NONE
RARE
VERY UNCOMMON
UNCOMMON TO FAIRLY COMMON
COMMON TO ABUNDANT

INCREASING
DECREASING
STABLE
IRRUPTIVE
BREEDS IN NH
OCCURS OFFSHORE
INLAND

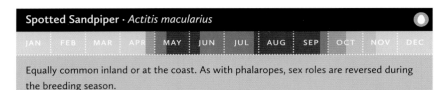

Spotted Sandpiper · *Actitis macularius*

| JAN | FEB | MAR | APR | MAY | JUN | JUL | AUG | SEP | OCT | NOV | DEC |

Equally common inland or at the coast. As with phalaropes, sex roles are reversed during the breeding season.

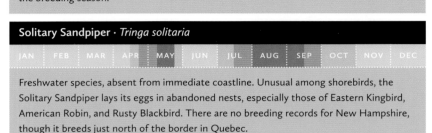

Solitary Sandpiper · *Tringa solitaria*

| JAN | FEB | MAR | APR | MAY | JUN | JUL | AUG | SEP | OCT | NOV | DEC |

Freshwater species, absent from immediate coastline. Unusual among shorebirds, the Solitary Sandpiper lays its eggs in abandoned nests, especially those of Eastern Kingbird, American Robin, and Rusty Blackbird. There are no breeding records for New Hampshire, though it breeds just north of the border in Quebec.

Greater Yellowlegs · *Tringa melanoleuca*

| JAN | FEB | MAR | APR | MAY | JUN | JUL | AUG | SEP | OCT | NOV | DEC |

Mainly coastal. March 21 early date; December 25 late date.

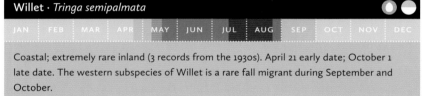

Willet · *Tringa semipalmata*

| JAN | FEB | MAR | APR | MAY | JUN | JUL | AUG | SEP | OCT | NOV | DEC |

Coastal; extremely rare inland (3 records from the 1930s). April 21 early date; October 1 late date. The western subspecies of Willet is a rare fall migrant during September and October.

Lesser Yellowlegs · *Tringa flavipes*

| JAN | FEB | MAR | APR | MAY | JUN | JUL | AUG | SEP | OCT | NOV | DEC |

Mainly coastal. March 30 early spring date; July 1 early fall date; December 19 late fall date.

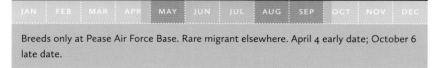

Upland Sandpiper · *Bartramia longicauda*

| JAN | FEB | MAR | APR | MAY | JUN | JUL | AUG | SEP | OCT | NOV | DEC |

Breeds only at Pease Air Force Base. Rare migrant elsewhere. April 4 early date; October 6 late date.

Whimbrel · *Numenius phaeopus*

| JAN | FEB | MAR | APR | MAY | JUN | JUL | AUG | SEP | OCT | NOV | DEC |

Coastal, mainly Hampton Harbor; extremely rare inland (6 records). July 2 early fall date.

Hudsonian Godwit · *Limosa haemastica*

JAN	FEB	MAR	APR	MAY	JUN	JUL	AUG	SEP	OCT	NOV	DEC

Mainly Hampton Harbor; almost unknown inland, with 1 record from Vermont side of Connecticut River near Hanover. July 14 early date; November 14 late date. Shorebirds are extremely strong fliers; some species, including the Hudsonian Godwit, are capable of covering staggering distances without stopping. The few individuals that we see in New Hampshire probably originate from the Hudson Bay population, most of which migrate straight to South America in a 3,000-mile nonstop journey over the western Atlantic.

Marbled Godwit · *Limosa fedoa*

JAN	FEB	MAR	APR	MAY	JUN	JUL	AUG	SEP	OCT	NOV	DEC

Coastal, mainly Hampton Harbor; 1 inland record. July 7 early date; September 21 late date.

Ruddy Turnstone · *Arenaria interpres*

JAN	FEB	MAR	APR	MAY	JUN	JUL	AUG	SEP	OCT	NOV	DEC

Coastal; very rare inland (15 records), primarily in fall. April 22 early spring date; July 10 early fall date; November 24 late fall date.

Red Knot · *Calidris canutus*

JAN	FEB	MAR	APR	MAY	JUN	JUL	AUG	SEP	OCT	NOV	DEC

Coastal; very rare away from immediate coast (3 inland records, all in spring). May 13 early spring date; July 15 early fall date; December 26 late fall date.

Sanderling · *Calidris alba*

JAN	FEB	MAR	APR	MAY	JUN	JUL	AUG	SEP	OCT	NOV	DEC

Found on sandy beaches along coast; rare inland, mainly in fall. June 24 late spring date; July 8 early fall date. The young of waterfowl and shorebirds such as Sanderling are precocial, which means they are born covered in down, with open eyes, and able to leave the nest within 1 or 2 days. This contrasts with songbirds, which are born naked, blind, and unable to leave the nest for several weeks. Sanderling are able to fly within 12 to 14 days of hatching.

Semipalmated Sandpiper · *Calidris pusilla*

JAN	FEB	MAR	APR	MAY	JUN	JUL	AUG	SEP	OCT	NOV	DEC

Mainly coastal. April 11 early spring date; July 4 early fall date; November 16 late fall date.

NONE
RARE
VERY UNCOMMON
UNCOMMON TO FAIRLY COMMON
COMMON TO ABUNDANT

INCREASING
DECREASING
STABLE
IRRUPTIVE
BREEDS IN NH
OCCURS OFFSHORE
INLAND

Western Sandpiper · *Calidris mauri*

JAN	FEB	MAR	APR	MAY	JUN	JUL	AUG	SEP	OCT	NOV	DEC

Coastal; very rare inland (8 records, all but 1 in fall). July 17 early fall date; November 2 late fall date.

Least Sandpiper · *Calidris minutilla*

JAN	FEB	MAR	APR	MAY	JUN	JUL	AUG	SEP	OCT	NOV	DEC

Coastal. Most common "peep" (small sandpiper) inland. Favors muddy pools with some vegetation. April 9 early spring date; November 11 late fall date.

White-rumped Sandpiper · *Calidris fuscicollis*

JAN	FEB	MAR	APR	MAY	JUN	JUL	AUG	SEP	OCT	NOV	DEC

Coastal; rare inland. May 10 early spring date; July 21 early fall date; November 27 late fall date. Like songbirds, many species of shorebirds have unique and identifiable calls, including the mouse-like squeaky note of the White-rumped Sandpiper. This species migrates over the western Atlantic en route to wintering grounds along the Atlantic coast of Argentina south to Tierra del Fuego.

Baird's Sandpiper · *Calidris bairdii*

JAN	FEB	MAR	APR	MAY	JUN	JUL	AUG	SEP	OCT	NOV	DEC

Mostly coastal; very few inland records. July 20 early fall date; October 17 late fall date.

Pectoral Sandpiper · *Calidris melanotos*

JAN	FEB	MAR	APR	MAY	JUN	JUL	AUG	SEP	OCT	NOV	DEC

Equally likely inland or at coast. March 19 early spring date; July 4 early fall date; December 1 late fall date.

Purple Sandpiper · *Calidris maritima*

JAN	FEB	MAR	APR	MAY	JUN	JUL	AUG	SEP	OCT	NOV	DEC

Coastal; very rare inland (5 records). Several summer records from the coast.

Dunlin · *Calidris alpina*

JAN	FEB	MAR	APR	MAY	JUN	JUL	AUG	SEP	OCT	NOV	DEC

Mainly coastal. June 25 late spring date; August 9 early fall date.

Stilt Sandpiper · *Calidris himantopus*

JAN	FEB	MAR	APR	MAY	JUN	JUL	AUG	SEP	OCT	NOV	DEC

Coastal; occasional inland in southeast coastal plain, very rare elsewhere. July 8 early fall date; November 15 late fall date.

Buff-breasted Sandpiper · *Tryngites subruficollis*

JAN	FEB	MAR	APR	MAY	JUN	JUL	AUG	SEP	OCT	NOV	DEC

Often in wrackline on coast; golf courses and sod farms inland. August 18 early fall date; October 27 late fall date. Unique among North American shorebirds, Buff-breasted Sandpiper uses a lek mating system. This species is one of the North American shorebirds that occasionally wanders to Western Europe, where it sometimes occurs in numbers that would be remarkable even in North America (for example, 45 individuals were observed in Ireland in the fall of 2011).

Short-billed Dowitcher · *Limnodromus griseus*

JAN	FEB	MAR	APR	MAY	JUN	JUL	AUG	SEP	OCT	NOV	DEC

Mainly coastal. April 26 early spring date; June 29 early fall date; October 29 late fall date. Majority are of the *griseus* subspecies. *Hendersoni* race recorded occasionally. The female Short-billed Dowitcher participates little in raising the young, a behavior shared by the phalaropes.

Long-billed Dowitcher · *Limnodromus scolopaceus*

JAN	FEB	MAR	APR	MAY	JUN	JUL	AUG	SEP	OCT	NOV	DEC

Coastal brackish habitat, especially Meadow Pond, and coastal saltmarshes; 2 inland records. July 23 early fall date; November 11 late fall date.

Wilson's Snipe · *Gallinago delicata*

JAN	FEB	MAR	APR	MAY	JUN	JUL	AUG	SEP	OCT	NOV	DEC

Freshwater sedge habitat; more common in North Country. March 3 early spring date.

American Woodcock · *Scolopax minor*

JAN	FEB	MAR	APR	MAY	JUN	JUL	AUG	SEP	OCT	NOV	DEC

February 23 early spring date.

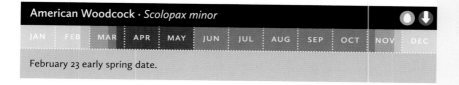

NONE
RARE
VERY UNCOMMON
UNCOMMON TO FAIRLY COMMON
COMMON TO ABUNDANT

INCREASING
DECREASING
STABLE
IRRUPTIVE
BREEDS IN NH
OCCURS OFFSHORE
INLAND

Wilson's Phalarope · *Phalaropus tricolor*

JAN	FEB	MAR	APR	MAY	JUN	JUL	AUG	SEP	OCT	NOV	DEC

Mainly coastal; very rare inland (14 records). May 8 early spring date; October 10 late fall date.

Red-necked Phalarope · *Phalaropus lobatus*

JAN	FEB	MAR	APR	MAY	JUN	JUL	AUG	SEP	OCT	NOV	DEC

Ocean; rare from coast or inland. May 2 early spring date; June 6 late spring date. Has occurred into December. Female phalaropes are larger and more brightly colored than the males. Phalaropes occasionally practice polyandry, in which the female mates with more than one male. This energy-intensive behavior, whereby the female produces several clutches of eggs, is probably facilitated by the remarkably abundant food supply in the phalarope's Arctic summer home.

Red Phalarope · *Phalaropus fulicarius*

JAN	FEB	MAR	APR	MAY	JUN	JUL	AUG	SEP	OCT	NOV	DEC

Ocean; rare from coast or inland. April 11 early spring date; June 11 late spring date.

Black-legged Kittiwake · *Rissa tridactyla*

JAN	FEB	MAR	APR	MAY	JUN	JUL	AUG	SEP	OCT	NOV	DEC

Ocean; less common on coast, occasionally following trawlers to entrance of Hampton Harbor; 5 inland records, mainly late fall.

Sabine's Gull · *Xema sabini*

JAN	FEB	MAR	APR	MAY	JUN	JUL	AUG	SEP	OCT	NOV	DEC

Presumed rare but annual offshore migrant, very rarely seen from the coast.

Bonaparte's Gull · *Chroicocephalus philadelphia*

JAN	FEB	MAR	APR	MAY	JUN	JUL	AUG	SEP	OCT	NOV	DEC

Mainly coastal; inland on larger lakes and impoundments. Bonaparte's Gull nests in trees, an unusual behavior for a gull. It is named in honor of Charles Lucien Bonaparte, an ornithologist and nephew to the Emperor Napoleon.

Black-headed Gull · *Chroicocephalus ridibundus*

JAN	FEB	MAR	APR	MAY	JUN	JUL	AUG	SEP	OCT	NOV	DEC

Coastal; very rare inland (6 records).

Little Gull · *Hydrocoloeus minutus*

JAN	FEB	MAR	APR	MAY	JUN	JUL	AUG	SEP	OCT	NOV	DEC

Coastal; very rare inland (3 records).

Laughing Gull · *Leucophaeus atricilla*

JAN	FEB	MAR	APR	MAY	JUN	JUL	AUG	SEP	OCT	NOV	DEC

Coastal; very rare inland (14 records). April 11 early date; December 14 late date.

Ring-billed Gull · *Larus delawarensis*

JAN	FEB	MAR	APR	MAY	JUN	JUL	AUG	SEP	OCT	NOV	DEC

Common coastal and inland.

Herring Gull · *Larus argentatus*

JAN	FEB	MAR	APR	MAY	JUN	JUL	AUG	SEP	OCT	NOV	DEC

Much more common coastally.

Iceland Gull · *Larus glaucoides*

JAN	FEB	MAR	APR	MAY	JUN	JUL	AUG	SEP	OCT	NOV	DEC

Coastal and inland at landfills on larger lakes and along major river valleys. May 27 late spring date; October 17 early fall date.

Lesser Black-backed Gull · *Larus fuscus*

JAN	FEB	MAR	APR	MAY	JUN	JUL	AUG	SEP	OCT	NOV	DEC

Coastal and inland at landfills, on larger lakes, and along major river valleys.

Glaucous Gull · *Larus hyperboreus*

JAN	FEB	MAR	APR	MAY	JUN	JUL	AUG	SEP	OCT	NOV	DEC

Coastal and inland at landfills. June 1 late spring date; August 16 early fall date.

NONE
RARE
VERY UNCOMMON
UNCOMMON TO FAIRLY COMMON
COMMON TO ABUNDANT

INCREASING
DECREASING
STABLE
IRRUPTIVE
BREEDS IN NH
OCCURS OFFSHORE
INLAND

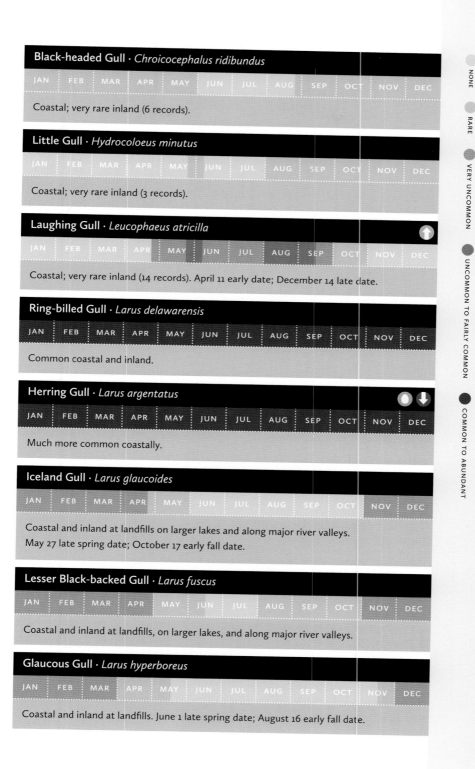

Great Black-backed Gull · *Larus marinus*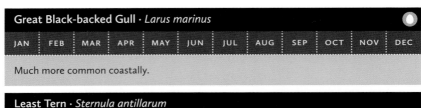

JAN	FEB	MAR	APR	MAY	JUN	JUL	AUG	SEP	OCT	NOV	DEC

Much more common coastally.

Least Tern · *Sternula antillarum*

JAN	FEB	MAR	APR	MAY	JUN	JUL	AUG	SEP	OCT	NOV	DEC

Exclusively coastal. May 7 early date; September 10 late date.

Caspian Tern · *Hydroprogne caspia*

JAN	FEB	MAR	APR	MAY	JUN	JUL	AUG	SEP	OCT	NOV	DEC

Coastal; very rare inland (5 records, mostly in the Connecticut River Valley). April 20 early spring date; October 28 late call date.

Black Tern · *Chlidonias niger*

JAN	FEB	MAR	APR	MAY	JUN	JUL	AUG	SEP	OCT	NOV	DEC

More likely inland in spring (especially Connecticut River Valley) and coastal in fall. May 1 early spring date; September 18 late fall date.

Roseate Tern · *Sterna dougallii*

JAN	FEB	MAR	APR	MAY	JUN	JUL	AUG	SEP	OCT	NOV	DEC

Exclusively coastal. A few dozen pairs nest on Seavey Island. Regular in fall from mainland coast. May 7 early date; October 1 late date.

Common Tern · *Sterna hirundo*

JAN	FEB	MAR	APR	MAY	JUN	JUL	AUG	SEP	OCT	NOV	DEC

Mainly coastal. About 2,500 pairs breed on White and Seavey Islands. Inland in spring, especially along Connecticut River. Rare inland in fall. April 22 early date; December 19 late date.

Arctic Tern · *Sterna paradisaea*

JAN	FEB	MAR	APR	MAY	JUN	JUL	AUG	SEP	OCT	NOV	DEC

Mainly coastal. Fewer than 10 pairs breed on White and Seavey Islands. Rarely seen from mainland coast; 8 records inland, all but 1 in spring. May 8 early date; September 30 late date.

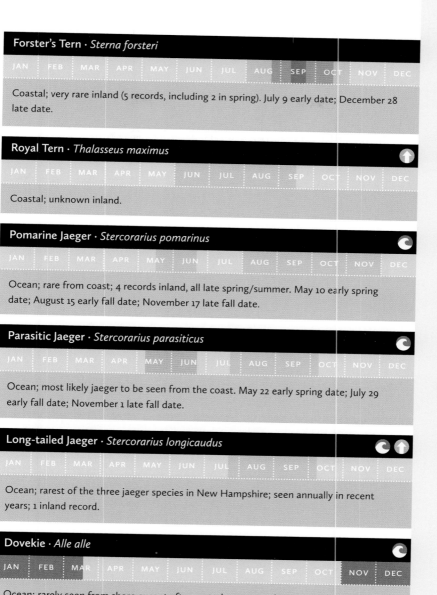

Forster's Tern · *Sterna forsteri*

JAN	FEB	MAR	APR	MAY	JUN	JUL	AUG	SEP	OCT	NOV	DEC

Coastal; very rare inland (5 records, including 2 in spring). July 9 early date; December 28 late date.

Royal Tern · *Thalasseus maximus*

JAN	FEB	MAR	APR	MAY	JUN	JUL	AUG	SEP	OCT	NOV	DEC

Coastal; unknown inland.

Pomarine Jaeger · *Stercorarius pomarinus*

JAN	FEB	MAR	APR	MAY	JUN	JUL	AUG	SEP	OCT	NOV	DEC

Ocean; rare from coast; 4 records inland, all late spring/summer. May 10 early spring date; August 15 early fall date; November 17 late fall date.

Parasitic Jaeger · *Stercorarius parasiticus*

JAN	FEB	MAR	APR	MAY	JUN	JUL	AUG	SEP	OCT	NOV	DEC

Ocean; most likely jaeger to be seen from the coast. May 22 early spring date; July 29 early fall date; November 1 late fall date.

Long-tailed Jaeger · *Stercorarius longicaudus*

JAN	FEB	MAR	APR	MAY	JUN	JUL	AUG	SEP	OCT	NOV	DEC

Ocean; rarest of the three jaeger species in New Hampshire; seen annually in recent years; 1 inland record.

Dovekie · *Alle alle*

JAN	FEB	MAR	APR	MAY	JUN	JUL	AUG	SEP	OCT	NOV	DEC

Ocean; rarely seen from shore except after easterly storms, when can occasionally be found far inland. October 25 early date; April 7 late date.

Common Murre · *Uria aalge*

JAN	FEB	MAR	APR	MAY	JUN	JUL	AUG	SEP	OCT	NOV	DEC

Ocean; rare from coast.

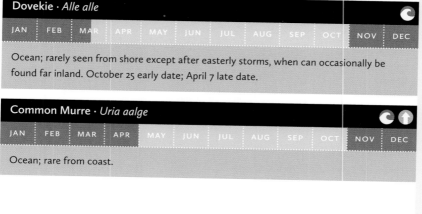

NONE

RARE

VERY UNCOMMON

UNCOMMON TO FAIRLY COMMON

COMMON TO ABUNDANT

INCREASING

DECREASING

STABLE

IRRUPTIVE

BREEDS IN NH

OCCURS OFFSHORE

INLAND

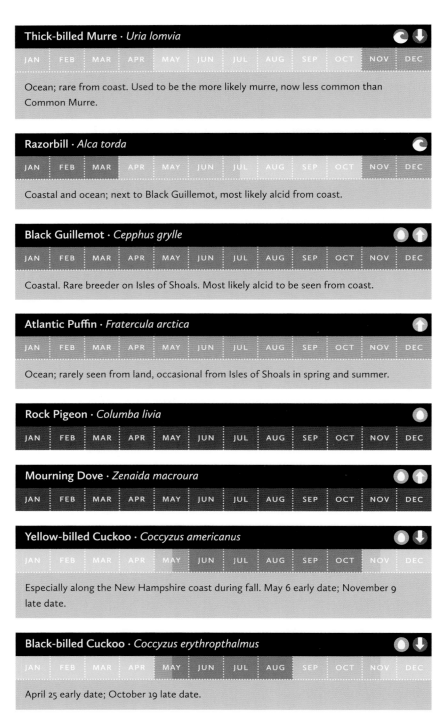

Thick-billed Murre · *Uria lomvia*

JAN	FEB	MAR	APR	MAY	JUN	JUL	AUG	SEP	OCT	NOV	DEC

Ocean; rare from coast. Used to be the more likely murre, now less common than Common Murre.

Razorbill · *Alca torda*

JAN	FEB	MAR	APR	MAY	JUN	JUL	AUG	SEP	OCT	NOV	DEC

Coastal and ocean; next to Black Guillemot, most likely alcid from coast.

Black Guillemot · *Cepphus grylle*

JAN	FEB	MAR	APR	MAY	JUN	JUL	AUG	SEP	OCT	NOV	DEC

Coastal. Rare breeder on Isles of Shoals. Most likely alcid to be seen from coast.

Atlantic Puffin · *Fratercula arctica*

JAN	FEB	MAR	APR	MAY	JUN	JUL	AUG	SEP	OCT	NOV	DEC

Ocean; rarely seen from land, occasional from Isles of Shoals in spring and summer.

Rock Pigeon · *Columba livia*

JAN	FEB	MAR	APR	MAY	JUN	JUL	AUG	SEP	OCT	NOV	DEC

Mourning Dove · *Zenaida macroura*

JAN	FEB	MAR	APR	MAY	JUN	JUL	AUG	SEP	OCT	NOV	DEC

Yellow-billed Cuckoo · *Coccyzus americanus*

JAN	FEB	MAR	APR	MAY	JUN	JUL	AUG	SEP	OCT	NOV	DEC

Especially along the New Hampshire coast during fall. May 6 early date; November 9 late date.

Black-billed Cuckoo · *Coccyzus erythropthalmus*

JAN	FEB	MAR	APR	MAY	JUN	JUL	AUG	SEP	OCT	NOV	DEC

April 25 early date; October 19 late date.

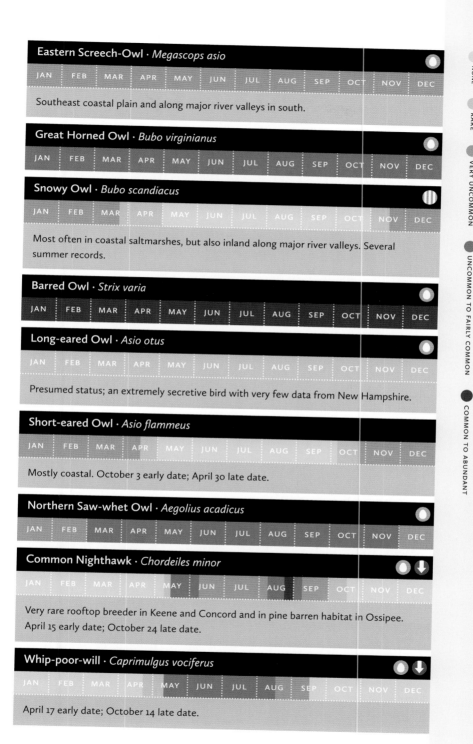

Eastern Screech-Owl · *Megascops asio*

| JAN | FEB | MAR | APR | MAY | JUN | JUL | AUG | SEP | OCT | NOV | DEC |

Southeast coastal plain and along major river valleys in south.

Great Horned Owl · *Bubo virginianus*

| JAN | FEB | MAR | APR | MAY | JUN | JUL | AUG | SEP | OCT | NOV | DEC |

Snowy Owl · *Bubo scandiacus*

| JAN | FEB | MAR | APR | MAY | JUN | JUL | AUG | SEP | OCT | NOV | DEC |

Most often in coastal saltmarshes, but also inland along major river valleys. Several summer records.

Barred Owl · *Strix varia*

| JAN | FEB | MAR | APR | MAY | JUN | JUL | AUG | SEP | OCT | NOV | DEC |

Long-eared Owl · *Asio otus*

| JAN | FEB | MAR | APR | MAY | JUN | JUL | AUG | SEP | OCT | NOV | DEC |

Presumed status; an extremely secretive bird with very few data from New Hampshire.

Short-eared Owl · *Asio flammeus*

| JAN | FEB | MAR | APR | MAY | JUN | JUL | AUG | SEP | OCT | NOV | DEC |

Mostly coastal. October 3 early date; April 30 late date.

Northern Saw-whet Owl · *Aegolius acadicus*

| JAN | FEB | MAR | APR | MAY | JUN | JUL | AUG | SEP | OCT | NOV | DEC |

Common Nighthawk · *Chordeiles minor*

| JAN | FEB | MAR | APR | MAY | JUN | JUL | AUG | SEP | OCT | NOV | DEC |

Very rare rooftop breeder in Keene and Concord and in pine barren habitat in Ossipee. April 15 early date; October 24 late date.

Whip-poor-will · *Caprimulgus vociferus*

| JAN | FEB | MAR | APR | MAY | JUN | JUL | AUG | SEP | OCT | NOV | DEC |

April 17 early date; October 14 late date.

NONE · RARE · VERY UNCOMMON · UNCOMMON TO FAIRLY COMMON · COMMON TO ABUNDANT

INCREASING · DECREASING · STABLE · IRRUPTIVE · BREEDS IN NH · OCCURS OFFSHORE · INLAND

Chimney Swift · *Chaetura pelagica*

JAN	FEB	MAR	APR	MAY	JUN	JUL	AUG	SEP	OCT	NOV	DEC

April 9 early date; November 8 late date.

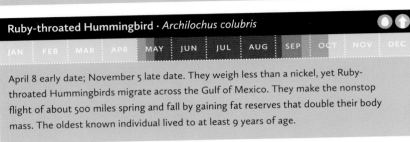

Ruby-throated Hummingbird · *Archilochus colubris*

JAN	FEB	MAR	APR	MAY	JUN	JUL	AUG	SEP	OCT	NOV	DEC

April 8 early date; November 5 late date. They weigh less than a nickel, yet Ruby-throated Hummingbirds migrate across the Gulf of Mexico. They make the nonstop flight of about 500 miles spring and fall by gaining fat reserves that double their body mass. The oldest known individual lived to at least 9 years of age.

Belted Kingfisher · *Megaceryle alcyon*

JAN	FEB	MAR	APR	MAY	JUN	JUL	AUG	SEP	OCT	NOV	DEC

Red-headed Woodpecker · *Melanerpes erythrocephalus*

JAN	FEB	MAR	APR	MAY	JUN	JUL	AUG	SEP	OCT	NOV	DEC

Very rarely breeds in New Hampshire.

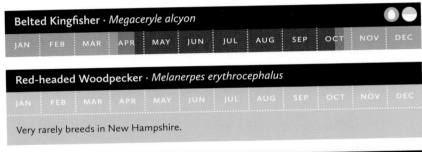

Red-bellied Woodpecker · *Melanerpes carolinus*

JAN	FEB	MAR	APR	MAY	JUN	JUL	AUG	SEP	OCT	NOV	DEC

More common along major river valleys and in southeast. Relatively recent arrival to New Hampshire from the south; first confirmed breeding in 2002.

Yellow-bellied Sapsucker · *Sphyrapicus varius*

JAN	FEB	MAR	APR	MAY	JUN	JUL	AUG	SEP	OCT	NOV	DEC

More common in North Country. March 5 early date.

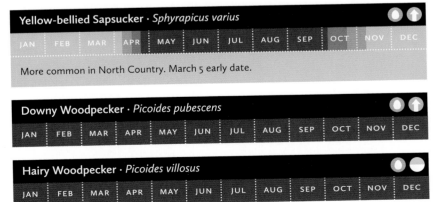

Downy Woodpecker · *Picoides pubescens*

JAN	FEB	MAR	APR	MAY	JUN	JUL	AUG	SEP	OCT	NOV	DEC

Hairy Woodpecker · *Picoides villosus*

JAN	FEB	MAR	APR	MAY	JUN	JUL	AUG	SEP	OCT	NOV	DEC

American Three-toed Woodpecker · *Picoides dorsalis*

JAN	FEB	MAR	APR	MAY	JUN	JUL	AUG	SEP	OCT	NOV	DEC

Very rare breeder in New Hampshire (White Mountains and North Country only).

Black-backed Woodpecker · *Picoides arcticus*

JAN	FEB	MAR	APR	MAY	JUN	JUL	AUG	SEP	OCT	NOV	DEC

Found in White Mountains and North Country only.

Northern Flicker · *Colaptes auratus*

JAN	FEB	MAR	APR	MAY	JUN	JUL	AUG	SEP	OCT	NOV	DEC

Pileated Woodpecker · *Dryocopus pileatus*

JAN	FEB	MAR	APR	MAY	JUN	JUL	AUG	SEP	OCT	NOV	DEC

American Kestrel · *Falco sparverius*

JAN	FEB	MAR	APR	MAY	JUN	JUL	AUG	SEP	OCT	NOV	DEC

Merlin · *Falco columbarius*

JAN	FEB	MAR	APR	MAY	JUN	JUL	AUG	SEP	OCT	NOV	DEC

More common in North Country, April through August.

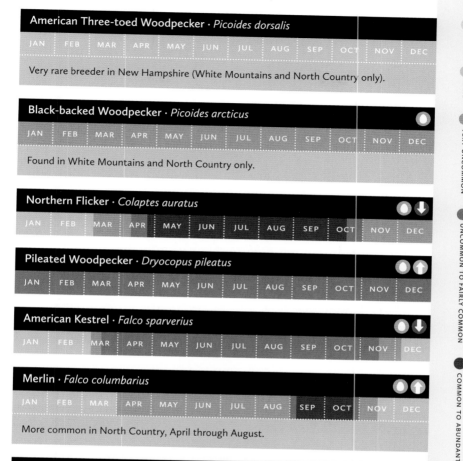

Peregrine Falcon · *Falco peregrinus*

JAN	FEB	MAR	APR	MAY	JUN	JUL	AUG	SEP	OCT	NOV	DEC

From 1980 to 2010, the New Hampshire population increased from 0 to 16 territorial pairs. Peregrine Falcon is a cosmopolitan species found on all continents except Antarctica. Known for attaining very high speeds when stooping on prey, a trained bird was clocked at 200 mph as it accompanied its trainer, a free-fall parachutist.

Olive-sided Flycatcher · *Contopus cooperi*

JAN	FEB	MAR	APR	MAY	JUN	JUL	AUG	SEP	OCT	NOV	DEC

Breeds from White Mountains north; migrant elsewhere. April 10 early date; October 18 late date.

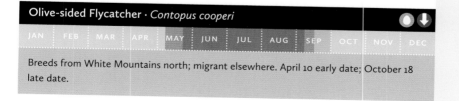

NONE
RARE
VERY UNCOMMON
UNCOMMON TO FAIRLY COMMON
COMMON TO ABUNDANT

INCREASING
DECREASING
STABLE
IRRUPTIVE
BREEDS IN NH
OCCURS OFFSHORE
INLAND

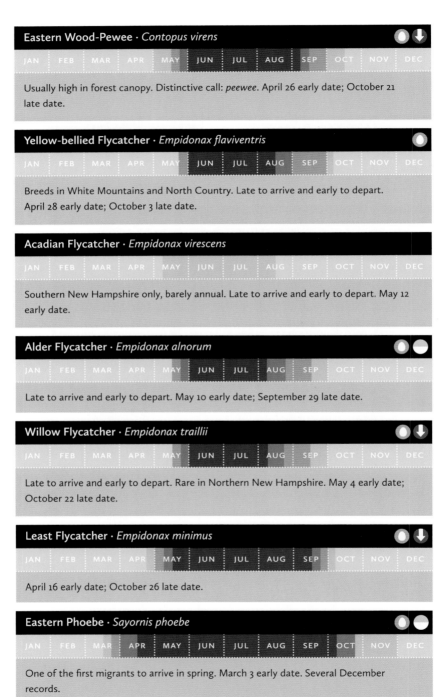

Eastern Wood-Pewee · *Contopus virens*

JAN	FEB	MAR	APR	MAY	JUN	JUL	AUG	SEP	OCT	NOV	DEC

Usually high in forest canopy. Distinctive call: *peewee*. April 26 early date; October 21 late date.

Yellow-bellied Flycatcher · *Empidonax flaviventris*

JAN	FEB	MAR	APR	MAY	JUN	JUL	AUG	SEP	OCT	NOV	DEC

Breeds in White Mountains and North Country. Late to arrive and early to depart. April 28 early date; October 3 late date.

Acadian Flycatcher · *Empidonax virescens*

JAN	FEB	MAR	APR	MAY	JUN	JUL	AUG	SEP	OCT	NOV	DEC

Southern New Hampshire only, barely annual. Late to arrive and early to depart. May 12 early date.

Alder Flycatcher · *Empidonax alnorum*

JAN	FEB	MAR	APR	MAY	JUN	JUL	AUG	SEP	OCT	NOV	DEC

Late to arrive and early to depart. May 10 early date; September 29 late date.

Willow Flycatcher · *Empidonax traillii*

JAN	FEB	MAR	APR	MAY	JUN	JUL	AUG	SEP	OCT	NOV	DEC

Late to arrive and early to depart. Rare in Northern New Hampshire. May 4 early date; October 22 late date.

Least Flycatcher · *Empidonax minimus*

JAN	FEB	MAR	APR	MAY	JUN	JUL	AUG	SEP	OCT	NOV	DEC

April 16 early date; October 26 late date.

Eastern Phoebe · *Sayornis phoebe*

JAN	FEB	MAR	APR	MAY	JUN	JUL	AUG	SEP	OCT	NOV	DEC

One of the first migrants to arrive in spring. March 3 early date. Several December records.

NONE · RARE · VERY UNCOMMON · UNCOMMON TO FAIRLY COMMON · COMMON TO ABUNDANT

INCREASING · DECREASING · STABLE · IRRUPTIVE · BREEDS IN NH · OCCURS OFFSHORE · INLAND

Great Crested Flycatcher · *Myiarchus crinitus*

| JAN | FEB | MAR | APR | MAY | JUN | JUL | AUG | SEP | OCT | NOV | DEC |

April 23 early date; December 1 late date (similar-looking Ash-throated Flycatcher more likely species in late fall). This species frequently uses old snakeskin in the construction of its nest. They can be enticed to nest by hanging up strips of clear polyethylene plastic—fake snakeskin—in the spring.

Western Kingbird · *Tyrannus verticalis*

| JAN | FEB | MAR | APR | MAY | JUN | JUL | AUG | SEP | OCT | NOV | DEC |

August 19 early date; December 3 late date.

Eastern Kingbird · *Tyrannus tyrannus*

| JAN | FEB | MAR | APR | MAY | JUN | JUL | AUG | SEP | OCT | NOV | DEC |

April 13 early date; October 5 late date.

Northern Shrike · *Lanius excubitor*

| JAN | FEB | MAR | APR | MAY | JUN | JUL | AUG | SEP | OCT | NOV | DEC |

September 2 early date; May 19 late date.

White-eyed Vireo · *Vireo griseus*

| JAN | FEB | MAR | APR | MAY | JUN | JUL | AUG | SEP | OCT | NOV | DEC |

Southern New Hampshire only, mainly coastal. April 30 early date; November 16 late date.

Yellow-throated Vireo · *Vireo flavifrons*

| JAN | FEB | MAR | APR | MAY | JUN | JUL | AUG | SEP | OCT | NOV | DEC |

April 28 early date; October 27 late date.

Blue-headed Vireo · *Vireo solitarius*

| JAN | FEB | MAR | APR | MAY | JUN | JUL | AUG | SEP | OCT | NOV | DEC |

Most often in mixed hardwood-softwood forest. March 31 early date; November 17 late date.

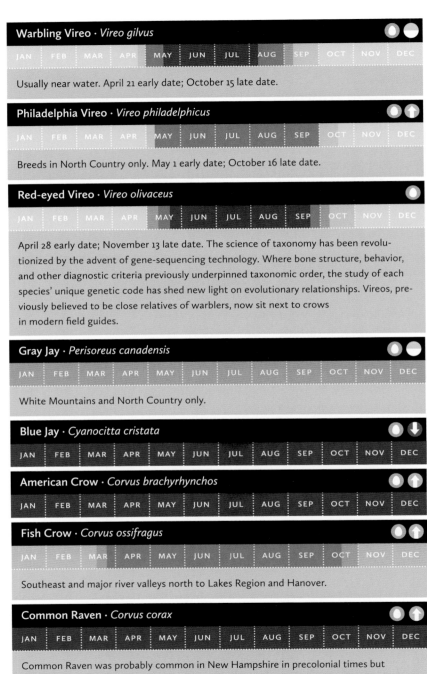

Warbling Vireo · *Vireo gilvus*

JAN	FEB	MAR	APR	MAY	JUN	JUL	AUG	SEP	OCT	NOV	DEC

Usually near water. April 21 early date; October 15 late date.

Philadelphia Vireo · *Vireo philadelphicus*

JAN	FEB	MAR	APR	MAY	JUN	JUL	AUG	SEP	OCT	NOV	DEC

Breeds in North Country only. May 1 early date; October 16 late date.

Red-eyed Vireo · *Vireo olivaceus*

JAN	FEB	MAR	APR	MAY	JUN	JUL	AUG	SEP	OCT	NOV	DEC

April 28 early date; November 13 late date. The science of taxonomy has been revolutionized by the advent of gene-sequencing technology. Where bone structure, behavior, and other diagnostic criteria previously underpinned taxonomic order, the study of each species' unique genetic code has shed new light on evolutionary relationships. Vireos, previously believed to be close relatives of warblers, now sit next to crows in modern field guides.

Gray Jay · *Perisoreus canadensis*

JAN	FEB	MAR	APR	MAY	JUN	JUL	AUG	SEP	OCT	NOV	DEC

White Mountains and North Country only.

Blue Jay · *Cyanocitta cristata*

JAN	FEB	MAR	APR	MAY	JUN	JUL	AUG	SEP	OCT	NOV	DEC

American Crow · *Corvus brachyrhynchos*

JAN	FEB	MAR	APR	MAY	JUN	JUL	AUG	SEP	OCT	NOV	DEC

Fish Crow · *Corvus ossifragus*

JAN	FEB	MAR	APR	MAY	JUN	JUL	AUG	SEP	OCT	NOV	DEC

Southeast and major river valleys north to Lakes Region and Hanover.

Common Raven · *Corvus corax*

JAN	FEB	MAR	APR	MAY	JUN	JUL	AUG	SEP	OCT	NOV	DEC

Common Raven was probably common in New Hampshire in precolonial times but disappeared from the state in the nineteenth century largely through persecution by humans. It has recolonized New Hampshire since the 1950s and is now quite common in most parts of the state, with the exception of the seacoast area.

Horned Lark · *Eremophila alpestris*

JAN	FEB	MAR	APR	MAY	JUN	JUL	AUG	SEP	OCT	NOV	DEC

Found in stubble fields, dunes, and saltmarsh. Mainly coastal from early November through February.

Northern Rough-winged Swallow · *Stelgidopteryx serripennis*

JAN	FEB	MAR	APR	MAY	JUN	JUL	AUG	SEP	OCT	NOV	DEC

Found near freshwater. April 3 early date; October 16 late date.

Purple Martin · *Progne subis*

JAN	FEB	MAR	APR	MAY	JUN	JUL	AUG	SEP	OCT	NOV	DEC

April 3 early date; September 22 late date.

Tree Swallow · *Tachycineta bicolor*

JAN	FEB	MAR	APR	MAY	JUN	JUL	AUG	SEP	OCT	NOV	DEC

February 25 early date; November 11 late date.

Bank Swallow · *Riparia riparia*

JAN	FEB	MAR	APR	MAY	JUN	JUL	AUG	SEP	OCT	NOV	DEC

April 15 early date; October 16 late date.

Barn Swallow · *Hirundo rustica*

JAN	FEB	MAR	APR	MAY	JUN	JUL	AUG	SEP	OCT	NOV	DEC

March 28 early date; December 1 late date.

Cliff Swallow · *Petrochelidon pyrrhonota*

JAN	FEB	MAR	APR	MAY	JUN	JUL	AUG	SEP	OCT	NOV	DEC

April 8 early date; November 7 late date.

Black-capped Chickadee · *Poecile atricapillus*

JAN	FEB	MAR	APR	MAY	JUN	JUL	AUG	SEP	OCT	NOV	DEC

Boreal Chickadee · *Poecile hudsonicus*

JAN	FEB	MAR	APR	MAY	JUN	JUL	AUG	SEP	OCT	NOV	DEC

White Mountains and North Country.

NONE
RARE
VERY UNCOMMON
UNCOMMON TO FAIRLY COMMON
COMMON TO ABUNDANT

INCREASING
DECREASING
STABLE
IRRUPTIVE
BREEDS IN NH
OCCURS OFFSHORE
INLAND

Tufted Titmouse · *Baeolophus bicolor*

JAN	FEB	MAR	APR	MAY	JUN	JUL	AUG	SEP	OCT	NOV	DEC

More common in the south.

Red-breasted Nuthatch · *Sitta canadensis*

JAN	FEB	MAR	APR	MAY	JUN	JUL	AUG	SEP	OCT	NOV	DEC

More common in the North Country. Somewhat irruptive.

White-breasted Nuthatch · *Sitta carolinensis*

JAN	FEB	MAR	APR	MAY	JUN	JUL	AUG	SEP	OCT	NOV	DEC

More common in south.

Brown Creeper · *Certhia americana*

JAN	FEB	MAR	APR	MAY	JUN	JUL	AUG	SEP	OCT	NOV	DEC

House Wren · *Troglodytes aedon*

JAN	FEB	MAR	APR	MAY	JUN	JUL	AUG	SEP	OCT	NOV	DEC

April 19 early date; November 27 late date.

Winter Wren · *Troglodytes hiemalis*

JAN	FEB	MAR	APR	MAY	JUN	JUL	AUG	SEP	OCT	NOV	DEC

Abundant in North Country during summer.

Marsh Wren · *Cistothorus palustris*

JAN	FEB	MAR	APR	MAY	JUN	JUL	AUG	SEP	OCT	NOV	DEC

April 25 early date.

Carolina Wren · *Thryothorus ludovicianus*

JAN	FEB	MAR	APR	MAY	JUN	JUL	AUG	SEP	OCT	NOV	DEC

Mainly in the south.

Blue-gray Gnatcatcher · *Polioptila caerulea*

JAN	FEB	MAR	APR	MAY	JUN	JUL	AUG	SEP	OCT	NOV	DEC

Southern New Hampshire only. April 13 early date; November 20 late date.

Golden-crowned Kinglet · *Regulus satrapa*

JAN	FEB	MAR	APR	MAY	JUN	JUL	AUG	SEP	OCT	NOV	DEC

More common in North Country. Weighing 6 grams (less than a quarter of an ounce), the Golden-crowned Kinglet is one of North America's smallest birds—only the hummingbirds are smaller. Small bodies lose heat more quickly than large bodies, and the kinglet has a very small body to endure temperatures down to –40 degrees Celsius in its boreal forest home. It does this by subsisting on spiders, mites, and their egg masses, which it finds at the tips of branches, among needles, and under bark.

Ruby-crowned Kinglet · *Regulus calendula*

JAN	FEB	MAR	APR	MAY	JUN	JUL	AUG	SEP	OCT	NOV	DEC

Breeds North Country only.

Eastern Bluebird · *Sialia sialis*

JAN	FEB	MAR	APR	MAY	JUN	JUL	AUG	SEP	OCT	NOV	DEC

Veery · *Catharus fuscescens*

JAN	FEB	MAR	APR	MAY	JUN	JUL	AUG	SEP	OCT	NOV	DEC

April 21 early date; October 9 late date. One December record. The Veery produces sound from its syrinx, which is structurally different than the human larynx. The syrinx enables the Veery to harmonize with itself by singing two notes at the same time, producing the ethereal song that is a familiar sound in our summer forests.

Gray-cheeked Thrush · *Catharus minimus*

JAN	FEB	MAR	APR	MAY	JUN	JUL	AUG	SEP	OCT	NOV	DEC

Most often detected by call during nocturnal migration.

NONE · RARE · VERY UNCOMMON · UNCOMMON TO FAIRLY COMMON · COMMON TO ABUNDANT

INCREASING · DECREASING · STABLE · IRRUPTIVE · BREEDS IN NH · OCCURS OFFSHORE · INLAND

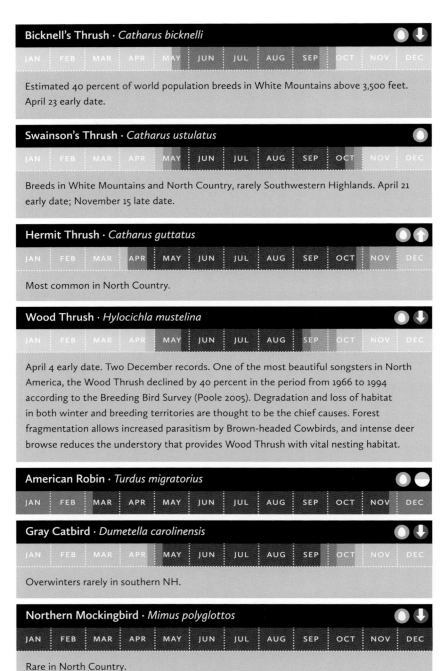

Bicknell's Thrush · *Catharus bicknelli*

JAN	FEB	MAR	APR	MAY	JUN	JUL	AUG	SEP	OCT	NOV	DEC

Estimated 40 percent of world population breeds in White Mountains above 3,500 feet. April 23 early date.

Swainson's Thrush · *Catharus ustulatus*

JAN	FEB	MAR	APR	MAY	JUN	JUL	AUG	SEP	OCT	NOV	DEC

Breeds in White Mountains and North Country, rarely Southwestern Highlands. April 21 early date; November 15 late date.

Hermit Thrush · *Catharus guttatus*

JAN	FEB	MAR	APR	MAY	JUN	JUL	AUG	SEP	OCT	NOV	DEC

Most common in North Country.

Wood Thrush · *Hylocichla mustelina*

JAN	FEB	MAR	APR	MAY	JUN	JUL	AUG	SEP	OCT	NOV	DEC

April 4 early date. Two December records. One of the most beautiful songsters in North America, the Wood Thrush declined by 40 percent in the period from 1966 to 1994 according to the Breeding Bird Survey (Poole 2005). Degradation and loss of habitat in both winter and breeding territories are thought to be the chief causes. Forest fragmentation allows increased parasitism by Brown-headed Cowbirds, and intense deer browse reduces the understory that provides Wood Thrush with vital nesting habitat.

American Robin · *Turdus migratorius*

JAN	FEB	MAR	APR	MAY	JUN	JUL	AUG	SEP	OCT	NOV	DEC

Gray Catbird · *Dumetella carolinensis*

JAN	FEB	MAR	APR	MAY	JUN	JUL	AUG	SEP	OCT	NOV	DEC

Overwinters rarely in southern NH.

Northern Mockingbird · *Mimus polyglottos*

JAN	FEB	MAR	APR	MAY	JUN	JUL	AUG	SEP	OCT	NOV	DEC

Rare in North Country.

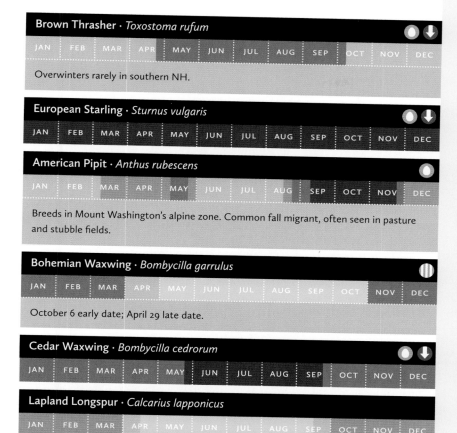

Brown Thrasher · *Toxostoma rufum*

JAN	FEB	MAR	APR	MAY	JUN	JUL	AUG	SEP	OCT	NOV	DEC

Overwinters rarely in southern NH.

European Starling · *Sturnus vulgaris*

JAN	FEB	MAR	APR	MAY	JUN	JUL	AUG	SEP	OCT	NOV	DEC

American Pipit · *Anthus rubescens*

JAN	FEB	MAR	APR	MAY	JUN	JUL	AUG	SEP	OCT	NOV	DEC

Breeds in Mount Washington's alpine zone. Common fall migrant, often seen in pasture and stubble fields.

Bohemian Waxwing · *Bombycilla garrulus*

JAN	FEB	MAR	APR	MAY	JUN	JUL	AUG	SEP	OCT	NOV	DEC

October 6 early date; April 29 late date.

Cedar Waxwing · *Bombycilla cedrorum*

JAN	FEB	MAR	APR	MAY	JUN	JUL	AUG	SEP	OCT	NOV	DEC

Lapland Longspur · *Calcarius lapponicus*

JAN	FEB	MAR	APR	MAY	JUN	JUL	AUG	SEP	OCT	NOV	DEC

Often with Snow Buntings, especially along coast and major river valleys. September 10 early date; May 13 late date.

Snow Bunting · *Plectrophenax nivalis*

JAN	FEB	MAR	APR	MAY	JUN	JUL	AUG	SEP	OCT	NOV	DEC

More common along coast and major river valleys. August 31 early date; June 1 late date.

Ovenbird · *Seiurus aurocapilla*

JAN	FEB	MAR	APR	MAY	JUN	JUL	AUG	SEP	OCT	NOV	DEC

Very loud song *teacher, teacher, teacher* distinctive sound of NH forests. April 26 early date. Several winter records.

NONE · RARE · VERY UNCOMMON · UNCOMMON TO FAIRLY COMMON · COMMON TO ABUNDANT

INCREASING · DECREASING · STABLE · IRRUPTIVE · BREEDS IN NH · OCCURS OFFSHORE · INLAND

Louisiana Waterthrush · *Parkesia motacilla*

JAN	FEB	MAR	APR	MAY	JUN	JUL	AUG	SEP	OCT	NOV	DEC

Breeds in southern New Hampshire only, near fast-flowing streams. Early to arrive and early to leave. April 5 early date; October 12 late date.

Northern Waterthrush · *Parkesia noveboracensis*

JAN	FEB	MAR	APR	MAY	JUN	JUL	AUG	SEP	OCT	NOV	DEC

Much more common in North Country. April 12 early date; November 27 late date. One winter record.

Blue-winged Warbler · *Vermivora cyanoptera*

JAN	FEB	MAR	APR	MAY	JUN	JUL	AUG	SEP	OCT	NOV	DEC

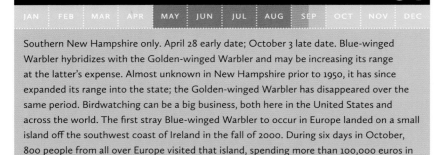

Southern New Hampshire only. April 28 early date; October 3 late date. Blue-winged Warbler hybridizes with the Golden-winged Warbler and may be increasing its range at the latter's expense. Almost unknown in New Hampshire prior to 1950, it has since expanded its range into the state; the Golden-winged Warbler has disappeared over the same period. Birdwatching can be a big business, both here in the United States and across the world. The first stray Blue-winged Warbler to occur in Europe landed on a small island off the southwest coast of Ireland in the fall of 2000. During six days in October, 800 people from all over Europe visited that island, spending more than 100,000 euros in the process.

Black-and-White Warbler · *Mniotilta varia*

JAN	FEB	MAR	APR	MAY	JUN	JUL	AUG	SEP	OCT	NOV	DEC

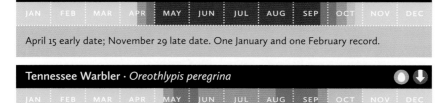

April 15 early date; November 29 late date. One January and one February record.

Tennessee Warbler · *Oreothlypis peregrina*

JAN	FEB	MAR	APR	MAY	JUN	JUL	AUG	SEP	OCT	NOV	DEC

Breeds White Mountain region and North Country only. May 1 early date; November 23 late date.

Orange-crowned Warbler · *Oreothlypis celata*

JAN	FEB	MAR	APR	MAY	JUN	JUL	AUG	SEP	OCT	NOV

Very rarely, spring and winter. August 23 early fall date.

Nashville Warbler · *Oreothlypis ruficapilla*

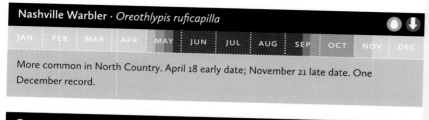

JAN	FEB	MAR	APR	MAY	JUN	JUL	AUG	SEP	OCT	NOV	DEC

More common in North Country. April 18 early date; November 21 late date. One December record.

Connecticut Warbler · *Oporornis agilis*

JAN	FEB	MAR	APR	MAY	JUN	JUL	AUG	SEP	OCT	NOV	DEC

August 23 early date. Fewer than 10 spring records.

Mourning Warbler · *Geothlypis philadelphia*

JAN	FEB	MAR	APR	MAY	JUN	JUL	AUG	SEP	OCT	NOV	DEC

Breeds in North Country only. May 10 early date; October 21 late date.

Common Yellowthroat · *Geothlypis trichas*

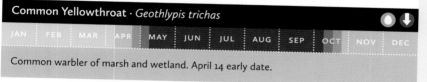

JAN	FEB	MAR	APR	MAY	JUN	JUL	AUG	SEP	OCT	NOV	DEC

Common warbler of marsh and wetland. April 14 early date.

American Redstart · *Setophaga ruticilla*

JAN	FEB	MAR	APR	MAY	JUN	JUL	AUG	SEP	OCT	NOV	DEC

April 20 early date; December 7 late date.

Cape May Warbler · *Setophaga tigrina*

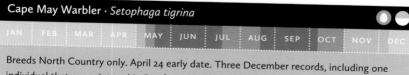

JAN	FEB	MAR	APR	MAY	JUN	JUL	AUG	SEP	OCT	NOV	DEC

Breeds North Country only. April 24 early date. Three December records, including one individual that overwintered in Rye from October 2011 to late March 2012.

Cerulean Warbler · *Setophaga cerulea*

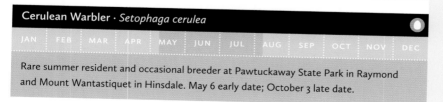

JAN	FEB	MAR	APR	MAY	JUN	JUL	AUG	SEP	OCT	NOV	DEC

Rare summer resident and occasional breeder at Pawtuckaway State Park in Raymond and Mount Wantastiquet in Hinsdale. May 6 early date; October 3 late date.

NONE
RARE
VERY UNCOMMON
UNCOMMON TO FAIRLY COMMON
COMMON TO ABUNDANT

INCREASING
DECREASING
STABLE
IRRUPTIVE
BREEDS IN NH
OCCURS OFFSHORE
INLAND

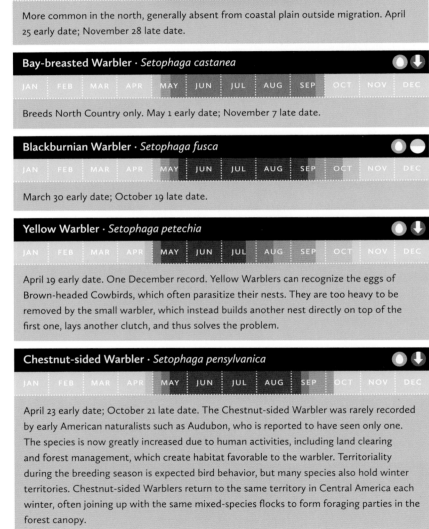

Northern Parula · *Setophaga americana*

JAN	FEB	MAR	APR	MAY	JUN	JUL	AUG	SEP	OCT	NOV	DEC

Breeds mainly in North Country. April 19 early date. One December record.

Magnolia Warbler · *Setophaga magnolia*

JAN	FEB	MAR	APR	MAY	JUN	JUL	AUG	SEP	OCT	NOV	DEC

More common in the north, generally absent from coastal plain outside migration. April 25 early date; November 28 late date.

Bay-breasted Warbler · *Setophaga castanea*

JAN	FEB	MAR	APR	MAY	JUN	JUL	AUG	SEP	OCT	NOV	DEC

Breeds North Country only. May 1 early date; November 7 late date.

Blackburnian Warbler · *Setophaga fusca*

JAN	FEB	MAR	APR	MAY	JUN	JUL	AUG	SEP	OCT	NOV	DEC

March 30 early date; October 19 late date.

Yellow Warbler · *Setophaga petechia*

JAN	FEB	MAR	APR	MAY	JUN	JUL	AUG	SEP	OCT	NOV	DEC

April 19 early date. One December record. Yellow Warblers can recognize the eggs of Brown-headed Cowbirds, which often parasitize their nests. They are too heavy to be removed by the small warbler, which instead builds another nest directly on top of the first one, lays another clutch, and thus solves the problem.

Chestnut-sided Warbler · *Setophaga pensylvanica*

JAN	FEB	MAR	APR	MAY	JUN	JUL	AUG	SEP	OCT	NOV	DEC

April 23 early date; October 21 late date. The Chestnut-sided Warbler was rarely recorded by early American naturalists such as Audubon, who is reported to have seen only one. The species is now greatly increased due to human activities, including land clearing and forest management, which create habitat favorable to the warbler. Territoriality during the breeding season is expected bird behavior, but many species also hold winter territories. Chestnut-sided Warblers return to the same territory in Central America each winter, often joining up with the same mixed-species flocks to form foraging parties in the forest canopy.

Blackpoll Warbler · *Setophaga striata*

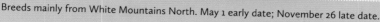

JAN	FEB	MAR	APR	MAY	JUN	JUL	AUG	SEP	OCT	NOV	DEC

Breeds mainly from White Mountains North. May 1 early date; November 26 late date.

Black-throated Blue Warbler · *Setophaga caerulescens*

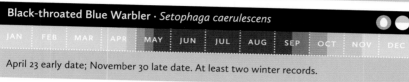

JAN	FEB	MAR	APR	MAY	JUN	JUL	AUG	SEP	OCT	NOV	DEC

April 23 early date; November 30 late date. At least two winter records.

Palm Warbler · *Setophaga palmarum*

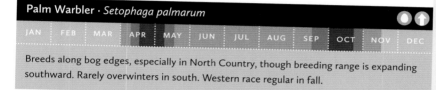

JAN	FEB	MAR	APR	MAY	JUN	JUL	AUG	SEP	OCT	NOV	DEC

Breeds along bog edges, especially in North Country, though breeding range is expanding southward. Rarely overwinters in south. Western race regular in fall.

Pine Warbler · *Setophaga pinus*

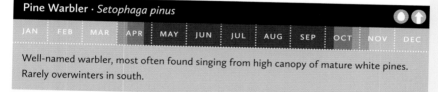

JAN	FEB	MAR	APR	MAY	JUN	JUL	AUG	SEP	OCT	NOV	DEC

Well-named warbler, most often found singing from high canopy of mature white pines. Rarely overwinters in south.

Yellow-rumped Warbler · *Setophaga coronata*

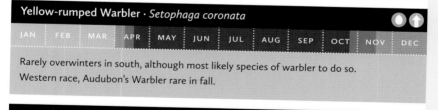

JAN	FEB	MAR	APR	MAY	JUN	JUL	AUG	SEP	OCT	NOV	DEC

Rarely overwinters in south, although most likely species of warbler to do so. Western race, Audubon's Warbler rare in fall.

Prairie Warbler · *Setophaga discolor*

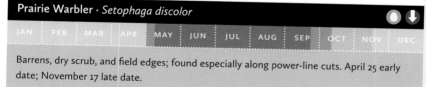

JAN	FEB	MAR	APR	MAY	JUN	JUL	AUG	SEP	OCT	NOV	DEC

Barrens, dry scrub, and field edges; found especially along power-line cuts. April 25 early date; November 17 late date.

Black-throated Green Warbler · *Setophaga virens*

JAN	FEB	MAR	APR	MAY	JUN	JUL	AUG	SEP	OCT	NOV	DEC

April 19 early date; December 22 late date.

 INCREASING

 NONE

 DECREASING

 RARE

 STABLE

VERY UNCOMMON

 IRRUPTIVE

UNCOMMON TO FAIRLY COMMON

 BREEDS IN NH

COMMON TO ABUNDANT

OCCURS OFFSHORE

INLAND

Canada Warbler · *Cardellina canadensis*

JAN	FEB	MAR	APR	MAY	JUN	JUL	AUG	SEP	OCT	NOV	DEC

Forest undergrowth and streamside thickets. April 29 early date; October 6 late date.

Wilson's Warbler · *Cardellina pusilla*

JAN	FEB	MAR	APR	MAY	JUN	JUL	AUG	SEP	OCT	NOV	DEC

Breeds in dense, moist thickets in North Country only. April 22 early date; November 28 late date.

Yellow-breasted Chat · *Icteria virens*

JAN	FEB	MAR	APR	MAY	JUN	JUL	AUG	SEP	OCT	NOV	DEC

Most often seen at or near coast, especially Star Island and Odiorne Point. April 28 early date.

Eastern Towhee · *Pipilo erythrophthalmus*

JAN	FEB	MAR	APR	MAY	JUN	JUL	AUG	SEP	OCT	NOV	DEC

Occurs most often along power lines and in pine barrens.

American Tree Sparrow · *Spizella arborea*

JAN	FEB	MAR	APR	MAY	JUN	JUL	AUG	SEP	OCT	NOV	DEC

Damp tangles and brushy thickets. October 2 early date; May 24 late date.

Chipping Sparrow · *Spizella passerina*

JAN	FEB	MAR	APR	MAY	JUN	JUL	AUG	SEP	OCT	NOV	DEC

Vast majority have departed prior to arrival of similar-looking American Tree Sparrow in late October.

Clay-colored Sparrow · *Spizella pallida*

JAN	FEB	MAR	APR	MAY	JUN	JUL	AUG	SEP	OCT	NOV	DEC

May 14 early date. Very rarely into December.

Field Sparrow · *Spizella pusilla*

JAN	FEB	MAR	APR	MAY	JUN	JUL	AUG	SEP	OCT	NOV	DEC

Field habitat with scattered trees, especially barrens, airports.

Vesper Sparrow · *Pooecetes gramineus*

JAN	FEB	MAR	APR	MAY	JUN	JUL	AUG	SEP	OCT	NOV	DEC

Southern New Hampshire only; grasslands, especially airports. March 30 early date.

Lark Sparrow · *Chondestes grammacus*

JAN	FEB	MAR	APR	MAY	JUN	JUL	AUG	SEP	OCT	NOV	DEC

Savannah Sparrow · *Passerculus sandwichensis*

JAN	FEB	MAR	APR	MAY	JUN	JUL	AUG	SEP	OCT	NOV	DEC

Grassland, stubble, and farm fields on migration.
An uncommon subspecies, the "Ipswich" Sparrow, winters along the coast, especially
in the dune systems of Hampton and Seabrook; has occurred rarely inland during fall
migration, as far west as Connecticut River. September 21 early date; April 18 late date.

Grasshopper Sparrow · *Ammodramus savannarum*

JAN	FEB	MAR	APR	MAY	JUN	JUL	AUG	SEP	OCT	NOV	DEC

Breeding almost exclusively confined to airport grasslands, southern New Hampshire
only. May 2 early date. Several winter records.

Nelson's Sparrow · *Ammodramus nelsoni*

JAN	FEB	MAR	APR	MAY	JUN	JUL	AUG	SEP	OCT	NOV	DEC

Strictly on the coast and around Great Bay, except for interior race (*Ammodramus nelsoni
nelsoni* or *Ammodramus nelsoni alter*), which occurs almost annually inland in fall.

Saltmarsh Sparrow · *Ammodramus caudacutus*

JAN	FEB	MAR	APR	MAY	JUN	JUL	AUG	SEP	OCT	NOV	DEC

Strictly on the coast and around Great Bay. May 4 early date; November 15 late date.

NONE
RARE
VERY UNCOMMON
UNCOMMON TO FAIRLY COMMON
COMMON TO ABUNDANT

INCREASING
DECREASING
STABLE
IRRUPTIVE
BREEDS IN NH
OCCURS OFFSHORE
INLAND

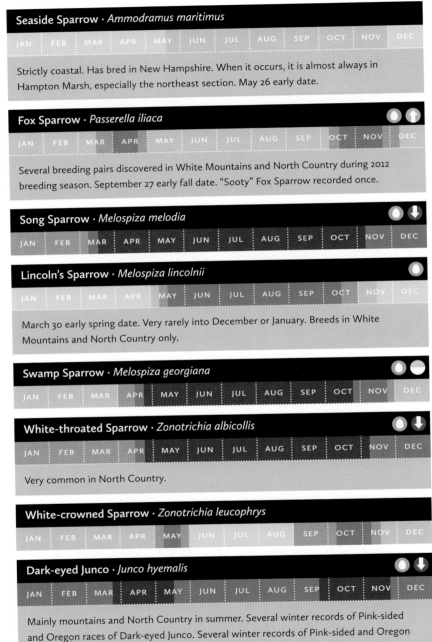

Seaside Sparrow · *Ammodramus maritimus*

JAN	FEB	MAR	APR	MAY	JUN	JUL	AUG	SEP	OCT	NOV	DEC

Strictly coastal. Has bred in New Hampshire. When it occurs, it is almost always in Hampton Marsh, especially the northeast section. May 26 early date.

Fox Sparrow · *Passerella iliaca*

JAN	FEB	MAR	APR	MAY	JUN	JUL	AUG	SEP	OCT	NOV	DEC

Several breeding pairs discovered in White Mountains and North Country during 2012 breeding season. September 27 early fall date. "Sooty" Fox Sparrow recorded once.

Song Sparrow · *Melospiza melodia*

JAN	FEB	MAR	APR	MAY	JUN	JUL	AUG	SEP	OCT	NOV	DEC

Lincoln's Sparrow · *Melospiza lincolnii*

JAN	FEB	MAR	APR	MAY	JUN	JUL	AUG	SEP	OCT	NOV	DEC

March 30 early spring date. Very rarely into December or January. Breeds in White Mountains and North Country only.

Swamp Sparrow · *Melospiza georgiana*

JAN	FEB	MAR	APR	MAY	JUN	JUL	AUG	SEP	OCT	NOV	DEC

White-throated Sparrow · *Zonotrichia albicollis*

JAN	FEB	MAR	APR	MAY	JUN	JUL	AUG	SEP	OCT	NOV	DEC

Very common in North Country.

White-crowned Sparrow · *Zonotrichia leucophrys*

JAN	FEB	MAR	APR	MAY	JUN	JUL	AUG	SEP	OCT	NOV	DEC

Dark-eyed Junco · *Junco hyemalis*

JAN	FEB	MAR	APR	MAY	JUN	JUL	AUG	SEP	OCT	NOV	DEC

Mainly mountains and North Country in summer. Several winter records of Pink-sided and Oregon races of Dark-eyed Junco. Several winter records of Pink-sided and Oregon races of Dark-eyed Junco.

Scarlet Tanager · *Piranga olivacea*

JAN	FEB	MAR	APR	MAY	JUN	JUL	AUG	SEP	OCT	NOV	DEC

April 19 early date; November 11 late date.

Northern Cardinal · *Cardinalis cardinalis*

JAN	FEB	MAR	APR	MAY	JUN	JUL	AUG	SEP	OCT	NOV	DEC

Rose-breasted Grosbeak · *Pheucticus ludovicianus*

JAN	FEB	MAR	APR	MAY	JUN	JUL	AUG	SEP	OCT	NOV	DEC

March 18 early spring date. Several winter records.

Blue Grosbeak · *Passerina caerulea*

JAN	FEB	MAR	APR	MAY	JUN	JUL	AUG	SEP	OCT	NOV	DEC

Barely annual (41 records since 1954). Mainly southern New Hampshire. April 19 early date; October 18 late date.

Indigo Bunting · *Passerina cyanea*

JAN	FEB	MAR	APR	MAY	JUN	JUL	AUG	SEP	OCT	NOV	DEC

More often along power lines, field and forest boundaries. April 6 early date; November 9 late date. Many birds owe their colorful feathers to the presence of carotenoids and melanins, the pigments that produce the reds and yellows of Northern Cardinals and American Goldfinches. These pigments absorb certain wavelengths of light, and the feather takes on the color of the remaining wavelengths. Indigo Buntings and Blue Jays, however, get their blue not from pigment but from the physical properties of the feather. Light is scattered by the feather's structure, leaving only wavelengths in the blue spectrum to be observed by the eye. When you hold such a feather up to the light, the blue disappears.

Dickcissel · *Spiza americana*

JAN	FEB	MAR	APR	MAY	JUN	JUL	AUG	SEP	OCT	NOV	DEC

Farm fields in fall, sometimes associating with House Sparrows. August 15 early fall date. Dickcissels form winter flocks in Venezuela that may number in excess of a million birds. Cereal farmers regard them as a pest, and as a consequence they are the subject of lethal control measures which have had a significant negative impact on their numbers.

NONE · RARE · VERY UNCOMMON · UNCOMMON TO FAIRLY COMMON · COMMON TO ABUNDANT

INCREASING · DECREASING · STABLE · IRRUPTIVE · BREEDS IN NH · OCCURS OFFSHORE · INLAND

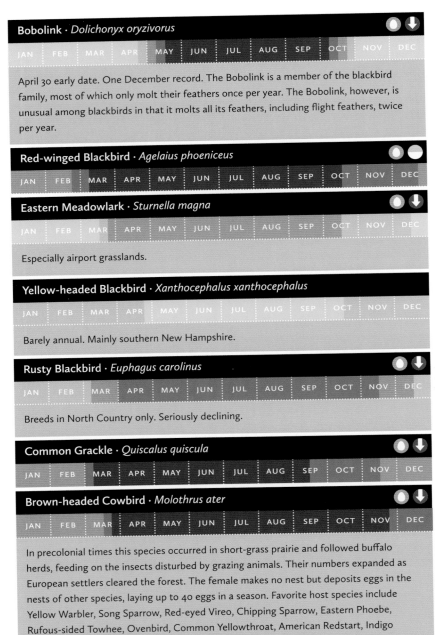

Bobolink · *Dolichonyx oryzivorus*

JAN	FEB	MAR	APR	MAY	JUN	JUL	AUG	SEP	OCT	NOV	DEC

April 30 early date. One December record. The Bobolink is a member of the blackbird family, most of which only molt their feathers once per year. The Bobolink, however, is unusual among blackbirds in that it molts all its feathers, including flight feathers, twice per year.

Red-winged Blackbird · *Agelaius phoeniceus*

JAN	FEB	MAR	APR	MAY	JUN	JUL	AUG	SEP	OCT	NOV	DEC

Eastern Meadowlark · *Sturnella magna*

JAN	FEB	MAR	APR	MAY	JUN	JUL	AUG	SEP	OCT	NOV	DEC

Especially airport grasslands.

Yellow-headed Blackbird · *Xanthocephalus xanthocephalus*

JAN	FEB	MAR	APR	MAY	JUN	JUL	AUG	SEP	OCT	NOV	DEC

Barely annual. Mainly southern New Hampshire.

Rusty Blackbird · *Euphagus carolinus*

JAN	FEB	MAR	APR	MAY	JUN	JUL	AUG	SEP	OCT	NOV	DEC

Breeds in North Country only. Seriously declining.

Common Grackle · *Quiscalus quiscula*

JAN	FEB	MAR	APR	MAY	JUN	JUL	AUG	SEP	OCT	NOV	DEC

Brown-headed Cowbird · *Molothrus ater*

JAN	FEB	MAR	APR	MAY	JUN	JUL	AUG	SEP	OCT	NOV	DEC

In precolonial times this species occurred in short-grass prairie and followed buffalo herds, feeding on the insects disturbed by grazing animals. Their numbers expanded as European settlers cleared the forest. The female makes no nest but deposits eggs in the nests of other species, laying up to 40 eggs in a season. Favorite host species include Yellow Warbler, Song Sparrow, Red-eyed Vireo, Chipping Sparrow, Eastern Phoebe, Rufous-sided Towhee, Ovenbird, Common Yellowthroat, American Redstart, Indigo Bunting, Red-winged Blackbird, Kentucky Warbler, Willow Flycatcher, Yellow-throated Vireo, and Field Sparrow.

Orchard Oriole · *Icterus spurius*

JAN	FEB	MAR	APR	MAY	JUN	JUL	AUG	SEP	OCT	NOV	DEC

Southern New Hampshire only, especially riparian habitat. April 25 early date; September 21 late date.

Baltimore Oriole · *Icterus galbula*

JAN	FEB	MAR	APR	MAY	JUN	JUL	AUG	SEP	OCT	NOV	DEC

April 16 early date.

Pine Grosbeak · *Pinicola enucleator*

JAN	FEB	MAR	APR	MAY	JUN	JUL	AUG	SEP	OCT	NOV	DEC

Will visit backyard crab apple trees during invasion years. August 20 early date. Several summer records.

Purple Finch · *Carpodacus purpureus*

JAN	FEB	MAR	APR	MAY	JUN	JUL	AUG	SEP	OCT	NOV	DEC

More common in the North Country.

House Finch · *Carpodacus mexicanus*

JAN	FEB	MAR	APR	MAY	JUN	JUL	AUG	SEP	OCT	NOV	DEC

More common in southern New Hampshire. House Finch was originally a bird of the Western United States. A small number were released on New York's Long Island in 1940; from there they colonized the eastern states and moved into Canada. It is one of the most abundant birds in North America, with population estimates ranging as high as 1 billion individuals.

Red Crossbill · *Loxia curvirostra*

JAN	FEB	MAR	APR	MAY	JUN	JUL	AUG	SEP	OCT	NOV	DEC

More likely in the North Country and Southern Highlands.

White-winged Crossbill · *Loxia leucoptera*

JAN	FEB	MAR	APR	MAY	JUN	JUL	AUG	SEP	OCT	NOV	DEC

More likely in the North Country and Southern Highlands in spruce-fir forest.

NONE
RARE
VERY UNCOMMON
UNCOMMON TO FAIRLY COMMON
COMMON TO ABUNDANT

INCREASING
DECREASING
STABLE
IRRUPTIVE
BREEDS IN NH
OCCURS OFFSHORE
INLAND

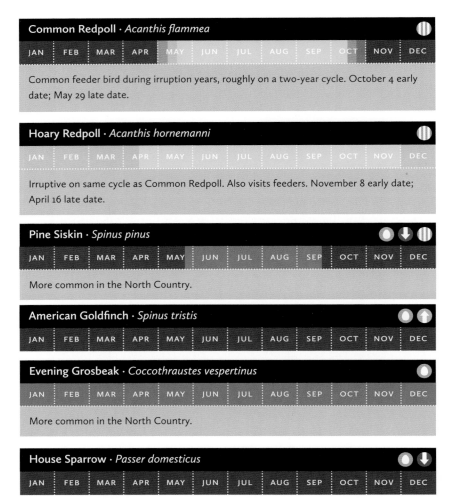

Common Redpoll · *Acanthis flammea*

JAN	FEB	MAR	APR	MAY	JUN	JUL	AUG	SEP	OCT	NOV	DEC

Common feeder bird during irruption years, roughly on a two-year cycle. October 4 early date; May 29 late date.

Hoary Redpoll · *Acanthis hornemanni*

JAN	FEB	MAR	APR	MAY	JUN	JUL	AUG	SEP	OCT	NOV	DEC

Irruptive on same cycle as Common Redpoll. Also visits feeders. November 8 early date; April 16 late date.

Pine Siskin · *Spinus pinus*

JAN	FEB	MAR	APR	MAY	JUN	JUL	AUG	SEP	OCT	NOV	DEC

More common in the North Country.

American Goldfinch · *Spinus tristis*

JAN	FEB	MAR	APR	MAY	JUN	JUL	AUG	SEP	OCT	NOV	DEC

Evening Grosbeak · *Coccothraustes vespertinus*

JAN	FEB	MAR	APR	MAY	JUN	JUL	AUG	SEP	OCT	NOV	DEC

More common in the North Country.

House Sparrow · *Passer domesticus*

JAN	FEB	MAR	APR	MAY	JUN	JUL	AUG	SEP	OCT	NOV	DEC

Rarities

Rarities are defined here as birds that occur regularly, but less than annually, or those that are likely to appear in New Hampshire at least once every 10 years. In the following list, the number in parentheses signifies the average period (in years) between occurrences. Birders can reasonably expect these species to recur in New Hampshire on a similar timeframe, adjusting the probabilities depending on whether a bird has been noted as increasing or decreasing in frequency.

Pink-footed Goose, *Anser brachyrhynchus*—only 1 record but pattern of occurrence in New England region suggests that it will likely be recorded with greater frequency, most likely late March to early April.

Ross's Goose, *Chen rossii*—only 1 record but situation similar to that of Pink-footed Goose; increasing.

Barnacle Goose, *Branta leucopsis*—4 records, with situation similar to that of Pink-footed Goose; increasing.

Eared Grebe, *Podiceps nigricollis* (5)—most likely at the coast, fall through winter.

Western Grebe, *Aechmophorus occidentalis* (3)—most likely at the coast, November through May.

American White Pelican, *Pelecanus erythrorhynchos* (3)—equally likely to occur in any month.

White-faced Ibis, *Plegadis chihi*—2 records but of sufficient and increasing regional occurrence to suggest likely regular recurrence; expected April through July.

King Rail, *Rallus elegans* (2)—late April through September, in brackish or freshwater marshes.

Purple Gallinule, *Porphyrio martinica* (8)—spring or fall.

American Avocet, *Recurvirostra americana* (8)—exclusively coastal, primarily in fall.

Ruff, *Philomachus pugnax* (5)—spring and fall, coast or inland.

Franklin's Gull, *Leucophaeus pipixcan* (7)—primarily coastal, June through November.

Thayer's Gull, *Larus thayeri*—becoming almost an annual winter vagrant in recent years, as understanding of gull identification has improved; all records at Rochester Wastewater Treatment Plant; recent practices

American Avocet, Hampton Harbor, August 20, 2011. This species is rare in the eastern states north of the Carolinas (this bird represented only the fifth record for New Hampshire).
Jason Lambert

to discourage gulls at the plant will perhaps mean fewer records of this species in future.

Slaty-backed Gull, *Larus schistisagus*—situation similar to that of Thayer's Gull.

Black Skimmer, *Rynchops niger* (4)—primarily August through September.

Great Skua, *Stercorarius skua*—several sightings of skuas likely refer to Great Skua, but it has yet to be definitively recorded in the state; based on regional patterns, it is presumed to be annual in fall and spring (and perhaps winter) at far offshore sites such as Cashes Ledge.

Northern Hawk Owl, *Surnia ulula* (5)—a winter visitor; invasion years include multiple occurrences.

Great Gray Owl, *Strix nebulosa* (7)—a winter visitor; invasion years include multiple occurrences.

Boreal Owl, *Aegolius funereus* (10)—a winter visitor, with recent breeding records from the White Mountains; invasion years include multiple occurrences; much more difficult to detect than previous two species.

Black Skimmer at Jenness Beach in Rye, September 10, 2010. *Len Medlock*

Rufous Hummingbird, *Selasphorus rufus* (1–2)—primarily October through November at feeders.

Gyrfalcon, *Falco rusticolus* (5)—primarily December through March.

Ash-throated Flycatcher, *Myiarchus cinerascens* (3)—primarily October through November.

Scissor-tailed Flycatcher, *Tyrannus forficatus* (6)—May to June, and October.

Cave Swallow, *Petrochelidon fulva*—November, most likely at the coast; almost annual since first record in 2003.

Sedge Wren, *Cistothorus platensis* (3)—May to July and October to November; decreasing.

Northern Wheatear, *Oenanthe oenanthe* (5)—September and October; increasing.

Townsend's Solitaire, *Myadestes townsendi* (4)—primarily December and January.

Varied Thrush, *Ixoreus naevius* (1–2)—primarily December through February at feeders.

Great Gray Owl, Durham, April 4, 2009. This owl is a rare winter visitor from the Great North Woods. *Jason Lambert*

Worm-eating Warbler, *Helmitheros vermivorum* (2)—primarily May and September to October.

Golden-winged Warbler, *Vermivora chrysoptera* (3)—primarily May and June; decreasing.

Prothonotary Warbler, *Protonotaria citrea* (6)—primarily occurs as spring overshoot in May.

Kentucky Warbler, *Geothlypis formosa* (4)—primarily occurs as spring overshoot in May.

Hooded Warbler, *Setophaga citrina* (2)—broad pattern of occurrence; April to June and August to November.

Yellow-throated Warbler, *Setophaga dominica* (3)—primarily occurs as spring overshoot in May; occasional fall vagrant, persisting through winter at feeders.

Townsend's Warbler, *Setophaga townsendi* (6)—5 records, all in November.

Summer Tanager, *Piranga rubra* (2)—primarily occurs as spring overshoot in May.

Western Tanager, *Piranga ludoviciana* (2)—spring and fall vagrant, with birds persisting through winter at feeders.

Painted Bunting, *Passerina ciris* (5)—late spring and early fall vagrant; persists through winter at feeders.

Bullock's Oriole, *Icterus bullockii* (4)—primarily late fall (November) vagrant, with individuals persisting through winter at feeders.

Accidentals

Through a combination of extreme rarity of occurrence and low likelihood of repeat occurrence within a 10-year period, the following species are classed as accidental vagrants to the state. These birds have occurred in New Hampshire 10 or fewer times or have declined from former numbers to a functionally equivalent status.

Species shown in orange are so reduced from their former status that they are now functionally accidental. The occurrence of species shown in green is hypothetical only (either we have no photograph of them or they have been seen only by a single observer). Occurrences of species shown in blue are associated with hurricane events.

Black-bellied Whistling-Duck, *Dendrocygna autumnalis*—1 record: Salem, June 28, 2011

Trumpeter Swan, *Cygnus buccinator*—Belknap (1792) hypothetical, based on vocalization and status at the time; now much reduced in abundance and extremely unlikely to occur in New Hampshire.

Yellow-nosed Albatross, *Thalassarche chlororhynchos*—at least 1 record: Hampton, June 6, 2006

Black-browed Albatross, *Thalassarche melanophris*—at least 1 record: Near Isles of Shoals, August 1, 1976;

Black-capped Petrel, *Pterodroma hasitata*—1 record in Chichester, August 31, 1893; future occurrence directly related to hurricane activity.

White-tailed Tropicbird, *Phaethon lepturus*—1 record: Claremont, August 29, 2011

Red-billed Tropicbird, *Phaethon aethereus*—1 record on White Island, June 23, 2009.

Wood Stork, *Mycteria Americana*—1 record in Lancaster, spring 1922.

Anhinga, *Anhinga anhinga*—3 records: Stratham, May 14, 2001; Chester, May 19, 2004; Portsmouth, May 17, 2005.

Brown Pelican, *Pelecanus occidentalis*—2 records: Newfound Lake, ca. 1880; Hampton Beach, May 1, 1907.

Little Egret, *Egretta garzetta*—3 records: Rye, April 28–May 1, 1990; Hampton Falls, August 2, 1992; Newmarket, June 30–August 14, 1998.

Western Reef-heron, *Egretta gularis*—1 record: Rye, New Castle, and Portsmouth, August 9–September 20, 2006.

White Ibis, *Eudocimus albus*—2 records: East Andover, September 11, 1969; Rye, August 6–8, 1984.

Swainson's Hawk, *Buteo swainsoni*—at least 2 records: Bristol, April 13, 1984; Peterborough, September 10, 2012

Swallow-tailed Kite, *Elanoides forficatus*—4 records: Franklin, 1875 (Allen); New Hampton, May 15–25, 1965; Danville, May 5, 1979; Hinsdale, April 26, 2011.

Yellow Rail, *Coturnicops noveboracensis*—5 records: Hampton Beach, September 1913 or 1914; Wolfeboro, October 2, 1952; Wilmot, October 21, 1961; North Hampton, September 4, 1963; Nottingham, September 23, 1985; possibly regular fall migrant through Hampton Marsh system en route from small breeding population in New Brunswick, but extremely secretive and difficult to detect.

Black Rail, *Laterallus jamaicensis*—1 record in Greenland, May 19, 2003.

Northern Lapwing, *Vanellus vanellus*—Rye, March 2, 1988.

Curlew Sandpiper at Plaice Cove in North Hampton, September 17, 2011. This species is a rare migrant from Eurasia. *Len Medlock*

Wilson's Plover, *Charadrius wilsonia*—2 records: Hampton Harbor, May 15–16, 1993; Seabrook Beach, May 1–8, 2005; possibly under-recorded based on regional patterns of occurrence.

Black-necked Stilt, *Himantopus mexicanus*—1 record in Rye, May 23, 1998.

Long-billed Curlew, *Numenius americanus*—2 records: Rye Beach, August 25, 1871; August 12 and 17, 1872.

Little Stint, *Calidris minuta*—1 record in Rye, August 7–11, 2003.

Curlew Sandpiper, *Calidris ferruginea*—6 records: Rye, August 9, 1930; Seabrook, October 31, 1953; Rye, July 23, 1961; Great Bay, November 9, 1980; Hampton Harbor, September 7, 1994; Rye, September 17, 2011.

Ivory Gull, *Pagophila eburnean*—4 records: Hampton, December 1948; Hampton, January 1, 1971; Portsmouth, January 15–21, 1983; Hampton, January 11, 2010.

Mew Gull, *Larus canus*—1 record in Exeter, March 2–15, 2010.

Glaucous-winged Gull, *Larus glaucescens*—1 record in Rochester, January 10, 2009.

Sooty Tern, *Onychoprion fuscatus*—7 records: Newmarket, September 14, 1878; Hinsdale, August 14–17, 1955; Hancock, August 15–16, 1955; Hampton, September 9, 1979; Rye, September 9, 1979; Seavey Island, August 11, 2000; Stoddard, August 30, 2011.

Gull-billed Tern, *Sterna nilotica*—Rye, July 23, 1998.

Sandwich Tern, *Thalasseus sandvicensis*—1 record at Hampton Harbor, August 20, 1991.

Band-tailed Pigeon, *Patagioenas fasciata*—2 records: Keene, January 3–15, 1972; Conway, March 24–30, 1991.

White-winged Dove, *Zenaida asiatica*—2 records: Dover, July 1–3, 2006; Jeffreys Ledge, May 28, 2011.

Barn Owl, *Tyto alba*—7 records: Belmont, August 10, 1948; Wolfeboro, August 17–18, 1960; Windsor, April 2, 1966; Meredith, October 16, 1971; Plainfield, December 20, 1972; Hollis, August–September 1977 (nesting); Alstead, February 10, 1999.

Burrowing Owl, *Athene cunicularia*—2 records: Dover, February 20, 1922; Star Island, May 14, 1978.

Say's Phoebe, *Sayornis saya*—1 record: Penacook, November 17–23, 2012

Chuck-will's-widow, *Caprimulgus carolinensis*—Star Island, May 21, 1966.

Tropical/Couch's Kingbird, *Tyrannus sp.*—1 record in Claremont, November 2, 2003.

Fork-tailed Flycatcher, *Tyrannus savanna*—1 record in Rye, November 18–20, 2006.

Loggerhead Shrike, *Lanius ludovicianus*—1 record during the past 20 years, in Newington, July 18, 1997.

Bell's Vireo, *Vireo bellii*—3 records: Durham, November 19, 1897; Exeter, November 1–9, 2003; Rye, October 1–5, 2009.

Black-billed Magpie, *Pica hudsonia*—8 records: Franklin, March 16, 1959; Plymouth, March 19–20, 1959; New Hampton, March 22–23, 1959; Dover, April 2, 1959; Lyme, October 15–17, 1962; Piermont, November 4, 1966; Lyme, January 20–February 10, 1969; Plymouth, April 20–24, 1981.

Violet-green Swallow, *Tachycineta thalassina*—New Durham, September 15, 1965; offshore, August 23, 1985.

Bewick's Wren, *Thryomanes bewickii*—5 records: Alton, April 2, 1890; Monroe, April 24–May 3, 1954; Epsom, June 13–September 11, 1966; Greenland, October 22, 1967; Portsmouth, August 30, 1985.

Chestnut-collared Longspur, *Calcarius ornatus*—1 record in Deering, November 29, 1992.

MacGillivray's Warbler, *Geothlypis tolmiei*—1 record in Gilford, October 1, 2005.

Kirtland's Warbler, *Setophaga kirtlandii*—2 singing males in Lancaster, on date prior to 1920.

Black-throated Gray Warbler, *Dendroica nigrescens*—1 record on Star Island, September 21–22, 1999.

Painted Redstart, *Myioborus pictus*—1 record in New Hampton, May 22–23, 1981.

Green-tailed Towhee, *Pipilo chlorurus*—2 records: North Haverhill, December 13, 1978; Keene, December 10, 1992.

Spotted Towhee, *Pipilo maculates*—3 records: Concord, December 14–February 29, 2004; Grafton, December 20–January 17, 2004; Peterborough, January–March 2011.

Lark Bunting, *Calamospiza melanocorys*—3 records: Twin Mountain, May 6, 1965; Bristol, July 22, 1972; North Hampton, October 11, 2008.

Henslow's Sparrow, *Ammodramus henslowii*—formerly a rare summer visitor and breeder in southern counties; declining but annual until 1950s, now very rare, recorded during breeding seasons of 1952, 1953, 1955, 1958, 1959, 1963, 1971, 1983, but not recorded since 1983.

Le Conte's Sparrow, *Ammodramus leconteii*—2 records: Seavey Island, May 16, 2000; Conway, October 18, 2008.

Harris's Sparrow, *Zonotrichia querula*—7 records: Tilton, December 30, 1964–April 21, 1965; Greenland, December 13, 1970–February 11, 1971; Plymouth, November 11–14, 1973; Dover, October 21, 1974; Moultonborough, November 10–17, 1975; Berlin, December 22–24, 2000; Campton, November 16–22, 2002.

Golden-crowned Sparrow, *Zonotrichia atricapilla*—2 records: Tamworth, April 27–29, 1985; Derry, October 17–19, 2010.

Black-headed Grosbeak, *Pheucticus melanocephalus*—3 records: Durham, January 27, 1976; Plymouth, May 16, 1978; Derry October 31–November 3, 2003.

Western Meadowlark, *Sturnella neglecta*—4 records: Newport, July 20–22, 1960; New Hampton, October 19, 1964; Hampton, June 16–July 25, 1969; Greenland, April 20, 1970.

Common Chaffinch, *Fringilla coeleb*—1 record in Orford, May 7, 1989.

Brambling, *Fringilla montifringilla*—1 record in Plymouth, October 23, 1987.

Captive or Reared Species

Any sighting of one of the following four species should be presumed to relate to a bird of captive origin.

Northern Bobwhite, *Colinus virginianus*—common in the eighteenth century, largely gone by the early twentieth century due to a combination of habitat change and harsh winters; restocking efforts result in frequent sightings of this species, though no evidence of a self-sustaining population is known.

Chukar, *Alectoris chukar*—gamebird, native to Eurasia.

Gray Partridge, *Perdix perdix*—gamebird, native to Eurasia.

Common Quail, *Coturnix coturnix*—gamebird, native to Eurasia.

Extinct Species

Labrador Duck, *Camptorhynchus labradorius*—presumed winter visitor to coastal New Hampshire until mid-nineteenth century.

Eskimo Curlew, *Numenius borealis*—regular migrant into the late nineteenth century.

Great Auk, *Pinguinus impennis*—known from bone fragments found in Seabrook.

Passenger Pigeon, *Ectopistes migratorius*—common to abundant resident and breeder into the nineteenth century.

Bibliography

Andrews, R. 1996. "Birding the Nashua NH area." *Bird Observer,* Vol. 24, No. 2, pp. 72–77.

Berry, J. 2003. "Birding the Brookside Wildlife Sanctuary in South Hampton." *New Hampshire Bird Records,* Vol. 22. No. 2.

Brickner-Wood, D. and P. Wellenberger. 2006–2010. *Great Bay National Estuarine Research Reserve Management Plan.* New Hampshire Fish and Game, Durham, NH. 63 pp.

Bronson, T. 2006. "Birding the Brentwood Mitigation Area." *New Hampshire Bird Records,* Vol. 25, No. 1, pp. 46–51.

Clements, J. F., T. S. Schulenberg, M. J. Iliff, B.L. Sullivan, C. L. Wood, and D. Roberson. 2011. "The Clements Checklist of Birds of the World: Version 6.6." Retrieved at http://www.birds.cornell.edu/clementschecklist/downloadable -clements-checklist.

Delorey, A. 1996. *A Birder's Guide to New Hampshire.* American Birding Association, Colorado Springs, CO.

Foss, C. R. 1994. *Atlas of Breeding Birds in New Hampshire.* Audubon Society of New Hampshire, Concord, NH.

Fox, R. 2006. "Spotlight on Kentucky Warbler." *New Hampshire Bird Records,* Vol. 25, No. 3, pp. 52–54.

Govatski, D. 2010. "Checklist of Birds of the Pondicherry National Wildlife Refuge and Vicinity." Retrieved at http://www.fws.gov/r5soc/library/pondicherry /pondicherry_birds.pdf.

Hunt, P. D. "The Birds of Mascoma Lake." New Hampshire. Unpublished.

Hunt, P. D., 2007. "Spring Arrival Dates Revisited." *New Hampshire Bird Records,* Vol. 26, No. 1, pp. 57–62.

Hunt, P. D., et al. 2004. *A Checklist of the Birds of New Hampshire.* New Hampshire Audubon, Concord, NH.

Hunt, P. D., M. B. Watkins, and R. W. Suomala. 2011. *The State of New Hampshire's Birds—A Conservation Guide.* New Hampshire Audubon, Concord, NH.

Iliff, M. 2011. "The 2011 October Coastal Fallout." *New Hampshire Bird Records,* Vol. 30, No. 3, pp. 51–54.

Kaufman, K. 1996. *Lives of North American Birds.* Houghton Mifflin, New York, NY.

Keith, A. R., and R. P. Fox. "The Birds of New Hampshire." Proposed for publication to Nuttall Ornithological Club, Cambridge, MA.

Lehman, P.E. 2003. "A Weather Primer of Birders." *Birding,* Vol. 33, pp. 596–605.

Mirick, S. 2000. "Birding Great Bay." *New Hampshire Bird Records,* Vol. 19, No. 1, pp. 35–37.

Mirick, S. 2001. "The Trails at Pickering Ponds, Rochester, NH." *Bird Observer,* Vol. 29, No. 1, pp. 8–10.

New Hampshire Department of Health and Human Services, 2012. "Black-legged Ticks and Lyme Disease Map." Retrieved at http://www.dhhs.nh.gov/dphs/cdcs/lyme/documents/blacklegged.pdf.

Nielsen, E. 2005. "Birding the Far North—Pittsburg." *New Hampshire Bird Records,* Vol. 24, No. 2, pp. 48–53.

Poole, A. (ed.). 2005. *The Birds of North America Online.* Cornell Laboratory of Ornithology, Ithaca, NY. Retrieved at http://bna.birds.cornell.edu/BNA/.

Quinn, R. 1994. "Finding Birds in Pittsburg, New Hampshire." *Bird Observer,* Vol. 22, No. 3, pp. 124–134.

Quinn, R. 2011. "Spotlight on Orange-crowned Warbler." *New Hampshire Bird Records,* Vol. 29, No. 3, pp. 58–62.

Quinn, R., and D. Govatski. 2002. "Birding the Pondicherry Wildlife Refuge and Vicinity." *Bird Observer,* Vol. 30, No. 3, pp. 153–160.

Richards, T., and R. Quinn. 1998. "Birding Lake Umbagog." *Bird Observer,* Vol. 26, No. 3, pp. 120–129.

Snyder, E. 2006. "Greenland Conservation and Land Stewardship Plan." Prepared for the Town of Greenland. 77 pp.

Sperduto, D., and B. Kimball. 2011. *The Nature of New Hampshire.* University Press of New England, Hanover, NH.

Sullivan, B. L., C. L. Wood, M. J. Iliff, R. E. Bonney, D. Fink, and S. Kelling. 2009. "eBird: A Citizen-Based Bird Observation Network in the Biological Sciences." *Biological Conservation,* Vol. 142, pp. 2282–2292.

Vazzano, T. 1998. "Watching the Weather." *New Hampshire Bird Records,* Vol. 17, No. 3, pp. 42–44.

Vazzano, T. 2002. "Birding Thompson Wildlife Sanctuary and Vicinity—Part 1." *New Hampshire Bird Records,* Vol. 20, No. 4, pp. 37–39.

Vazzano, T. 2003. "Birding Thompson Wildlife Sanctuary and Vicinity—Part 2." *New Hampshire Bird Records,* Vol. 21, No. 1, pp. 38–41.

Index

Note: Page numbers in *italics* refer to photographs, illustrations, or species graphs.